7

ISLAM
the
NATURAL
Way

ISLAM
the
NATURAL
Way

AbdulWahid Hamid

In the name of God, most Gracious, most Merciful

"And so, set your face steadfastly towards the (one) ever-true faith, turning away from all that is false, in accordance with the natural disposition which God has instilled into man. Not to allow any change to corrupt what God has thus created — this is (the purpose of the one) ever-true faith."
(*The Qur'an*, Surah ar-Ruum, 30: 30)

"He, the Prophet, enjoins on them that which they themselves sense as right, and forbids them that which they themselves sense as wrong. He makes lawful for them all good things, and prohibits for them only the foul, and relieves them of their undue burden and of the many shackles that used to be on them."
(*The Qur'an*, Surah al-A'raaf, 7: 157)

First published 1989 by
MELS
61 Alexandra Road
Hendon
London NW4 2RX

ISBN 0 948196 09 2

Reprinted 1999
with the kind permission of the copyright holder by
A.S.Noordeen
Post Box No 10066
50704 Kuala Lumpur
Malaysia
Telephone 03 4236003 Fax 03 4213675

Printed in Malaysia by
Percetakan Zafar Sdn. Bhd. (97878-H)
Kuala Lumpur

CONTENTS

NOTE ON TRANSLITERATION OF ARABIC

Long vowels in Arabic words have been transliterated as follows:
  long vowel 'a' as 'aa' as in Shahaadah;
  long vowel 'i' as 'ii' as in Diin (pronounced Deen);
  long vowel 'u' as 'uu' as in Huduud (pronounced Hudood).
The above scheme is not applied to words whose form is now in common use, such as 'Islam' which should be pronounced Islaam.
  No attempt has been made to distinguish between light and heavy consonants. Arabic is very precise and if you are in doubt about the pronunciation of any Arabic word, do seek the help of an Arabic speaker.

Introduction

This book is an attempt to explain what Islam is and what it means for every person. It seeks to show that Islam is the natural way for all creation and for man in particular. To discover Islam is to return to one's natural disposition. To understand Islam properly is to understand something of the true meaning and purpose of life. To live by Islam is to live by natural universal values and to fulfil one's needs and obligations, naturally.

Of course, this is only an introduction to the subject. It is intended for anyone, Muslim or non-Muslim, who desires to have an understanding of the main concerns of Islam and of the foundations on which it is built.

Essentially, it is a personal book. It requires you to think of reality as a whole and to ask, as no doubt you have asked, such questions as: Who am I? Where do I come from? What am I doing here? Where do we all go from here? It requires you to think in ever expanding circles of your own condition, your livelihood and your leisure, your family relationships, your neighbourhood, community, the environment, people with differing worldviews, matters of global concern and beyond.

An attempt has been made to keep the language and style of this book as simple as possible. This may not always have succeeded and the result may be some unevenness in the text as a whole. The layout has been designed to make the book easy to use and follow.

Many sources in both Arabic and English have been used in preparing this book. Detailed references to these at each point were considered unnecessary in a text of this kind. However, the mention of some of these sources in the guide to *Further Reading* is also intended as acknowledgement.

I am grateful to Abdullah Omar Nasseef, Secretary General of the Muslim World League and Ziauddin Sardar for suggesting that I put together this book. They both share a deep concern for the human condition and they both work extremely hard. Sincere thanks are due to all those, including family and friends, who read the manuscript and suggested improvements and to others who supported the writing and publication of the book. I am particularly grateful to my wife Azieza for her constant encouragement and support.

I hope, God willing, that this modest effort will in some measure prove useful and I seek His forgiveness for any shortcomings. I pray that as human beings we grow to know and share the worldview which enables us to enjoy and, where necessary, to endure all that life has to offer, and that we may all live our lives, through His limitless providence and guidance, fully and naturally — in Islam.

Abdul Wahid Hamid
Hendon, London
Ramadan 1408/May 1988.

ONE

FACE *to* FACE *with* REALITY

Like countless millions before you, you must have asked yourself such questions as: Who am I? Where do I come from? How did the world and the universe come into being? What am I doing in this world? Can I do what I want to, how I want to, when I want to? Where do I go from here, from this seemingly earth-bound existence? Where do we all go from here?

These are questions about life and about the meaning and purpose of life. These are questions about the universe and our place in it.

WORLDVIEWS

The answers you give to these questions help to shape your worldview. A worldview is the way in which a person sees and explains the world and his place in it. Your worldview not only affects the way you think. It also affects the way you act or behave. Your worldview shapes the quality of your life.

In the long history of mankind, there have been many different ways of explaining the world, how it came about, how it works, and what is man's place in it.

Some people have seen the world as a mysterious place, with dark and evil forces at work. In such a worldview, a person's life is ruled by superstition and fear.

Others have seen the world as a bright, rich and beautiful place. They do not show concern about how it came about or about what will happen to it. They are happy "to make the most of it", to eat, drink and enjoy life. If they do think of life and death at all, they might just say, "We live and die and nothing causes our death except time."

Some people have seen the universe as a battleground of good and evil, of light and darkness, of positive and negative. Among some Chinese, for example, there are ideas of *yin* and *yang*. Yang is light and heat and goodness. Yin is dark and cold and damp and bad. In some forms of Zoroastrian religion, there is Ahura Mazda, the force of good, battling with Angra Mainyu, the force of evil, for control of the world.

Some people get their worldview from religions which hold that there is a creator or maker of the universe or a supreme being. Religions differ about the nature of this supreme being. Some say this being has absolute power — he can do whatever he wishes and no other has a share in his power. Others associate this being with other gods, demons and spirits.

Nowadays, many people have turned away from religions and a belief in God. Many feel that the idea of God and of a creator is an invention of man's imagination anyway. They feel that man has the power and the right to decide what is best for him. Such people are called atheists, agnostics or humanists. An atheist is one who denies the existence of God. An agnostic is one who says that he does not know whether God exists or not. He may even go further and say that he does not care. He is really quite close to the atheist. A humanist (who may be an atheist or an agnostic) insists that human beings alone must decide what is best for them for there is no such thing as Divine laws.

At the same time as they turn to humanism, many now turn to "Science" and the scientific method for their understanding of the world and man's place in it. They may have a notion of science as something exact and precise and of the scientific method — of gathering data, experimentation, observation and deduction — as the only way of gaining knowledge, of determining what is true and what is false.

Some people pick and choose to form their own worldview. For some questions they may turn to a religion, especially in times of distress. For other answers they may turn to an astrologer, the horoscope in their daily or weekly newspaper, a popular guru, or a fashionable ideology like Marxism. For certain questions they would invoke the name of science. And so on.

False and True

From this brief look at various worldviews, it would seem that human beings as a whole are totally mixed up and confused without any hope of finding out what is right or true. It may seem that we are groping in the dark, not really knowing where we are, from where we came and where we are going. In this situation we may well wonder if there is any way of knowing what is true from what is false.

Clearly, all the ways of looking at the world cannot all be true. Some appear to have some things in common but each is different from the other in important ways.

Of any worldview, we may ask:

● Does it portray the truth and is it at least reasonable? We should not be content with a worldview that is false and that is not supported by reason and logic.

- Is it capable of explaining reality as a whole? We should not be content with a worldview that can only explain or furnish knowledge on a part of reality.
- So far as human beings are concerned, does the worldview cater for and can it satisfy human needs and potentials?
- Does it provide proper values to live by and valid goals to strive for? Which of the worldviews that have shaped people's lives can thus be described as valid and reasonable, complete and logically satisfying?

Science — a limited worldview

No single person on his own, no matter how clever he is, can give complete, valid and satisfying answers to the questions about the origins of the world and man's place in it, about life and destiny. No group of persons can do so either. For example, all the knowledge of the world and the universe amassed by scientists throughout the ages is knowledge of only a small part of reality. However much scientists in the future may come to know, there will always be a point where they must say, "We do not know." From the standpoint of science, the universe is like an old book the first and last pages of which have been lost. Neither the beginning nor the end is known. Thus, the worldview of science is a knowledge of the part, not of the whole.

Science, as the word is now widely understood, acquaints us with the situation of some parts of the universe; it cannot explain the essential character of the whole universe, its origin or its destiny. The scientist's worldview is like the knowledge about the elephant gained by those who touched it in the dark. The one who felt the elephant's ear supposed the animal to be shaped like a fan; the one who felt its leg supposed it to be shaped like a column; and the one who felt its back supposed it to be shaped like a throne. Science it has been said is like a powerful searchlight in the long winter night, lighting up a small area in its beam but unable to shed light beyond its border. This is not to pronounce on its usefulness or otherwise; it is only to say that it is limited.

The Power of Reason

Fortunately, in our quest for a true and valid worldview, human beings do have a special gift or power — the power of reason and logic. Of course, we must realise that this power is in itself limited: it is like a precision balance which you might use for weighing gold but you would be vain and foolish to think of using it to weigh mountains. Still, if reason is properly used, it could point to some of the real answers about our place in this world. At the very least, this power of reason could be used to show which theory or which worldview is false or inadequate.

We shall thus try to use reason to answer the most important of the questions listed at the very beginning of this section, which is: Where do we come from?

WHERE DO WE COME FROM?

For everything, like man, that has a beginning in time, there can be only three ways of trying to explain how it came to be.

1. Either, it was made, or created, or caused by nothing at all. In other words, it came out of nothing.

2. Or, it created itself.

3. Or, it has a creator, cause, or maker outside itself.

The first and second explanations are obviously impossible. It is inconceivable for something that has a beginning in time to come out of or be made of nothing at all. It is also inconceivable that it should bring itself into being. The universe and all that is in it, therefore, could not have created itself nor did it come about by chance.

The conclusion then is clear. The universe and all that is in it owe its existence to a Creator or Maker outside itself. You, as a human being, as part of the universe, owe your existence to such a Creator.

To say, as many do, that human beings came from or evolved from other creatures or that they originated from water, or that there was a big bang and everything just happened to fall in place, does not really answer the question about the origin of the universe and all that is in it, including human beings.

We can therefore conclude that any worldview that denies or does not accept the existence of a Creator of the universe is a false worldview.

What is the nature of the Creator?

The Creator must be of a different nature from all that has been created. This is because if He is of the same nature as they are, He will need to have a beginning in time and will therefore need a maker. One word for "to have a beginning in time" is "temporal".

If the Maker or Creator is not temporal, He must be eternal. Eternal means to have no beginning or end in time.

If the Maker is eternal, He cannot be caused and if nothing caused him to come into existence, nothing outside Him causes Him to continue to exist, which means that he must be self-sufficient. Self-sufficient means that he does not depend on anyone or anything to exist.

And if he does not depend on anything to exist, then his existence can have no end. The Creator is therefore eternal and everlasting.

If the Creator is eternal and everlasting, then all His qualities must be eternal and everlasting. This means, for example, that if He is powerful, He must always be powerful. He cannot cease to be powerful. If He is all-knowing, He must always be all-knowing. If He is wise, He must always be wise. If He is kind and just, He must always be kind and just.

The Creator then does not lose or get any new qualities. Qualities that do not change and that last forever are absolute qualities. Another name for qualities are attributes.

THE NOMAD

A desert nomad was asked about the existence of God.
He said:

"Camel droppings point to the existence of a camel. Footprints on the sand tell of a traveller. The heavens with its stars, the earth with its mountains and valleys, and the sea with its waves — don't they point to the Maker, all-Powerful, Knowing, Wise and Caring?"

THE ATHEIST

A conversation took place between the leader and scholar, Ja'far as-Saadiq and an avowed atheist. Ja'far asked the person:

"Have you ever travelled on the sea?"

"Yes."

"Have you experienced its terrors?"

"Yes, indeed! One day while we were out at sea, a terrible hurricane blew up and smashed our ship. Several sailors perished. I clung to a rafter of the ship but it was soon snatched away. I was thrown about in the stormy sea but eventually was tossed up on the shore."

"When the storm broke," Ja'far commented, "perhaps you first relied on the ship and the sailors for your safety and then on the rafter which saved you for a while. But when all these went, did you resign yourself to death or did you still hope for safety?"

"I hoped for safety."

"On whom did you hope for safety?"

The man was silent and Ja'far said:

"The Creator is the one on whom you placed your hopes at that time. And He is the one who delivered you from drowning."

After this conversation, the atheist was no longer an atheist.

THE MULBERRY TREE

The famous jurist, Ash-Shaafi', was asked: "What is the proof for the existence of God?"

He replied:

"The leaf of the mulberry tree. Its colour, smell, taste and everything about it seem one and the same to you. But a caterpillar eats it and it comes out as fine silken thread. A bee feeds on it and it comes out as honey. A sheep eats it and it comes out as dung. Gazelles chew on it and it congeals producing the fragrance of musk.

"Who has made all these different things come from the same type of leaf?"

THE FORTRESS

Another famous jurist, Ahmad ibn Hanbal, was also asked the same question and he said:

"There is this strong, smooth fortress. It is completely enclosed. It has neither door nor window. It looks like white silver on the outside and like pure gold in the inside. While it is in this state, suddenly its walls begin to crack and crumble and out comes something alive which can hear and see. It looks beautiful and gives off a pleasing sound."

(He was of course speaking of an egg and the birth of a chick.)

Can there be more than one creator with such absolute attributes? Can there for example be two absolutely powerful creators? This is not possible. Why?

If a Maker is absolutely powerful, it follows that he is absolutely free to do whatever he likes. But if another maker with similar powers exists and they differ over the making of something, then one of two things can happen. Either, one will overcome the other, in which case the latter cannot be absolutely powerful. Or, they will neutralise each other , in which case the powers of both are limited.

Even if we assume that the two powers agree on everything or complement each other, they cannot both be absolutely powerful because in doing anything one at least will need to assume that the other will not interfere or is not capable of interfering. In other words, one will need to assume that the function of the other is redundant, or that the power of the other is limited.

The Creator then must be One. There cannot be any other like Him so He must be Unique. The Creator must be all Powerful and must be able to do whatever He wills.

From the above, it is valid and reasonable to assert that the Creator must be Eternal and Everlasting, Self-Sufficient and All-Powerful, One and Unique. These are some of the qualities or attributes of the Creator that we must have in mind when we use the word God. We must also remember that His attributes or qualities are absolute and do not change.

There must then be a clear separation between the Creator and the created. It follows that no man can be God. God cannot have a mother or a father. He cannot have a son or a daughter. The sun, the moon or the stars or any heavenly bodies cannot be God.

No part of creation whether it be a mountain, a tree or a fire can be God and does not deserve to be worshipped as God.

Any religion or any worldview which regards any human being or any part of creation as God or part of God must be a false religion or worldview.

Also, any religion or any worldview which regards God as having human characteristics, for example having a human shape and suffering from tiredness and needing rest and sleep, must be a false religion or worldview.

DECLARATION OF GOD'S PERFECTION

Say: He is the One God;
God is Eternal, the Everlasting, the Independent.
He begets not and neither is He begotten
And there is nothing that could be compared with Him.

(*The Qur'an*, 112: 1-4)

Natural to acknowledge the Creator

From what we have said and from what we shall detail later, it is reasonable and natural for man to acknowledge the existence and power of the Creator. It is natural and reasonable for man to acknowledge that all creation is preserved through God's will and grace — what is called in English "providence". If for an instance this providence were to be withdrawn from this world, it would cease to be. It is therefore natural and reasonable for the human being to give thanks or show gratitude to the Creator for all the favours of life.

ATTRIBUTES OF GOD

"God — there is no god but He; the One who knows all that is beyond the reach of a created being's perception, as well as all that can be witnessed by a creature's senses or mind. He is the most Gracious, the most Merciful.

God — there is no god but He; the Sovereign Supreme, the Holy, the One with whom all salvation rests, the Giver of Faith, the One who determines what is true and what is false, the Almighty, the One who subdues wrong and restores right, the One to whom all greatness belongs.

Glory be to God for He is remote from all that men may associate as partners unto Him!

He is God, the Creator, the Maker who shapes all forms and appearances!

His (alone) are the attributes of perfection. All that is in the heavens and on earth extols His limitless glory; for He alone is Almighty, truly Wise."

(*The Qur'an*, 59: 22-24)

"God — there is no god but He, the Ever-Living, the Self-Subsisting Source of all being.

Neither slumber overtakes him nor sleep. His is all that is in the heavens and all that is on earth. Who is there that can intercede with Him , unless it be by His permission?

He knows all that lies open before men and all that is hidden from them, whereas they cannot attain to any of His knowledge except that which He wills (them to attain).

His eternal power overspreads the heavens and the earth, and their upholding wearies Him not. And He alone is truly Exalted, Mighty."

(*The Qur'an*, 2: 255)

It is unreasonable and unnatural for the human being to think of himself as totally independent and self-sufficient. If a person thinks in this manner, he becomes proud and vain. He is thus inclined to be ungrateful for the bounties he enjoys–the air he breathes and the food he eats to sustain him, the wondrous eyes and ears he uses to perceive the world about him, the subtle tongue and lips he uses to express his wants and needs. And being ungrateful, he is inclined to forget or to reject the truth of the existence of God.

NATURAL OR INNATE VALUES

We shall deal with creation in more detail later. Here, we state that all creation has been created according to a measure and functions according to certain inbuilt laws and norms. The human being is endowed by the Creator with in-born or innate knowledge and values. We say that these innate values form a natural moral sense which makes a person recognise what is good and beautiful such as telling the truth, keeping promises and being grateful. This moral sense also makes a person recognise what is bad and morally ugly such as telling lies, deceit and arrogance. A child who says to another, "Come on, you promised", or a person who challenges a bully, "How'd you like it if someone did the same to you?" are both appealing to values and standards of behaviour — in these cases, honesty and justice, which people the world over will recognize because everyone is born with these natural values.

The natural moral sense is one way in which the Creator has provided for the guidance of human beings. He has granted us a conscience which registers right and wrong and a mind which has the ability to reason. He made the whole universe a natural book full of signs that lead a thinking person to existence of God, His power and bounty.

REVELATION AND PROPHETHOOD

However, to make matters clearer, to give man more detailed knowledge of God, and to show him in a more specific way how to relate to Him, God has since the creation of mankind sent messages to men through persons chosen and inspired by Him. Such persons have been the real leaders of mankind. They are called Prophets or messengers of God.

How do we know this? How do we know who these persons are? How do we know that these persons are true and what they said is true and not invented by themselves or others? And since many people have claimed and some still claim to be prophets, how do we know a true prophet from an impostor or a charlatan? Even if we can establish that a prophet is true, how can we be sure that the message he brought is preserved exactly as he brought it and has not been changed or distorted in any way? At this stage, we need to take a dip into history.

It is a fact that there exist many books in the world which are sometimes described as "holy". Various people derive their worldview from these writings or scriptures. There is the Vedas and the Bhagawat Gita among Hindus. There is the Avesta and its various parts among the Zoroastrians. There is the Bible and various versions of it used by Christians and partly by the Jews. There is the Kojiki and Nihon Shoki of the Shinto religion in Japan. There is the Qur'an. Closer to our own times are such writings as the Adi-Granth of the Sikhs or the Book of Mormon of the Church of Christ of Latter-Day Saints in the United States.

Some of these writings or scriptures are regarded as the message or the words of a Supreme Being, or at least inspired by this Being and transmitted by prophets or people chosen by God.

Criteria for a true scripture

We could try to use reason and logic to find out which of the existing messages or scriptures may be considered as being inspired by the true God. In doing so, we must remember the attributes of God are absolute, that He is and must be the One and Unique, all-Powerful, all-Knowing Creator of the universe.

For a scripture to be true and not false and for it to be God's message or inspired by God, it must logically meet certain standards or criteria:

1.   The scripture should not attribute to God anything which goes against His unique nature. It should not say, for example, that God was ever a man or that there existed other gods or goddesses with him, or that there is an evil being which has power equal to His.

2.   It should not attribute to any created being anything which pertains only to God. It should not say for example that any person knows or can know everything or that any person has the power to do anything and everything.

3.   It should completely deny to anyone or anything, apart from the Creator, the right to be worshipped and obeyed.

4.   No part of the scripture should contradict another part.

5.   The scripture should not attribute major sins or vices to the persons whom God chose for the task of conveying His guidance because this would be just like saying that the message conveyed was not worthy enough to be followed or that God was ignorant or stupid in choosing such a person.

6.   The person claiming to have received the scripture should be a person of whom no evil or sin is known and who is completely honest and truthful. He must be a person who claims no rewards or benefits for himself from people.

Most scriptures do not meet these standards. They contain many statements and stories which speak of God, man and the universe often in quite fantastic terms. Here is not the place to go into the details of the scriptures we have mentioned and others too. However, it can be safely said that the Qur'an is the only scripture existing which meets these standards. This will be shown as we go along.

Why do other scriptures not meet or fall short of these standards? How do we account for the fantastic statements and stories about God and his creation in these 'holy' scriptures? Is it because they belong to an earlier, more primitive stage in man's history when man might have been ignorant and searching about on his own for explanations about life and the universe?

The Qur'an itself mentions that from the beginning mankind has been given knowledge and guidance from God. It mentions that when God created the first man, Adam, He "taught Adam the names of all things" (2: 31). It also states that the most Gracious God "created man and imparted unto him articulate thought and speech" (55: 3-4).

PRIMITIVE RELIGION?

It is not therefore right to think of the first human being as ignorant and primitive, as worshipping the sun and trees and natural objects and that only as time passed and people allegedly became wiser they abandoned such beliefs and progressed to the belief in monotheism or in a "single High God".

The only way in which early people could be said to be primitive was in the skills they possessed and the tools they used for living and survival. Modern man may be developed in the skills he possesses and the tools he uses but in his worldview and beliefs he could be and is often ignorant, limited and misguided and far removed from the pure state in which he was created.

What is most important about an individual at any time is not whether he lives in a cave or at the top of a glass-steel-and-concrete tower, whether he uses a sickle or a combine harvester to gather his grain, whether he uses firewood or a microwave oven for cooking, or whether he uses a bow and arrow or a laser beam as a weapon. What is important, as we shall see, is whether he preserves his pure and original state by living in accordance with his natural moral sense and whether he acknowledges the Creator and follows His guidance.

Knowledge and human history

To return to the question of true and false scriptures: From the Qur'an, which fulfils the criteria for a true scripture or revelation, we learn that the first man was Adam and he was a Prophet. He had a correct knowledge of God and creation inasmuch as he was taught directly by God. He was not ignorant. His descendants make up the human race. Some descendants of Adam followed the guidance he brought from God. Some did not. Some added new things, some changed the original guidance. Some later went into the worship of the sun or idols they themselves had made. Some went against the natural moral sense and inclined towards obscenity, injustice and cruelty to others. God in His mercy continued to send prophets to guide these people back to the straight path and to correct their errant beliefs and ways.

To every people, we are told in the Qur'an, God sent a guide, a messenger or a prophet. They were the genuine leaders of mankind. All prophets taught the same message, the need to believe in the Oneness of God. It was their followers and later generations who changed or distorted this message. It is possible, for example, that Zoroaster was a true prophet but his teachings have been so corrupted that they cannot be recognised in the mixture of myths and legends that now form part of the Zoroastrian scriptures. In the case of Jesus, he was undoubtedly a true Prophet but his teachings have been so falsified by later Christians that his original message is unrecognizable. No doubt there are still elements of good in it but totally false teachings (for example that Jesus is God made flesh or that Jesus is the son of God) make the Bible unfit to be regarded as a true scripture.

Among the prophets mentioned in the Qur'an are Adam, Abraham, Noah, Moses, David, Jesus and Muhammad. The last of these prophets was Muhammad and the message revealed to him is the Qur'an. It still exists in the form it was revealed and remains the only true and authentic expression of God's guidance for mankind.

Realizing that our view of human history is part of our worldview, we can say from the above that history is not mainly a progression from simple and primitive to more developed and complex tools, skills, or life-styles. History must be viewed mainly in relation to a constant straight path. This path involves in essence acknowledging the Creator and living according to the natural moral sense with which man is endowed. People may stick to this straight path. Some may deviate and go astray but eventually come back to the straight path. Some may deviate and not only go astray but get lost altogether. The role of prophets and those who follow them has been to call people back to the straight path, to the belief in and worship of the One God—in other words, to right belief and right action according to that belief. The most instructive way to look at man and the history of mankind therefore is in relation to this natural moral constant or straight path. To look at the history of mankind from purely materialistic angles such as changes in tools and modes of production is fascinating but less meaningful.

THE QUR'ANIC WORLDVIEW

We can now proceed to get some idea of the guidance and the worldview offered by the Qur'an. A simple way to do this is to turn to the opening chapter of the Qur'an. It is made up of seven short verses and is the most repeated part of the Qur'an. (The word for "verses" of the Qur'an is "aayaat" which really means "signs" or "messages" pointing to the Oneness of the Creator and the purpose of His creation.)

The surah is composed of three parts.

The first part — verses 1-4 — describes the truth about God. He is the Maker, Owner, Lord and Sustainer of all creation. With all His might and glory, God is, above all, good and kind, full of grace and mercy to His creation.

He is also Master of the Day of Judgement which points to a part of reality which is beyond man's present perception. This day points to an existence beyond this present life. It also points to the fact that man has been created with a purpose and that he must answer to God for his life on earth. It also points to the absolute fairness and justice of the Creator.

For all these attributes and bounties, only God is worthy of all praise and thanks. *Al hamdu lillaah* — all praise and thanks is due to God alone.

The second part — verse 5 — follows logically from the first part and des-

---

SURAH AL-FAATIHAH

1 **"In the name of God, most Gracious, most Merciful.**

2 **All praise and thanks are due to God**
   The Lord and Sustainer of all the worlds

3 **Most Gracious, Most Merciful.**

4 **Master of the Day of Judgement.**

5 **You alone do we worship**
   And You alone do we ask for help.

6 **Guide us the straight way—**

7 **The way of those whom You have favoured**
   Not of those who deserve Your anger
   Nor of those who go astray."

The opening chapter of the Qur'an is called Surah al-Faatihah in Arabic. It is described as *"Umm al-Qur'an"* or the Essence of the Qur'an. It is known as *"Al-Kanz"* or *"The Treasure"* and *Al-Kaafiyah"* or *"The Sufficient"* because it is sufficient and complete as a description of reality and as a prayer. It is also called *"Al-Asaas"* or *"The Foundation"* on the basis of a saying of the Prophet Muhammad: *"There is a foundation for everything... and the foundation of the Qur'an is the Faatihah, and the foundation of the Faatihah is *"Bismillaahi-r Rahmaani-r Rahiim"* — in the name of God, Most Kind, Most Merciful."*

---

cribes the only proper and acceptable relationship between man the creature, and God the Creator. It is the relationship between the servants and the Served. Only God may be worshipped or served:

"You alone do we worship and You alone do we ask for help."

Everyone who utters these words must abandon the worship of all false gods, including his own desires and inclinations if these go against the will of God.

The third part — verses 6 and 7 — registers man's need for guidance and help from his Maker and Sustainer and ends with a plea and a supplication: "Guide us the Straight Way."

The rest of the Qur'an is an answer to this prayer. The way of the Qur'an is *the Straight Way*.

Purpose and Content of the Qur'an

The Qur'an presents itself as a "guidance for mankind" as a whole. It is not for any one race or class of people. It is not for any one place or period in time. It is addressed to all people. In particular, it is for "those who are conscious of God, who believe in the existence of that which is beyond the reach of human perception". From the beginning, it puts man face to face with reality as a whole.

Yet, the Qur'an does not require people to believe blindly. It is addressed to "people who think", who think about what they can see and hear and observe about themselves and the world about them; about the earth and mountains, clouds and sky, the sun, the moon and planets in their orbits, the alternation of night and day, or the parched earth brought to life after a shower of rain. It asks us to reflect on the beginning of our own life — from a drop of sperm mingled with an ovum, the clinging of the fertilised egg to the wall of the mother's womb, the growth of this embryo, the formation of bones, the clothing of the bones with flesh and after an appointed time, the birth of a new being. It asks us to reflect on the growth of this new being to maturity and strength and then its decline into old age, weakness and death. It asks us to watch and think about our eyes, our tongue, our lips. It asks us to think about the seeds we sow, the water we drink, the food we eat, the fire we light, and all the other innumerable "signs" of creation and the innumerable instances of the Creator's grace and bounty.

"FOR PEOPLE WHO USE THEIR REASON"

"Your god is One God;
There is no god but He;
The all-Merciful, the all-Compassionate.
Behold in the creation
of the heavens and the earth;
in the alternation
of night and day;
in the sailing of ships
through the ocean
for the profit of mankind;
in the rain which God
sends down from the skies,
and the life He gives therewith
to an earth that is dead;
in the creatures of all kinds
that He causes to multiply
through the earth;
in the change of the winds,
and the clouds which run
their appointed courses
between sky and earth;
in all this are signs indeed
for people who use their reason." *(The Qur'an, 2: 164)*

"Have you watched the seeds which you sow?" (56: 63), "the water you drink..." (56: 68), "...the fire you light" (56: 71).

Again and again, we are asked to observe and think and question: Why should man believe in a single Creator who is Eternal, Beneficent, Compassionate, Loving, Just? Why shouldn't it be one or several of the many other gods in which people believe? Why shouldn't the arguments of the materialists and those who deny the existence of God not be correct? Almost the whole of the Qur'an is addressed to these questions.

Throughout, the Qur'an stresses knowledge and reason as the valid way to faith and God-consciousness. It says: "Only those of the servants of God who possess knowledge are the ones who truly stand in awe of Him" (35: 28).

GOD AND HIS CREATION

We know that creation is amazingly vast and intricate. From the tiniest and invisible protons and neutrons to the vast galaxies, it inspires wonder and awe. It is not only vast; it is well-ordered.

However, Reality according to the Qur'an is not only made up of matter, of the things we can see and hear and smell and feel and taste. It is not only made up of the vast observable universe. There are parts of God's creation which is beyond the knowledge and experience of any human being. The Qur'an mentions the seven heavens, periods in time when man was not even a thing mentioned. It speaks of angels created from light and jinns made from fire. It speaks of another world — the Aakhirah — which is better and more lasting than this world. To disbelieve or reject the existence of all these simply because we cannot now perceive them is to doubt the creative power of the Creator. It is like looking down a single street and denying that anything exists around the street corners simply because that is outside our field of vision.

Creation is also not a one-off thing. God did not just create the world and go to rest or to sleep. He would not be God if He did so. God continues to sustain His creation and He has the power to bring to an end or to cause new life or creation as He wills.

The Qur'an speaks of everything in the universe as being created according to a measure which is set by the Creator. The sun moves in a path of its own and "may not overtake the moon". All heavenly bodies float through space according to the laws set by God. Plants need sunlight to grow and flourish. Birds and bees have been inspired by the Creator with amazing sense of direction to enable them to obtain food. People need oxygen to survive. Each creation follows or obeys the special laws or norms built into it. A bee cannot live in the sea. A fish cannot live on land. Each lives according to the laws set by the Creator. Each lives in a state of submission. This is precisely the meaning of the Arabic word *"islam"*. Anything which follows the laws measured out for it by the Creator lives in a state of submission or islam and is thus a *"muslim"* which literally means "one who submits".

We may use the world islam with a small "i" to denote the state of submission of all creation and the word "muslim" with a small "m" to refer to all creation submitting, as they must, to the laws by which each was created.

Every created being, whether it is the sun with its life-giving light and warmth or the moon in its orbit, daffodils shooting up in the spring, golden leaves falling in the autumn to merge in the earth once more, a Christian, a Jew, a Hindu, a Buddhist, a Muslim or any other person breathing air — each, in a fundamental sense, is a muslim, that is, one who submits to the laws and norms of God.

Human beings however are different from other creation in one respect. While they must obey natural laws relating to birth, life, and death, they have been given the power of intellect which gives them the capacity to understand the universe and to shape their environment. More than that, they have been given the freedom to choose, whether to acknowledge the Creator and follow the guidance He has provided or whether to go against their inherently good nature and the purpose for which they were created.

If human beings use this freedom to acknowledge God and follow his guidance, they then live consciously in a state of Islam. They are no longer just passive muslims like the rest of creation but conscious Muslims as well.

When we speak of Islam with a capital "I", we refer to the worldview described by the Qur'an in the first instance and the totality of guidance it contains. A Muslim (with a capital "M") is one who consciously accepts this worldview and follows the guidance it contains.

The most important quality of a person

Here we come to the most important quality or characteristic of an individual.

For many people in today's world, the most important characteristic of a person is the colour of his skin, whether he is black or white or brown. For others, it is his economic, social or political situation — whether he is rich or poor, whether he is ruler or ruled, oppressor or oppressed.

For some people, the most important fact about a person is his place of birth and the language he speaks, his nation or his "tribe".

For others, a person's main characteristic is his social standing — whether he is regarded as an aristocrat, a middle-class bourgeois, or a working class individual.

The most important characteristic of a person, however, is none of these. In Islam a person's language or colour, for example, has no social, economic or political significance. They are merely signs of the creative power of God to enable people to recognise one another.

The most important characteristic of a person is whether he is a believer in God or not.

Confronted with the full reality of existence, a person in complete knowledge and awareness acknowledges his dependence on the Creator for life and guidance. Such a person is described as a believer in God.

The Arabic word for belief is *"Imaan"*. It literally means "to know", "to believe", "to be convinced beyond the least shadow of a doubt". It does not mean blind, irrational belief.

The Arabic word for a believer is *"Mu'min"*. A Mu'min is one who knows and reposes unshakeable belief in the unity of God, in His attributes, in His law and guidance revealed to the prophets and in the Divine code of just recompense, of reward and punishment (to be discussed in chapter 10). Without Imaan there can be no true and complete Islam.

On the other hand, a person who refuses to acknowledge his dependence on the Creator or indeed the existence of a Creator is described as a disbeliever.

The word for disbelief in Arabic is *"Kufr"* which literally means "to cover" or "to conceal".

A person who denies God is called a *"Kaafir"* (concealer) because he conceals by his disbelief what is inherent in his nature.

A Kaafir also implies one who is ungrateful, one who refuses to acknowledge the favours of his Lord and Creator.

To disbelieve is therefore to be unnatural and unreasonable.

All this leads us to the most important statement in Islam and in the life of a believer — the *Shahaadah*.

THE SHAHAADAH

The word "Shahaadah" in Arabic means "witness" or "testimony". The first part of the Shahaadah is expressed in just four words in Arabic: *Laa ilaaha illa Allah* which means "There is no god except God".

Laa ilaaha illa Allah is a very simple, but very profound and far-reaching declaration. It is perhaps the most oft-repeated sentence in any language that has ever been spoken. It consists of two parts: one a negation, the other an affirmation.

The first part — *laa ilaaha* (there is no other god) — negates the existence of each and any false god and condemns false worship. The word *"ilaah"* means "god" or whatever is worshipped and could refer to any being, person, matter, or concept which is taken as an object of adoration or worship whether this is done out of love or fear.

In disobedience and ignorance, people have taken the sun, the moon, trees, stones, fire, rulers, prophets, priests, rabbis, saints and other men to be gods.

But "ilaah", as the Qur'an cautions us (25: 43), could also refer to our whims and desires. To succumb or surrender totally to whims and passions is in effect to worship them and take them as gods. The feeling of pride and vanity for example could become our "god" driving us to do totally selfish acts and causing us to trample on or destroy our natural moral inclinations and responsibilities.

The Qur'an speaks of *"shirk"* or worshipping other gods with God as the most atrocious act, "a tremendous wrong" and "a great sin" which will not be forgiven. The Prophet Muhammad was asked which is the gravest sin in the sight of God and he replied, "That you should associate a partner with God (despite the fact) that He has created you." This suggests that ingratitude to God is one of the reasons why *shirk* is such a grave sin.

The second part of the Shahaadah — *illa Allah* — stresses that only Allah,

---

THE PROPHET'S SADNESS

One of Prophet Muhammad's companions, Shaddaad ibn Aws, saw his noble face filled with sadness and wondered why.

"I am afraid," said the Prophet, "of one thing for my community — *shirk* (which means worshipping others with God)!"

"Would your community commit shirk after you, Messenger of God?" asked Shaddaad.

"Shaddaad, they will not worship a sun or an idol or a stone, but they would show off their deeds to people."

"Is this ostentation or pride (a form of) worshipping others besides God?" enquired Shaddaad.

"Yes," replied the Prophet who went on to warn people of this type of shirk because "it is more imperceptible than the crawling of an ant", he said.

---

the Arabic name for the One and Only God, the Creator and Sustainer of all being, deserves to be worshipped and His guidance followed.

Tawhiid

One word in Arabic for "saying or affirming that God is One" is the word *Tawhiid*. Tawhiid is the *affirmation* that there is only One Creator who deserves our praise and gratitude and whose guidance needs to be followed for our own good and benefit. Tawhiid has two main parts:

1. to believe in and affirm that there is only One Creator and Sustainer of the universe;

2. to affirm that only the One Creator deserves to be worshipped and obeyed.

Tawhiid is the basis of the worldview of a conscious Muslim. It is the only reasonable, sound, correct and natural position for any person to adopt.

Tawhiid ushers the individual into a haven of freedom, contentment and harmony that stems from total submission to the Creator Who is Beneficent, Compassionate, Loving, Forgiving, Mighty, Just and Worthy of all Praise.

Tawhiid is also a powerful liberating force.

Tawhiid liberates mankind from the worship of false gods.

Tawhiid liberates man from the tyranny and oppression of other men, in as much as there is no obedience due to another creature which involves disobedience to the Creator.

Tawhiid, by establishing a direct link between God and man, liberates man from the power of priests and clerical intermediaries and such degrading acts as the worship of saints.

Tawhiid liberates the human mind and conscience from all superstition and fancy, from the grip of horoscopes and fortune-tellers, from magic and the sinister grip of occult practices.

Tawhiid liberates a person from self-conceit, pride and the arrogance of self-sufficiency.

Tawhiid therefore creates a unique blend of submission to God and individual freedom and dignity.

The Last Messenger

We now come to the second part of the Shahaadah or the Muslim's testimony. This is to declare that Muhammad is the messenger of God. What does this declaration really mean and why is it so important for mankind?

This declaration affirms the historical fact that:

1. someone called Muhammad, who lived in the sixth-seventh century after the Prophet Jesus, was chosen by God to provide guidance to people;
2. he was not just one in the line of God's prophets chosen to guide people but that he was the last in this line of prophets;
3. his mission was for all mankind.

There will be no other prophet after Muhammad because the message or the revelation given to him — the Qur'an — is Divine guidance completed. There is the stated guarantee that it will be preserved in the form it was revealed; it will not be changed or corrupted like previous scriptures. The Qur'an has been preserved just as it was revealed. It will continue to be man's only source of authentic guidance to truth and his abiding link with Reality.

To declare that Muhammad is the messenger of God is to declare all this and more. It is to state that Islam as a system and a way of life is both a message and a method of implementing this message. Whereas the Qur'an is the final expression of God's message and guidance to mankind, the life and example of Muhammad as the last prophet of God to humanity represents the way or method in which God's message has been and can be implemented. The importance of the Prophet's example has been stressed in the Qur'an:

"Verily in the messenger of God, you will find an excellent example for whoever hopes for God and the Last Day."

"Whatever the messenger (Muhammad) has brought for you, adopt it; and from whatever he as prohibited you, keep away from it."

And the Prophet himself said shortly before he died:

"I am leaving behind me two things which if you hold fast to them, you will never go astray — the Book of God (the Qur'an) and my example (*Sunnah*)."

Whereas the Qur'an is essentially the message of God, the Sunnah or Example of the Prophet which includes what he said, did or agreed to, forms the method of implementing this message.

Message and Method

Some of the major concerns of the mission and method of the Prophet are eloquently presented in a speech which one of his companions, Ja'far ibn abii Taalib, made to the ruler of Abyssinia in Africa. Ja'far was the spokesman of a group of Muslims who had sailed across the Red Sea and sought refuge in Abyssinia from the persecution of the pagan Makkans:

"O King," he said, "We were a people of ignorance, worshipping idols, eating the flesh of dead animals, committing abominations, neglecting our relations, doing evil to our neighbours, and the strong among us would oppress the weak.

"We were in this state when God sent to us a messenger from among us, whose descent and sincerity, trustworthiness and honesty were known to us.

"He summoned us to worship the One True God and to divest ourselves of the stones and idols we and our fathers had been worshipping in addition to God.

"He ordered us to be truthful of speech, to fulfil all that is entrusted to us, to care for our relatives, to be kind to our neighbours, to refrain from unlawful food and the consumption of blood.

"He forbade us to engage in shameful acts and false speech. He commanded us to worship God alone and to assign no partners unto Him, to pray, to pay the purifying tax and to fast.

"We deemed him truthful and we believed him, and we followed the message he brought to us from God..."

From Ja'far's speech on the mission and method of the Prophet, we see that the first thing he stressed was the worldview of Tawhiid. To be on the straight and natural way, man's first duty is to gain or regain a correct knowledge of and belief in God. From this knowledge he will come to accept the wisdom and authority of God. From this will spring correct action.

As an indication of this method of the Prophet, peace be on him, his wife 'Aa'ishah is reported as saying that the Prophet did not start by telling people not to drink wine and not to commit fornication. He started by telling them about God and the Hereafter until they had firm belief in them. It is only then he told them not to drink or commit adultery and they obeyed him. "Had he started by telling them not to drink wine or not to commit adultery, they would have said, 'We will never abandon them.' "

From Ja'far's speech, we learn that the Prophet encouraged all the natural inbuilt moral virtues such as truth, kindness, generosity, and justice. And he condemned all the naturally repugnant vices such as false speech, shamelessness, ignorance, and oppression.

There is also the testimony of Ja'far on the truthfulness of the Prophet. Both before and after he became a prophet, Muhammad had the unchallenged reputation of a man who was always truthful and trustworthy. For this he was known as *As-Saadiq* and *Al-Amiin* respectively.

In fact, mission and method fused in the Prophet since we are told by

'Aa'ishah, his wife: "His character was the Qur'an." To reject the Prophet is to reject the Qur'an and to reject the Qur'an is to reject man's only authentic source of Divine guidance.

PROPHET MUHAMMAD

"Never has a man set for himself, voluntarily or involuntarily, a more sublime aim, since this aim was superhuman: to subvert superstitions which had been interposed between man and his Creator, to render God unto man and man unto God; to restore the rational and sacred idea of divinity amidst the chaos of the material and disfigured gods of idolatry, then existing.

"Never has a man undertaken a work so far beyond human power with so feeble means, for he (Muhammad) had in the conception as well as in the execution of such a great design no other instrument than himself, and no other aid, except a handful of men living in a corner of the desert. Finally, never has a man accomplished such a huge and lasting revolution in the world...

"If greatness of purpose, smallness of means, and astounding results are the true criteria of human genius, who could dare to compare any great man in modern history with Muhammad? The most famous men created arms, laws, and empires only. They founded, if anything at all, no more than material powers which often crumbled away before their eyes. This man moved not only armies, legislations, empires, peoples and dynasties, but millions of men in one-third of the inhabited world, and more than that, he moved the altars, the gods, the religions, the ideas, the beliefs, and the souls. On the basis of a Book, every letter of which has become law, he created a spiritual nationality which blended together peoples of every tongue and of every race. He has left us — as the indelible characteristic of this Muslim nationality — the hatred of false gods and the passion for the One and Immaterial God... The conquest of one-third of the earth to his dogma was his miracle; rather it was not the miracle of a man but that of reason.

"His life, his meditations, his heroic revilings against the superstitions of his country, and his boldness in defying the furies of idolatry, his firmness in enduring them for thirteen years at Makkah, his acceptance of the role of public scorn and almost of being a victim of his fellow countrymen: all these and finally, his migration, his incessant preaching, his wars against odds, his faith in his success and his superhuman security in misfortune, his forbearance in victory, his ambition, which was entirely devoted to one idea and in no manner striving for an empire, his endless prayers, his mystic conversations with God, his death and his triumph after death — all these ... (served) to affirm conviction which gave him the power to restore a creed...

"Philosopher, orator, apostle, legislator, warrior, conqueror of ideas, restorer of rational dogmas, of a cult without images; the founder of twenty terrestrial empires and of one spiritual empire, that is Muhammad. As regards all standards by which human greatness may be measured, we may well ask, is there any man greater than he?"

(Lamartine, "Histoire de la Turquie", Paris, 1854.)

We now have some idea of the importance of the Qur'an and the example of the Prophet Muhammad in forming a valid and satisfying worldview for man in whatever time or place he may live. Since the Qur'an is the final and complete message of God to humanity and since there will be no prophet after Muhammad, it is especially important for people everywhere to discover or rediscover the meaning and relevance of the Qur'an to their lives. Whether you live in the north or the south, the east or the west, whether you live in the so-called developed and advanced world or the underdeveloped and impoverished world, whether you are a male or female, young or old, the Qur'an has a message for you. In fact, it is *the* message for you.

We have only had a glimpse of the content of the Qur'an and its purpose for man. We have seen that it stresses the Oneness of God and man's duty to acknowledge and worship God alone. We now want to look a little more closely at what the Qur'an says about the nature of man, the purpose of his life and the various choices and destinies open to him. In other words: Who are we? What are we doing here on earth? And where do we go from here?

HUMAN NATURE

According to the Qur'anic or Islamic worldview, the human being — man and woman — is created by God in a naturally good and pure state, free from sin. This is called the state of *fitrah*. A babe at birth is totally innocent. He does not bear the sin or guilt of his parents or his ancestors. He starts off with a clean slate.

> "And so, set your face steadfastly towards the (one) ever-true faith, turning away from all that is false, in accordance with the natural disposition (*fitrah* which God has instilled into man, (for) not to allow any change to corrupt what God has thus created — this is the purpose of the ever-true faith, but most people know it not." (*The Qur'an*, 30: 30)
>
> "Each child is born in a natural state of goodness (*fitrah*). It is only his parents that later turn him into a Jew, a Christian or a Magian."
> (*Hadith* or Saying of the Prophet Muhammad.)
>
> **Note:** The term "parents" in the above hadith has the wider meaning of "social influences" or "environment". The religions named were the ones best known at time of the Prophet but refer to any religion or worldview which takes a person away from his natural disposition.

Good and Evil

The human being, as we mentioned earlier, was created with an inbuilt moral sense which allows him to recognise what is true and good from what is false and evil. "Good" may be defined as whatever is pleasing to God and therefore beneficial to man. "Evil" may be defined as whatever incurs the anger of God and is therefore harmful to man. Although God created mankind in a naturally good state, He also created him with the capacity or power to do both good and evil. He gave him the freedom to choose between doing good and doing evil. The existence of good and evil therefore is closely connected with man's freedom of choice and responsibility for his actions. Evil comes from the intentions and actions of man. Evil does not come from God and God is not responsible for evil.

To preserve the pure and sinless state in which he was born, one of man's main tasks is to keep away from or ward off evil. This is why *taqwa*, which is repeatedly stressed in the Qur'an, is the most important quality a person could develop in relation to good and evil. Taqwa means to be conscious of God and to be careful of not overstepping the limits set by God. It is a defence against evil and temptation. It keeps man within the boundaries of his natural state. It is often difficult to remain within these limits because man, as we have mentioned, has the capacity or the power to go against his naturally good nature. He has a certain weakness from which all his major ills spring. This weakness is described in the Qur'an as *da'f* which also connotes "pettiness" and "narrowness of mind".

Man, if he is sensible, ought to follow his good nature and confirm this good nature with good intentions and actions. But he is often foolish and, encouraged sometimes by other foolish creatures, succumbs to his weakness and narrow-mindedness. This is expressed in pride, selfishness, hatred of others and other forms of evil. This in turn gives rise to greed, plunder, destruction, rapacious wars and other forms of injustice.

The more a person indulges in evil, the more "rust" he accumulates on his pure heart until it may even become "sealed" and impenetrable to good influences. Before this state is reached, a person may still have the opportunity to "return" to his original good nature by repentance and good deeds. This is what the Qur'anic term "*tawbah*" signifies — to return to one's original good state. "Make tawbah," is the standard Islamic advice given to one who has erred.

Freedom and responsibility

We can see then that man was not created to be selfish and destructive. He was not created in vain, to live in hopelessness and despair. He was created with the noble and natural purpose of acknowledging and worshipping God. God favoured man with the power of intellect and honoured him by making him His *khaliifah* or steward on earth. Man thus enjoys an essential nobility and greatness over other creation. Being God's khaliifah, he has a special role and responsibility to creation. Everything in the heavens and on earth has been put at the disposal of man as a trust or *amaanah*.

This trust requires man to live in harmony with the will of the Creator, in harmony with his own natural self and with the needs of the rest of creation. When man works for this universal harmony, he is a Muslim in the complete sense of the word. He is virtuous. On the other hand, when man works against this natural order, he creates discord, injustice and evil. He is vicious.

By virtue of the intellect and the freedom of choice given to him, man is thus responsible for whatever he does.

The Future Life

It is unreasonable to expect that the virtuous and the vicious in this world should be treated in the same manner by the Wise, Just and Merciful Creator. This is why it is reasonable and natural to believe in a life after death and a judgement where all will be called to account for their deeds. Man's responsibility and accountability is thus a major theme of the Qur'an.

The Qur'an asserts that a future life is both desirable and possible. If there is no future life in which the virtuous are rewarded and the vicious punished, there would be no justice and there would be no purpose in creating men with a sense of responsibility and in sending prophets to them to remind them of their responsibilities. God says in the Qur'an:

"What, does man reckon he shall be left to roam at will?"

"What, did you think that We created you only for sport and that you would not be returned to Us?"

On the possibility of a future life and of resurrection, the Qur'an argues that if it is God who created man in the first place, why should it be impossible for Him to re-create him after he dies. Life after death is therefore an important part of the worldview of Islam.

From this brief description, we can therefore see that the Qur'an presents an integrated and harmonious view of reality. It describes the nature of God, the nature of the universe and the nature of man. It sets out the various choices and destinies open to man. It deals with the nature of good and evil. It deals with the causes of an individual's happiness and discontent. It treats of societies and civilizations and points to the real reasons for their rise, decline and fall. Over and over, it encourages man to be mindful of his nature and his responsibilities and holds out the promise of eternal peace and satisfaction. Equally it warns of pain and punishment for those who transgress the limits set by God.

The Qur'an is not content merely to ask people to do good and eschew evil in a general way. It specifies the ways in which people can do good for their spiritual, physical, social, political and economic good. It specifies the ways in which they bring loss and destruction to their individual and collective existence. This is what gives Islam a certain stability. Its Ethical and Legal Code or *Shari'ah* contains not only detailed laws but fixed principles which define what is lawful and what is prohibited . All that it prohibits can be shown to be injurious to man and society and his environment. People are not left forever groping and experimenting.

Islam is capable of solving many of the problems that afflict individuals and humanity today. However, it is not just a set of solutions for problems but the natural way to all that is good in this world and the Hereafter. It is the way open and available to all men at all times who wish to learn the truth and shape all aspects of their lives by it.

"For to God belong the East and the West and His mercy is near to all who call upon Him."

TWO

YOU and YOUR CONDITION

You have been created as a single being, in a state of nature, pure and free from sin. You have been blessed with the gifts of body and mind, with talents and resources. You will be raised up as a single being to account for the use of these talents and resources — resources such as time and health and wealth.

You are unique and have an identity or personality of your own. While your roles and obligations may be different from those of others, your main purpose is the same as that of everyone else: to live life fully and to make the best use of the resources and talents which God has given you.

Obviously some people have more resources than others and there are many who have hardly enough to live on. The more you have the more you have to account for. On no soul does God place a burden greater than it can bear, the Qur'an assures us.

"SO WIDE A SCOPE"

"And now indeed you have come to Us in a lonely state, even as We created you in the first instance; and you have left behind you all that We have bestowed on you (in your lifetime)." (6: 94)

"Leave Me alone (to deal) with him whom I have created alone and to whom I have granted resources vast...and to whose life I gave so wide a scope and yet, he greedily desires that I give him yet more." (74: 11-15)

You are not created by God in vain, without aim or purpose. God has placed a trust on the human being. This trust requires you to respect and fulfil the needs of your own body, mind and soul, as well as the needs and the rights of other creation — human beings, animals and the environment as a whole. It involves living in total harmony with God's laws. How do you go about fulfilling the trust which God has placed on you?

We are concerned in this section mainly with you as an individual, the duties you owe to yourself and the rights your body and mind have upon you.

ON BECOMING MUKALLAF

From the age of puberty onwards, according to Islam, you become *mukallaf*. This means that you come under the obligation to discharge all the duties and fulfil all the rights of an adult. To keep yourself physically clean is an obligation, to work is an obligation, to refrain from lying or the consumption of alcohol is an obligation; these are no less than the obligations of maintaining honour and chastity and performing Prayer.

The concept of individual responsibility, of being mukallaf, is a most dynamic one for individual fulfilment and social harmony. All obligations, whether on you as an individual or on a community as a whole, are designed to encourage and promote the good and beautiful, and to discourage and combat the bad and reprehensible.

The values, attitudes and habits encouraged by Islam are in conformity with the natural goodness of man. The values and habits it condemns go against the grain of man's innate goodness. This you must bear in mind whenever you consider the Islamic prescriptions for your intellectual and physical, spiritual and moral, emotional and psychological development.

HADITH: ON KNOWLEDGE

"To seek knowledge is a sacred duty on every Muslim, male and female."

"He who acquires knowledge acquires a vast portion."

"If anyone goes on his way in search of knowledge, God will, thereby, make easy for him the way to Paradise."

"There are still among us those who go to consult soothsayers," observed one of the Prophet's companions to him.
"You should not go to them," advised the Prophet.
"There are some among us who are guided by omens," said the companion.
"These are things they invent in their minds and they should not be influenced by them," cautioned the Prophet.

KNOWLEDGE

The first and most crucial obligation on you as an individual is to acquire knowledge. This is so because correct knowledge must come before correct action. The opposite is also true: that partial or false knowledge could, and does, lead to wrong or disastrous conduct. Also, action should not be based on blind imitation for this is not the mark of a thinking, sensible human being.

As we shall see more and more, it is impossible for you to be a Muslim, to live according to the requirements of Islam, and at the same time live in a state of ignorance and barbarity.

Our attitude to knowledge is an important part of our worldview. How well we understand and fulfil our role as human beings will depend on:

- the type of knowledge we acquire;
- the sources we depend on and the ways in which we gain knowledge,
- the purposes for which we use our knowledge.

Categories of Knowledge

True and False

To help us know what type of knowledge to acquire, we need to know some of the main ways in which knowledge can be classified. One way is to classify knowledge into that which is true and that which is false. For example, we have seen that there is knowledge of the Creator which can be classified as true and other knowledge which must be regarded as false. It is not worthwhile to spend time acquiring false knowledge except if you want to guide someone away from what is false.

Useful and Harmful

Another helpful approach is to distinguish between knowledge that is useful for the well-being of man, his society and environment and knowledge that is harmful for the well-being of man, his society and environment. The distinction between knowledge that is useful and knowledge that is not was made by the noble Prophet, may God bless him and grant him peace.

Knowledge that is useful, beneficial and even indispensable for the well-being of man includes:

- knowledge of the Creator;
- knowledge of man and his functioning that will bring him closer to the Creator — such knowledge is related to *'ibaadah* or worship;
- knowledge of nature which has been made subservient to man. This includes knowledge of the physical sciences, the use of reason, observation and experimentation to find out how the world works, to gain a knowledge of astronomy for navigation, agriculture, animal husbandry, medical sciences, oceanography for benefitting from the seas and so on;
- knowledge of history and geography for we are told in the Qur'an to travel through the earth and see what has been the fate of earlier peoples and civilizations;
- knowledge of the role of prophets and in particular of the last and final prophet, Muhammad, upon whom be peace;

- knowledge of what is right and wrong. Such knowledge is tied to *akhlaaq* or ethics and moral values and underpins the pursuit and practice of all knowledge.

Sources of knowledge

All these various types of knowledge are stressed in the Qur'an. Some types, knowledge of the physical world for example, may be gained through the use of the intellect or reason. Other types of knowledge, for example, in relation to the nature of prophesy and the hereafter and man's destiny, can only be gained from genuine Divine revelation, in particular the Qur'an. The two main sources of knowledge, therefore, are reason and revelation.

'Ilm

The totality of all true knowledge in Islam is called *'ilm* and a person who knows is called an *'aalim*. It is significant that the word for a legal scholar in Islam or for a physicist or for a philosopher is an 'aalim. All aspects of 'ilm are interconnected.

"Among the servants of God, the only ones who truly stand in awe of Him are those who have knowledge," says the Qur'an. The knowledge referred to here of course is true knowledge — knowledge that is motivated by worship ('ibaadah) and controlled by ethical values (akhlaaq).

Knowledge, worship and ethics

Knowledge is connected in Islam with worship. The acquiring of knowledge is worship, reading the Qur'an and pondering upon it is worship, travelling to gain knowledge is worship. The practice of knowledge is connected with ethics and morality — with promoting virtue and combatting vice, enjoining right and forbidding wrong. This is called in the Qur'an: *amr bi-l ma'ruuf wa nah-y 'ani-l munkar.*

Knowledge is pursued and practiced with modesty and humility and leads to beauty and dignity, freedom and justice.

The main purpose of acquiring knowledge is to bring us closer to God. It is not simply for the gratification of the mind or the senses. It is not knowledge for its own sake or science for its own sake. Knowledge accordingly must be linked with values and goals.

One of the purpose of acquiring knowledge is to gain the good of this world, not to destroy it through wastage, arrogance and shamelessness in the reckless pursuit of higher standards of material comfort.

Another purpose of knowledge is to spread freedom and dignity, truth and justice. It is not to gain power and dominance for its own sake.

We can thus say that:

Knowledge + Power + Arrogance = Tyranny and injustice

Knowledge + Power + Ethics = Justice and freedom.

According to this, even if a Muslim by name has knowledge and power and acts arrogantly, he would be creating injustice and tyranny, in the first instance to himself. Conversely, if a person who is not Muslim but has knowledge and power and uses it according to his natural ethical inclinations, he is likely to create a state of justice and freedom.

Obviously, what we may call the reservoir of knowledge is deep and unfathomable. It is a vast and open field that is not limited to the world of nature and observation.

It is impossible for anyone to gain anything more than a fraction of what there is to know in the short span of one life. We must therefore decide what is most important for us to know and how to go about acquiring this knowledge.

Fundamental Knowledge and Professional Knowledge

For our purposes here, it may be convenient to divide knowledge into two parts:

1. Fundamental or Essential knowledge. This is knowledge which everyone must have to fulfil his natural functions as a human being, i.e. the functions of being a Muslim;

2. Professional knowledge. Knowledge which a person would need in order to earn a living. This would require knowledge of a particular discipline or skills. The choice of profession may be decided by a person's individual talents and interests or the needs of his community; both the choice of profession and the manner in which it is conducted are also shaped by aspects of fundamental knowledge.

Fundamental knowledge

1. From what we have learnt in the previous chapter, the Qur'an is our most important link with reality. You must therefore acquire a knowledge of the Qur'an and its essential guidance.

2. You need to have a knowledge of the *Sunnah* of the Prophet Muhammad. This is because his Sunnah is the practical method or path for implementing Islam. The Sunnah includes what the noble Prophet said, what he did and what he agreed to.

3. In order to really understand the Qur'an, you need to acquire a knowledge of Arabic. A sufficient knowledge of Arabic is also necessary in order to perform obligatory duties like Salaat or Prayer.

4. From the Qur'an and the Sunnah you need to have a knowledge of the Shari'ah or the Islamic Moral and Legal System which regulates man's actions. We need to know the sources of the Shari'ah, its purposes and how it categorises life's transactions, that is, what is lawful (*halaal*) and what is unlawful (*haraam*) and the principles and values that govern each.

Let us look at each of these briefly in turn.

The Qur'an

The Qur'an is now the only authentic way to come nearer and closer to your Creator. It tells you of Him, of His attributes, of how He rules over the cosmos and history, of how He relates Himself to you, and how you should relate to Him, to yourself and to your fellowmen and to every other being.

Read, understand, follow

Your obligations to the Qur'an are mainly three: to read it, to understand it and to follow it.

At the outset, you should realise and treat the process of reading, understanding and following the Qur'an as a single unified process.

Reading the Qur'an

You need to learn to read the Qur'an in its original Arabic, correctly, fluently and beautifully. At the beginning you may not understand what you read. However, reading the Qur'an knowing that it is the word of God is certainly one of the best ways of remembering Him. It will bring you closer to Him and give you psychological peace. You should read the Qur'an daily. It is better to read regularly, even if it is only a small portion, than to read long parts but only occasionally. Aim to read the whole Qur'an at least once every year in addition to reading it once during Ramadan, the month in which it was first revealed to the Prophet Muhammad.

The Qur'an should not be read in haste. 'Aa'ishah once heard a man babbling over the Qur'an and said, "He has neither read the Qur'an, nor kept silent."

You need to memorize the opening chapter, the Faatihah, since it is an essential part of Prayer, and some other portions as well. Memorizing should not be a mechanical, ritual act. Memorizing makes the Qur'an flow on your tongue, reside in your heart and dwell in your mind. "One who has nothing of the Qur'an inside him is like a desolate or ruined house," said the noble Prophet. He also said that the person whose recitation and voice is most beautiful is the one who, when you hear him recite, you think he fears God."

Understanding the Qur'an

To understand the Qur'an properly, you should aim to understand Arabic. This could be a life-long process but a start has to be made. This you may do through self-study, through joining a study circle or pursuing a course of study at an institution.

It is advisable to have a reliable and experienced teacher in this regard, to take you through the language and the specialised knowledge that is required to understand the Qur'an in some depth.

However, you need to remember that "the people who understood the Qur'an most and benefitted from it the greatest were its first hearers. They were men and women — merchants, farmers, shepherds, camel riders, nomads and labourers. They did not have at their elbows great libraries of books relating to Qur'anic sciences. Yet they were the most successful in understanding the Qur'an. This is because they took the message of the Qur'an to their heart and lived it. This approach to understanding the Qur'an ought to be and is available to every person. How much you understand depends on your sincerity and the amount of effort you put into it.

Side by side with understanding the grammar, structure and vocabulary of the Qur'an, you could benefit a great deal from the many translations that are available. You need to understand that all translations are limited and can never convey the full force, power and great richness of the original. A word like *Rabb* might be translated as Lord for example when it means also Owner, Sustainer, and Cherisher.

Following the Qur'an

As you read and understand what you read, you need to respond emotionally and in practice to the words of the Qur'an:

• When you hear God's name and His attributes, your heart should be filled with awe, gratitude, love and other appropriate feelings.

• When you read of God's messengers, your heart should have an urge to follow them, and an aversion for those who opposed them.

• When you read of the Day of Judgement, your heart should long for Paradise, and tremble at the very thought of Hell-fire.

• When you read of disobedient persons and nations who went astray and earned God's punishment, you should intensely dislike being as they were.

• When you read of the righteous whom God loves and rewards, you should be eager to be like them.

• When you read of the promises of good and honour in this world, of forgiveness and mercy, of His pleasure in the Hereafter, let your heart be filled with a desire to work for them and deserve them.

• When you read of those who are indifferent to the Qur'an, who turn away from it, who do not accept it, who do not live by it - you must fear lest you be one of them, and resolve not to be.

• And when you hear the summons to obey God and strive in His way, you should be determined to respond and achieve the peace and happiness that come from responding.

HADITH: ATTITUDES TO THE QUR'AN

"Many of the hypocrites in my Ummah will be from among the readers of the Qur'an."

"He is not a true believer in the Qur'an who treats as permissible what it has prohibited."

LAMENT OF THE QUR'AN

As an ornament do they adorn me,
Yet they keep me and sometimes kiss me.
In their celebrations they recite me,
In disputes they swear by me,
On shelves do they securely keep me
Till another celebration or dispute, when
they need me.

Yes, they read me and memorize me,
Yet only an ornament am I.
My message lies neglected, my treasure
untouched,
The field lies bare, where blossomed once
true glory.
Wrong is the treatment that I receive
So much to give have I, but none is there to
perceive.

Mahir-ul-Qadri

The Qur'an is above all a guide to those who are prepared to keep their naturally pure state intact, who are vigilant and act to save themselves from the harm that comes from living against God's will. Such people are called in Arabic the *muttaqiin*–those who have taqwa or deep consciousness and awareness of God. Taqwa has been described as the single most important quality of a person mentioned in the Qur'an. Those who possess it live the natural way, the Qur'anic way.

The Sunnah

The word Sunnah means method, example or path. It refers to what the noble Prophet said, did and agreed to.

You need to study the Sunnah, not from the point of view of merely verifying dates and events in his life and the lives of his companions, but to see how beautiful an example the Prophet set in all the full and varied aspects of his life. As you follow the course of his life, you cannot fail to see his complete trust and dependence on God, his truthfulness and sincerity, his constant devotion and struggle to make the word of God supreme, his strength and wisdom, his compassion and concern for the human condition. So noble was his person and example that his companions loved him more than themselves. To so love the Prophet and desire to follow his example should be our main purpose in studying his Sunnah.

Because Muhammad, peace be on him, is the last messenger of God, his life and works have a validity beyond his time. The Prophet's Sunnah emphasises the natural needs and dispositions of every human being. The Qur'an makes this clear:

"He the Prophet enjoins on them that which they themselves sense as right, and forbids them that which they themselves sense as wrong. He makes lawful for them all good things and prohibits for them only the foul, and relieves them of their undue burden and of the many shackles that used to be on them."
(7:157)

At a straightforward level, we need to know the Sunnah to learn how to perform the major duties like Salaat, Fasting, and Hajj. To such acts of worship, there can be no addition to or subtraction from the Sunnah. Moreover, without the Prophet's detailed instructions and example, we would not be able to follow the Qur'an in all respects.

For example, the Qur'an commands us to perform Salaat or Prayer. The Prophet shows us how and commanded: "Pray as you see me praying." There can be no addition to or subtraction from the manner of performing the Prayer.

The Qur'an commands us to perform the Hajj and to experience its benefits. The Prophet shows us how to perform the Hajj and commanded: "Take from me your rites in performing the pilgrimage." The pilgrimage must therefore be performed as he did it with only the variations and allowances as he permitted.

The Qur'an tells us that Muslims are those who use consultation to manage their affairs. The Sunnah shows how this was and can be done.

The Qur'an commanded us to do good for God loves those who do good. While it gives many ways of doing good, the Sunnah of the Prophet provides more detailed guidance on doing good and the practice of charity or *sadaqah*.

There are certain things that the Prophet did which were incidental to the place or the time in which he lived. The fact that he, for example, often wore a headcovering or rode a camel, does not mean that all Muslims must wear turbans or ride camels. But when he insisted that the clothes a person wears must be clean and must cover certain parts of the body, or that he must feed, water, rest and treat animals with kindness, this is his Sunnah which must be followed.

We therefore need to know from the Sunnah not only what the Prophet did, but why he did it and how he did it.

Because the Sunnah is valid for all times to come, there is scope provided in it for dealing with issues that people at the time of the Prophet did not face. When the Prophet appointed his companion, Mu'aadh ibn Jabal, as a judge in the Yaman , before Mu'aadh set out, the Prophet asked him:

"According to what will you judge?"
"According to the Book of God."

"And if you find nothing therein?"
"According to the Sunnah of the Prophet of God."

"And if you find nothing therein?"
"Then I will exert myself to form my own judgement."

The Prophet was pleased and said:
"Praise be to God Who has guided the messenger of His Prophet to that which pleases His Prophet."

From the above dialogue, you can see that you may form your own judgement on an issue only if there is no relevant text in the Qur'an and the Sunnah and only if your judgement does not go against the Qur'an and the Sunnah. When these conditions are met, you are expected to use your judgement and initiative.

The Hadith

What the Prophet said also forms part of his Sunnah. The Hadith are the sayings of the Prophet. Knowledge of the authentic sayings of the Prophet must form part of the essential knowledge of all Muslims. The Hadith is a vast storehouse of guidance on all aspects of life and reflect the rich and varied life of the Prophet himself.

You may start with a small collection like Nawawi's *Forty Hadith* and go on to other major compilations like those of Al Bukhari and Muslim who were two of the great scholars of Hadith. Some of these compilations are now available in computer databases which make it easy to access Hadith on a particular subject.

The study of Hadith require specialist knowledge not only of the text and the circumstances in which they were spoken but also of the transmitters of hadith. This is a highly developed science which is concerned with the soundness of Hadith. In every Muslim community there is need for people to study this science.

THE SHARI'AH

From the Qur'an and the Sunnah, the Islamic Moral and Legal System has been formulated. Each person needs to know:
• the sources of the Shari'ah

- the purposes of the Shari'ah
- the basic principles of the Shari'ah.

Sources of the Shari'ah

The Shari'ah is derived above all from the Qur'an and Sunnah. We have also seen that when required the Sunnah sanctions the use of one's own judgement and initiative in reaching decisions. This use of individual reason and judgement is known as *ijtihaad* and is one of the factors which give the Shari'ah its essential flexibility and dynamism.

The Shari'ah also recognizes local customary law of any place so long as it is not in conflict with the Qur'an and the Sunnah.

The purposes of the Shari'ah

The main purpose of the Shari'ah is to realise and secure the general good or the interests (*masaalih*) of people by promoting their welfare as individuals and as a collective body and keeping harm and injury away from them. This it seeks to do, in order of priority, by:

1.   guaranteeing their 'vital needs' *(duruuriyaat)*
2.   catering for their 'requirements' or exigencies *(haajiyaat)*
3.   allowing for 'betterment', enhancement or improvements *(tahsiiniyaat)* in the quality of their life.

An example of a vital need is housing, to protect people from heat or cold and provide for sleep and rest.

An example of a requirement is windows in the house to allow for light and privacy.

An example of an improvement or enhancement is furniture or beds to make life easy and comfortable.

'Requirements' and 'improvements' can only be catered for if vital needs are met or satisfied. If a vital need is threatened then a lesser need can be dispensed with. For example, under normal circumstances a person must keep his or her private parts covered. Keeping your private parts covered is important for the enhancement of your life and conduct but it may not be absolutely vital for the preservation of health and life. If, therefore, a person has to have medical treatment which is a vital need and which requires his or her private parts to be examined, the vital need takes precedence. In such a situation, the Shari'ah allows a person to uncover his or her private parts to the view of a medical professional.

Vital needs

The vital needs which the Shari'ah is concerned to protect are those on which the life of man depend. If any of these needs are threatened, corruption, disorder and injustice will result in individual and collective life. These vital needs, in order of priority, are five:

1. the *Diin* or the natural system of beliefs and way of life of Islam;
2. the life or *nafs* of the individual human being and of the human species;
3. the mind or the *'aql* of the individual;
4. the honour and chastity or *'ird* of the individual;
5. wealth or property.

The protection of each of these is necessary for the welfare of individuals and society.

By Diin is meant the totality of beliefs, practices and laws by which Islam regulates the relationship between man and his Creator and between man and man. Preservation of Diin implies keeping it free from deviation and error, inviting others to accept and live according to it, and defending it from hostile forces.

By the preservation of life is meant measures to preserve the human species in the best possible way and this includes laws relating to marriage and reproduction. It also includes providing the vital needs of food, drink, clothing, shelter and security. It also includes laws relating to the prohibition of suicide and abortion (except when the mother's life is in danger) and the need for just retaliation against those who commit murder.

The safeguarding of the mind is the concern of such provisions of the Shari'ah which forbid the consumption of alcohol and all intoxicating substances.

Preserving honour and chastity is the goal of such Shari'ah laws which punish sexual relations outside marriage and false accusations against people who are chaste.

By the preservation of wealth is meant the laws in the Shari'ah which encourage people to work and earn a living lawfully and which prohibit exploitation and injustice.

Requirements or exigencies

These pertain to laws of the Shari'ah which provide ease in case of difficulty and which eliminate or reduce hardship from people's lives. For example, a person is not required to fast in the month of Ramadaan if he is ill or on a journey. In business transactions, the Shari'ah has allowed a variety of contracts and trading practices. It allows any local custom in meeting needs so long as it is not otherwise prohibited. It allows divorce in case of need. Such allowances receive sanction in the verses of the Qur'an:

"God has not created any hardship over you in matters of religion."

"God desires ease for you. He does not desire hardship for you."

Moreover, the noble Prophet said:

"I was sent with the true and tolerant Religion."

Improvements or Enhancements

These pertain to all the laws of the Shari'ah that relate to improving the quality of human life, conduct and morals and beautifying the conditions under which life is lived.. These include laws pertaining to cleanliness of the body, clothes, and environment, the covering of the private parts or *'awrah*, the method of getting rid of impurities, the performance of extra acts of worship such as voluntary fasting and charity and so on.

The above categories relate to the general objectives or concerns of the Shari'ah. From these, we can see that the concerns of the Shari'ah are not only with aspects of personal religion or worship but deal with all aspects of life. Moreover, the Shari'ah is not just 'law' as many understand the term; it is concerned with morals and worship as well.

Specific guidance and basic principles

In order to realise its objectives, more detailed guidance is then provided in the Shari'ah by dividing all life's transactions into that which is lawful and that which is prohibited. In many cases, this guidance is explicit for Islam is not vague and it does not simply ask people to be good and morally upright and to keep away from evil, and then leaves them to their own devices. More than this, it provides basic principles which give the Islamic system a strength and a flexibility to deal with new problems and situations and which help to promote goodness, justice and fairness at all times.

The LAWFUL AND THE PROHIBITED

All a person's activities and transactions are divided into two main categories according to the Shari'ah: the *Halaal* and the *Haraam*.

Halaal literally means that which is lawful or permissible. All that is beneficial for an individual, his society and the environment comes under the category of halaal.

The basic principle in Islam is that every act or transaction is allowed unless it is prohibited. This principle emphasises growth and development rather than meanness, hardness and constriction.

Haraam means that which is unlawful or prohibited. Only that which is destructive for a person as an individual, his society and his environment — destructive in the physical, mental and spiritual senses — is regarded as haraam or forbidden.

Categories of Halaal

Of the things that are halaal, you need to know what is *fard* or compulsory, *mustahabb* or recommended, *mubaah* or tolerated, *makruuh* or disliked.

What is compulsory is so because its neglect renders a person blameworthy. For example, to deliberately abandon the compulsory daily Salaat is to rebel against the wisdom of the Qur'an and the Prophet.

One classification of knowledge relating to what is compulsory is the distinction between *fard 'ayn* and *fard kifaayah*.

Fard 'Ayn is a duty imposed on the individual, like the daily Salaat or the payment of Zakaat if he or she is eligible. Noone can do this duty for you. If you neglect it, you alone are blameworthy.

Fard kifaayah is a duty imposed on the whole Muslim community. If this duty is performed by a few in the community, it is considered discharged. If it is not performed by anyone, then the whole community is blameworthy.

Mustahabb refers to those acts which are recommended in the Sunnah of the Prophet. The doing of such acts — such as smiling to your fellow Muslim or using the toothbrush regularly and before Prayer — is rewarded while not doing them is not punished.

Mubaah or tolerated refers to those acts which may be done but which do not attract either reward or merit punishment.

Makruuh refers to that which is detested but allowed and there is no punishment for it. Something like divorce is detested but allowed only in the last resort as the least of other evils.

Haraam and the principles governing it

A person needs to know what is haraam and the principles governing it:

- What has been declared haraam is because of its impurity and harmfulness.
- What leads to haraam is itself haraam;
- What is haraam in large quantities is also haraam in small quantities.
- Good intentions are not an excuse for indulging in haraam activities. A good end does not justify a wrong means in Islam.
- What is haraam is prohibited to everyone alike.
- In case of necessity, the haraam may be allowed but only so long as the necessity lasts.
- It is unlawful to declare something which is lawful haraam and it is haraam to declare what is unlawful to be lawful.

The doing of anything that is haraam is punishable.

Doubtful areas

A person needs to know that there are areas where there is no precise pronouncements in the Shari'ah. It is better to avoid these doubtful areas in as much as it may lead in the end to what is unlawful. One should not also place oneself in situations of temptation or go near to what is prohibited.

More basic principles

In addition to the categories mentioned above and the principles governing them, there are a number of principles for understanding and applying the Shari'ah under varying circumstances which make it a sound and effective problem-solving system at all times. Some of these principles are:

1. *Actions are judged according to intentions.* This principle distinguishes between conduct based on knowledge and sincerity on the one hand and mere habitual actions, conscious wrongdoing or hypocritical behaviour on the other. It applies to the administration of justice in a Muslim community or state as well as to the judging of deeds in the Hereafter. It is the basis for judging accountability. For example, a person is not accountable if he is forced to say or do something like renouncing faith or drinking wine under duress. He is not accountable if he does something in ignorance, like selling a defective article without knowing it is defective. He is not accountable if he forgets, like drinking water unintentionally during fasting: this does not break the fast.

2. *Harm or injury must not be allowed to exist or persist.* This rule for example gives a buyer the right to return defective goods to the seller. It also allows the killing of harmful pests. It allows for punishments to be meted out to criminals. Some of these punishments are fixed. Others are discretionary and involve censure in public.

3. *What is harmful cannot be used to combat another harm.* For example, a person is not allowed to prevent flooding of his land by flooding another person's land.

4. *The need to stop a particular act, which may on its own be lawful, in order to prevent general hardship or injury.* For example, refusing to permit the setting up of a foundry or a blacksmith's shop in the midst of shops trading in clothes; the compulsory selling of food which is hoarded by one person but which is needed by people;

5. *Adopting the lesser of two evils to avoid the more serious of the two.* If a person wants to perform Salaat and is sick and cannot make wuduu, or cannot cover his 'awrah, or cannot face the Ka'bah, he must still perform Salaat because not fulfilling these conditions of Salaat is less serious than abandoning the Salaat.

6. *Meeting vital needs allows what is normally forbidden.* This allows the eating of forbidden foods like pork if life is threatened. As soon as proper food becomes available, the allowance is cancelled. This principle has also been used by some scholars to allow the buying of a house in which to live — a vital need — with a loan obtained on interest which is normally forbidden. However, the attempt should be made to come out of what is forbidden as soon as possible. Also, if non-interest funds become available, this allowance is cancelled.

7. *Hardship gives rise to relaxation of laws.* Certain laws, for example laws relating to Salaat and fasting, are relaxed for persons who are sick or travelling.

From these and other principles, it could be seen that there is nothing in the Shari'ah that imposes undue hardship and difficulty on people.

It is also appropriate to emphasise again that there is nothing in the Shari'ah that is not suited to or in conformity with human nature. The concerns of the Shari'ah, its basic principles, its detailed laws and sanctions are all meant to create the conditions under which man can preserve and safeguard all that is noble and just from all that is false, vicious and destructive.

The search for knowledge

It is important to remember that knowledge is the not the preserve of a priestly class, a group of 'ulamaa', the intelligentsia or any body of intellectuals. There are of course people who have acquired more knowledge than others and we need to go in search of these people or their writing and benefit from them. We should never let our admiration or reverence for such persons lead us into following any obnoxious practices.

It is also important to remember that the search for knowledge is a life-long process and does not end with the receiving of a certificate.

KNOWLEDGE IS SOUGHT – IT DOES NOT JUST COME

In spite of his youth, 'Abdullah ibn 'Abbaas, a cousin of the Prophet, became one of the most learned companions. He was only thirteen when the Prophet died.

The collection and study of hadith was one of his many specialisations. It is said that he committed to memory about 1,660 sayings of the Prophet which have been authenticated.

Whenever he heard of someone who knew a hadith which he did not know, he would quickly go to him and record it. He would closely scrutinise whatever he heard and check it against other reports. He would go to as many as thirty companions to verify a single matter.

'Abdullah described what he once did on hearing that a companion of the Prophet knew a hadith unknown to him:

"I went to him during the time of the afternoon siesta and spread my cloak in front of his door. The wind blew dust on me (as I sat waiting for him). If I wished, I could have sought his permission to enter and he would certainly have given me permission. But I preferred to wait on him so that he could be completely refreshed. Coming out of his house and seeing me in that condition he said:

'O cousin of the Prophet! What's the matter with you? If you had sent for me I would have come to you.'

'I am the one who should come to you, for knowledge is sought – it does not just come,' I said. I asked him about the hadith and learnt from him."

Professional Knowledge

It is important for a Muslim to acquire the knowledge of a skill in order to obtain a livelihood.

The more skills you acquire, the better it would be for your freedom of choice and independence. It may be good in this context to remember the saying of the noble Prophet: "Place no hope on what is at the hands of men." It would be better for your community as well.

If a particular community lacks essential expertise in any given area, it becomes fard kifaayah or compulsory on the community to get people trained in that particular field. If a community needs more farmers, or more doctors or more teachers or more munitions manufacturers, it should create the facilities for the training and employment of such skills.

In pursuing professional knowledge and skills, it is important to realise that the use of any technologies should be subjected to the requirements of what is halaal and haraam. If nuclear arms, chemical or biological weapons are deemed to be haraam because their use would inevitably involve the killing of innocents and non-combatants which is forbidden in the Sunnah, then such knowledge and skills would not be acquired.

Intellectual Pursuits

"Whoever is not concerned with the situation of Muslims is not one of them," said the noble Prophet.

Over and above knowledge that is necessary for individual practices and needs, the Muslim needs to have knowledge of the times in which he lives.

We now live in a complex and difficult world and are dominated by forces — systems of knowledge, technologies and economics — which have marginalised Islam and Muslims, and created much destruction and havoc in the world.

Muslims have a duty to themselves and to others to know the contemporary world intimately, to be able to analyse it using principles and concepts from the Islamic worldview, from the Qur'an and the Sunnah, and to offer alternatives for the future direction of man.

If you have the talents, the capacity and the resources, and especially if you are in position of authority and responsibility, it is your duty to take on the challenge of contemporary knowledge. This applies particularly if you are a student or teacher at an institution of higher learning. The Muslim ummah and indeed mankind as a whole have a right upon you.

There are many principles and concepts in the Qur'an and the Sunnah which need to be looked at anew and applied to contemporary human needs. When, for example, the Qur'an speaks of man's *khilaafah* (stewardship) and *amaanah* (trust and responsibility), it is important to ask how these concepts shape our attitude to politics, to economic development, to the environment and ecological balance. When, for example, the Prophet says that "Purity is half of faith" and "Cleanliness is part of faith" — how does this affect health and sanitation requirements of people living in overcrowded cities and slums in many parts of the world? When the Prophet warned that non-combatants should not be killed in a war, how do we allow the use of bombs and the growth of the nuclear armament industry?

Such knowledge and strategies to bring about a better, more just, more caring, and in the end a safer world for ourselves and generations to come may be classified as fard kifaayah on the Muslim community. If such knowledge is not pursued and put into action by scholars and rulers, the whole ummah would be held to be blameworthy. The task before you is not merely the collection of data and the elaboration of theories. It is the task of developing communication networks from the family and neighbourhood to global levels and disseminating this knowledge with such vigour that the present dominance of what is false or *baatil* is eclipsed and marginalised. The tendency of many scholars to concentrate almost exclusively on minor issues and on certain rituals is a sign of fatal escapism.

There are other aspects of knowledge, of the study of man and the universe, which are worthy of continuous research. Man needs always to reflect on and delve more into the "signs" of God and join the ranks of those "steeped in knowledge" according to the Qur'an. If you have the talents and resources such pioneering research at the frontiers of knowledge must be part of your vocation. Such research is not to be determined solely by the needs of commercial corporations or arms manufacturers, for example, but should lead to a greater awareness of the power and wisdom of God and your utter dependence on Him.

YOUR PHYSICAL NEEDS

"Your body has a right over you," said the noble Prophet to one of his companions who was keen on observing long periods of fast.

On the other hand, for example, he said, "No man fills a vessel which is worse than his stomach. Sufficient for the son of Adam are a few mouthfuls to keep his back straight."

From these two sayings, we can see that Islam is the moderate or balanced way. Islam prohibits you from neglecting your body or from harming it by over-indulgence. Moreover, according to the Prophet, "A strong believer is better than a weak one, but in each is good." Islam requires you to keep a strong and healthy body by:

- proper eating and drinking habits
- exercise, work and activity
- proper sleep and rest
- cleanliness and personal hygiene.

Eating and drinking

While you are encouraged to eat of the good and wholesome things which God has provided, the Prophet stressed that overeating and gluttony are harmful. We now know that overeating and resulting obesity give rise to many diseases. If you are afflicted by this problem, fasting is recommended . The Prophet recommends natural foods like milk and honey, honey being at once a laxative and a treatment for diarrhoea. Excessive abstinence from food is also discouraged since it leads to weakness and incapacity.

All harmful food and drink are prohibited. Chief among these are alcoholic drinks. In addition to consuming alcohol, you are forbidden to make, sell, buy, give or even transport the stuff. We know the harmful effects of alcohol consumption on the body and the mind and its destructive impact on home and society. It has been well said that when Islam prohibits alcohol it functions as a science, not as a religion as the term is often understood.

The abuse of drugs such as hashish and cocaine is also prohibited because of their harmful effects on the mind. Some scholars also regard smoking tobacco as haraam because of its harmful effects on the lungs and on health generally and because it involves a waste of wealth or *israaf* which is condemned in the Qur'an.

The prohibition on the consumption of blood requires you, in preparing animals for food, to perform clinical slaughter or *dhabh* in a particular manner to allow for the maximum drainage of blood from meat tissue. Pork and pork products are also prohibited.

Other things which have been declared haraam in Islam, like marriage within the prohibited categories, all have a bearing on the health of the individual.

Exercise, work and activity

The Qur'an commends work and activity and frowns on inactivity and sluggishness. Those who strive and exert themselves *(mujaahiduun)* are better than those who remain idle or indolent. The Prophet himself prayed for God's protection against laziness and incompetence. He stressed regular physical activity and exercise — horseriding, swimming, archery, wrestling and running. He himself was a good rider and a good wrestler. He even had races with his wife. When we look at his life and consider the thousands of kilometres he travelled all over peninsular Arabia, which is often a harsh and mountainous terrain, we cannot but be impressed by the extraordinary physical fitness of the man.

Nonetheless, it is important to remember that physical fitness and strength is not an end in itself and the body is not venerated and worshipped, neither in life nor in art. "God does not look to your bodies and appearances but to your hearts and deeds," said the noble Prophet.

It is important to point out that many of the devotions in Islam like Salaat and Hajj require a body that is physically fit.

Proper sleep and rest

Sleep and what happens during sleep remain very much a mystery to human beings. What we do know is that adequate rest and sleep are of vital importance for reactivating and strengthening body functions and for mental and emotional stability.

Partly because of the unnatural life-style that many people now adopt, sleeplessness or insomnia has become a major problem. This often leads not only to physical incapacity but also to mental disorders. To deal with the problem of sleeplessness, some people have resort to sleeping tablets. The dependence on drugs and tranquilizers then becomes part of such persons' lifestyle. A temporary cure then becomes a permanent problem.

Sleeplessness can also be caused by unusual or unhealthy sleeping hours. Many people now regularly go to bed very late at night because of such habits as late television viewing. They then remain asleep late into the day. This then has a further knock-on effect making it difficult to sleep early at night. The night according to the Qur'an is naturally made by God "as a cloak" and "for resting" while the day is naturally made "for living". However, it also describes the late hours of night (after some sleep has been taken) as well suited for contemplation and clarity of thought.

'YOUR EYES HAVE A RIGHT OVER YOU'

The young 'Abdullah, son of the famous 'Amr ibn al-'Aas, and a companion of the Prophet, became known for his extreme self-denial. The Prophet came to know of the punishing routine he had set himself and asked him:

"Has it not been said that you fast during the day and stay awake at night, O 'Abdullah?"

"Yes, O Messenger of God," he replied.

"Do not do so," cautioned the Prophet. "Fast and break your fast. Stay up (for some time) and sleep (for some time). Your body certainly has a right over you. Your eyes have a right over you. Your wife has a right over you. Your visitors have a right over you."

At the other extreme of insomnia is too much sleep which is also bad as it leads to sluggishness and inactivity.

To sleep well, a person should be able to relax. Relaxation comes from having a feeling of satisfaction and contentment and an attitude of equanimity in facing problems of life. All this can come from having true faith in God. The Prophet's daughter, Faatimah, once requested him to provide her with a servant because both she and her husband were overworked. He replied by saying to her:

"Shall I tell you of something that is better for you than a servant? When you go to bed, say SubhaanAllah (Glory be to God) thirty three times; say Alhamdulillaah (All praise is due to God) thirty three times; and say Allahu Akbar (God is Most Great) thirty four times at the time of going to your bed."

Thus, an attitude of mind which is characterised by contentment and satisfaction in God's wisdom and grace; a life-style that is not motivated by the desire to possess more and more material things and which appreciates the wisdom of the Prophet's saying that "the little but sufficient is better than the abundant but alluring''; a life-style that is free from the burdens of debt and unnatural behaviour like lying and deceit; a life-style that generally uses the day for earning a living and the night for resting—this is the type of life-style that is likely to ensure peace of mind, reduce agitation and worry and make for restful sleep and happiness.

The noble Prophet has given directions on how to prepare for sleep. He recommended recitations from the Qur'an (like the Aayat al-Kursi, 2: 255) and certain supplications on going to bed and on waking up which all serve to make us conscious of our Creator, of the purpose of life and of the reality of death. He recommended sleeping on the right side and this is now known to help in the processes of proper respiration and digestion. He also recommended performing wuduu before going to sleep. All this adds up to a general condition of cleanliness, relaxation and awareness of reality.

Cleanliness and personal hygiene

There is no doubt that cleanliness and personal hygiene form a major part of bodily health. "Purity is half of the faith," and "Cleanliness is part of the faith," declared the noble Prophet and stressed the importance of regular baths, ablutions and the use of the toothbrush. This is all the more remarkable in an environment where water was at a premium.

Cleanliness and personal hygiene are maintained as part of religious devotion and as part of a natural daily routine. A Muslim is required to wash his private parts after going to the toilet. He is required to be in a state of *wuduu*, for wuduu is a condition for Salaat and Salaat is performed five times a day. Wuduu cleans parts of the body which are not normally cleaned such as the nostrils and behind the ears. *Ghusl* is a particular method of having a bath. It involves first of all pereneal toilet or washing the private parts, which confirms the clinical principle of washing the dirty parts first and then the cleaner. This is then followed by wuduu and then the washing of the entire body from head to toe. Ghusl is compulsory on every Muslim, male and female on attaining puberty; it is also compulsory after sexual contact between spouses, after menstruation and after the emission of semen. It is recommended before the congregational prayer on Friday and at least once in seven days by the Prophet.

Cleanliness remains the chief factor inhibiting the spread of disease. Wherever you live and no matter how poor you are, Islam requires of you to remain clean and develop habits of cleanliness.

All that has been mentioned concerning eating habits, physical exercise, rest and sleep, fasting, and personal hygiene point to a sophisticated system of balance and an emphasis on preventive medicine. For major ailments and infectious diseases, the search for curative medicines is encouraged. The noble Prophet is reported to have said: "For every disease there is a cure," thus providing motivation and optimism for medical researchers.

One of the major problems of our age is sexually transmitted diseases.

These can have a disastrous effect on bodily health. The regulation of sexual behaviour in Islam—its firm stand against adultery and fornication, homosexuality, prostitution and promiscuity—works against the spread of such diseases.

Mental health also affects bodily health. Worry, anxiety, loneliness and despair are mental states which not only affect mental health but may give rise to physical disorders like migraine, high blood pressure and digestive disorders. Illnesses in which disturbance of the mind causes physical changes in the body are referred to as psychosomatic diseases.

Mental illnesses and disorders in themselves are among the most disturbing and perplexing of illnesses and often elude treatment. There is no doubt, however, that belief in God, in His knowledge, wisdom and grace should serve to reduce worry and anxiety. Optimism, reflected in a cheerful and smiling face, is part of the normal outlook of the believer who knows that life is not vain and futile. Even when confronted with difficulties and ordeals, the believer does not abandon God but finds strength in the quality of *sabr* or patience and steadfastness which He recommends:

"And bear with patient constancy whatever befalls you for that is firmness of purpose in the conduct of affairs." (31: 17)

The capacity to enjoy and endure whatever an existence has to offer are all part of the meaning of Islam or submission. These should serve to banish despair and frustration.

"Despair not and grieve not, for you are bound to rise high if indeed you are believers," says the Qur'an (3: 139).

"There is no fear on them and neither do they grieve," is how the Qur'an often describes believers.

MORAL AND SPIRITUAL DEVELOPMENT

Bodily needs normally come before other needs of man. This is why the Prophet warned that poverty may lead to unbelief or why a person who steals food while facing starvation is not to be punished according to the Shari'ah. However, as we have seen, physical strength and fitness is not an end in itself. Man has other basic and crucial needs.

Side by side with looking after his bodily needs, man has the need to keep his *imaan* (faith and awareness) alive and to strengthen it. He must strive to preserve and develop his innate goodness. Quite clearly, it is not enough for you to say, "I believe" and expect that your moral sense will remain sharp. It is easy to be forgetful and become engrossed in the business and cares of life. Through neglect or even deliberate disobedience, the moral sense can also become so blunt that the ugliness of vice may seem beautiful and attractive. There is need then for a code or pattern of behaviour that is a natural outcome of your beliefs, a code or pattern that will not leave you to grope or wander about aimlessly.

Throughout the day and throughout the year, Islam provides such a pattern of behaviour and the institutions of control and dynamism to strengthen the innate goodness of the human being and keep him on the straight way. The most important institution in this regard is the Salaat.

Salaat

There is no word in English to translate Salaat. It is not merely "prayer" in the limited sense of the random turning to God in invocation and supplication. The Arabic word for supplication is *du'aa*. For the sake of convenience and to denote its special character we refer to Salaat in this book as "Prayer" with a capital "P" but usually we would use the term Salaat itself.

Salaat may only be performed in a prescribed form and under certain conditions as assigned to it by the Prophet Muhammad. Any change in its form nullifies it.

Salaat must be preceded by ablutions. "The key to Paradise is Salaat and the key to Salaat is wuduu or ablution."

The compulsory Salaat is connected to definite times of day — between dawn and sunrise, early afternoon, mid-afternoon, sunset, and night. It is also connected to a fixed geographical direction — the Ka'bah in Makkah. Salaat is thus bound to nature and its movements, to space and time. It creates a natural rhythm in one's lifestyle. We may note that the development of astronomy among Muslims was conditioned by the need for accurate definition of space and time. Again you can see in this the truth that it is impossible to be a Muslim and live in a state of ignorance and barbarity.

Salaat needs to be performed on time. It should not be delayed or abandoned deliberately. The abandoning of Salaat puts a person outside the pale of Islam.

Salaat consists of units or rakaats. Each rakaat consists of the pronouncement of *Allahu Akbar* (God is Most Great), of the Opening Surah of the Qur'an, of praising and glorifying God and invoking His blessings on Prophet Muhammad and on His righteous servants in specific terms. All words in the Salaat are always recited in Arabic.

Salaat also consists of precise bodily postures - standing, bowing, prostrating and sitting. The sight of a person in a crouched position with his forehead, hands, knees and toes touching the ground may sometimes be perplexing and amusing to a non-Muslim. But the postures of Salaat is a vivid indication of man's relation to his Creator — a relation of uprightness, reverence, submission and gratitude.

In the midst of your daily activities and preoccupations, Salaat comes as a regular reminder of your relationship with God, your place in the scheme of things, your responsibilities and your ultimate goal. Through the prescribed reading of the Qur'an in Salaat, you link yourself constantly with the Source of all creation and you stand firmly within the worldview of Islam. Salaat requires you to recite the Faatihah at least seventeen times in the day.

Salaat keeps your moral sense sharp and prevents it from being blunted and corrupted. It is a protection or an insulation from obnoxious and destructive acts and practices. This is clearly stated in the Qur'an: "Salaat indeed prevents a person from shameful and reprehensible deeds." (29: 45)

Salaat is a regular means of purifying both body and soul. The ablutions before the Prayer with fresh water act as a refresher and cleanser. The Salaat itself, properly performed, purifies the soul of arrogance and hypocrisy, shirk and kufr. The Prophet, peace be on him, likened a person who regularly performs Salaat to a person who washes himself regularly in a stream of clean running water five times a day.

Salaat leads to success or felicity in this world and the next. This is the meaning of the resounding phrases in the *Adhan* or Call to Prayer: *Hayya ala-s Salaat, Hayya ala-l Falaah* — Come to Prayer, Come to Felicity. It brings mental satisfaction and emotional fulfilment.

Despite all these possible benefits, there is a risk of Salaat becoming merely repetitive, a series of motions and the uttering of set phrases in which the heart and mind are not present. This is a risk which you should guard against by spending some more time in preparing for Salaat, for example by sitting quietly before the Salaat reading the Qur'an. One way of focussing the mind on Salaat is to perform each Salaat, in the words of the Prophet, as if it is your last Prayer, your farewell Prayer on this earth.

Fasting

Every year, for one complete lunar month — the ninth month in the Islamic calendar, you as an adult Muslim are required to fast. From dawn to sunset in the month of Ramadaan, you are required to refrain from all food and drink and sexual relations with your spouse. If you are sick or on a journey you are allowed not to fast but you must make up for it by fasting the same number of days missed during Ramadaan.

The main purpose of fasting is described in the Qur'an as "so that you may attain taqwa or God-consciousness". Fasting is thus yet another instrument for bringing us closer to our natural state, our state of fitrah and for cleansing this state from the dross of any disobedience and corruption.

"Fasting is a shield," said the noble Prophet so simply and eloquently. And he also said: "Whoever spends the month of Ramadaan in complete faith and self-rectification, his previous sins will be forgiven."

Ramadaan is a month of heightened devotion. In it, Salaat is performed with greater intensity. There are extra Sunnah Salaat on Ramadaan nights called *Salaat at-Tarawiih*. In the last ten days of Ramadaan, some retreat to the mosque to perform *I'tikaaf*, a period of intense reflection and devotion, seeking guidance and forgiveness, and reading the Qur'an.

Ramadaan is a great opportunity to get closer to the blessed guidance of the Qur'an which was revealed in this month. Ramadaan is also called the month of the Qur'an.

The month of Ramadaan is an opportunity to develop qualities of endurance and self-restraint, to control anger and a fiery or malicious tongue. It is an opportunity to fine tune the body and shed it of obesity and sloth, and to benefit from any therapeutic effects fasting may have.

Ramadaan is a time to awaken compassion and solidarity with others and in particular with the poor. We are urged to be more liberal in giving during Ramadaan and are required at the end of fasting to give *Sadaqatu-l Fitr*, an amount to enable all to share in the spirit of warmth, affection and brotherhood.

Ramadaan is above all an opportunity to reorient oneself to the Creator and the natural path of goodness and God-consciousness.

Fasting in Islam is in no way related to penance for sins nor is it regarded as a means of appeasing God's wrath as in some religions.

Although Ramadaan may appear to be a hard and difficult month, it is in fact an enjoyable time. A special atmosphere prevails in homes, in mosques and in Muslim communities as a whole. Muslims look forward to the coming of Ramadaan with great longing and expectation and feel a certain sadness when the month is at an end.

It is possible that too much emphasis is sometimes placed on the preparation of food during Ramadaan. In fact a greater variety and quantity of food may be consumed during the month of Ramadaan at nights than in other periods. And some of us may end up weighing more at the end of the month than at the beginning.

It may also be possible that Ramadaan be taken as a time when normal work during the daytime is reduced or suspended. It should be borne in mind that normal work activities should continue during Ramadaan and it should not be taken as an excuse for sluggishness and idleness.

You need to be careful that the true benefits of fasting, of self-restraint and control, are not lost through gluttony on the one hand or idleness on the other.

Voluntary fasting

Outside of Ramadaan, the Muslim is also advised to fast voluntarily to maintain a state of self-control. It is Sunnah to fast six days in the month of Shawwaal after Ramadaan, the days of 'Aashuuraa (9th, 10th, 11th) in the month of Muharram, and in the month of Sha'baan in preparation for the month of Ramadaan. Voluntary fasts may also be observed on two days a week — Mondays and Thursdays, or three days a month. It is not recommended to fast voluntarily on Fridays as it is considered to be a day of Eid or celebration. Voluntary fasts may be broken if one has guests or for any reason without any requirement to make amends.

Other forms of Tazkiyyah (Purification and Personal Development)

Apart from the major institutions of Salaat and Fasting in Ramadaan, there are a number of practices recommended in the Qur'an and the example of the noble Prophet for strengthening man's awareness of God and moulding his thoughts and actions into the natural mould of 'ibaadah or worship of God.

Dhikr

One of these instruments is *Dhikr* which literally means the remembrance of God. This may be through the conscious repetition at any time of meaningful phrases like:

- *Alhamdu lillah* — All praise and thanks is due to God;
- *Laa ilaaha illa Allah* — There is no god but Allah;
- *SubhaanAllah* — Glory be to God;
- *Astaghfirullah* — I seek God's forgiveness;
- *Laa hawla wa laa quwwata illa billah* — There is no power or might except with God.

Dhikr is not difficult. While one is travelling, on a bus or on a train, while one is studying, eating, playing, working, a few minutes, a minute or even a few seconds, to say *Alhamdulillah* will provide a person with a natural mental climate and orientation.

However, apart from these phrases repeated orally, dhikr deals with all aspects of work and leisure. Every work that is done consciously in accordance with the guidance of God is dhikr. The difference between the one who makes dhikr and one who does not has been likened by the noble Prophet to the difference between the living and the dead. And God gives us the assurance in the Qur'an:

"As you remember Me so shall I remember you."

ON PIETY

'Aa'ishah, the wife of the Prophet, is reported to have said that one of the most pious persons she knew was 'Umar ibn al-Khatttaab. When he walked, he walked briskly, when he spoke he made his voice heard and when he beat his beating caused pain.

Du'aa

Du'aa which means literally "calling upon" or supplication is another instrument of purification and rectification. Your du'aa or calling upon God for knowledge and guidance, for health and strength, for sustenance and healing, for forgiveness for wrongs committed, or protection from such evils as anxiety and sadness, laziness and incompetence, cowardice and miserliness, over-powering debt and oppressive men — are all expressions of your human state of need and dependence and of your essential "human-ity" before your Creator.

Your du'aa may be couched in your own or any language. It is the outpouring of your heart to your Maker and an expression of your innermost aspirations and ambitions.

The du'aas of the Prophet and other supplications in the Qur'an however show us in the most beautiful and moving way possible what we should pray for and how. In fact there are du'aas of the Prophet for almost all occasions.

SUPPLICATIONS FROM THE QUR'AN

"O my Lord and Sustainer!
Grant me that I may be grateful for Your favour which You have bestowed upon me, and upon both my parents, and that I may work righteousness such as You may approve. And be gracious to me in my offspring. Truly, I have turned to You and truly I am of those who submit to You." (46: 15)

"O my Lord and Sustainer!
Bestow wisdom on me, and join me
With the righteous. (26:83)

"Our Lord and Sustainer!
Let not our hearts deviate now after You have guided us,
But grant us blessings and mercy from Your own presence,
For You are the Grantor of bounties without measure." (3: 8)

SUPPLICATIONS OF THE NOBLE PROPHET

"O God! We seek Your help and ask Your forgiveness. We seek Your guidance and affirm our faith in You. We turn to You in repentance and put our trust in You. We give praise to You in the goodliest manner and offer our thanks to You and are not ungrateful to You...
"O God! You alone do we worship and unto You do we pray and prostrate ourselves. Towards You do we strive and hasten. We hope for Your mercy and dread Your chastisement. Indeed, Your chastisement shall overtake the disbelievers."

"O Lord! I seek Your protection
against knowledge that profits not
and a heart which fears not God
and a mind that is not satisfied
and a prayer that is not answered."

"O Lord! I beseech You
for guidance,
righteousness,
chastity
and self-sufficiency."

Personal qualities and habits

"I was sent to perfect the best in moral characteristics," said the noble Prophet describing his mission. While this points to the fact that the message he brought was not a new one, it also shows that the main purpose of this message is to make man live according to the highest moral standards which he is capable of.

This saying of the Prophet may be linked to many verses in the Qur'an such as:

> "Consider the human self and how it is formed in accordance with what it is meant to be.
> And how it is imbued with moral failings as well as with consciousness of God.
> He shall indeed attain to a happy state who causes this self to grow in purity.
> And truly lost is he who buries it (in darkness)." (*The Qur'an*, 91: 7-10)

From this we can see that each person has a duty to cultivate good and desirable qualities which are part of his natural make-up. Some of these qualities which are stressed in the Qur'an and the Sunnah are:

Truthfulness, honesty, reliability in fulfilling trusts
Gentleness, politeness, courtesy
Generosity, compassion and forgiveness
Purity, modesty and decency
Humility, patience and steadfastness, courage, thankfulness
Dignity, honour, self-respect
Warmth and lovingness, cheerfulness and good temper
Striving and hard work.

> "Verily, men and women who submit;
> And men and women who believe:
> And men and women who are patient;
> And men and women who are truthful;
> And men and women who are humble before God;
> And men and women who give in charity;
> And men and women who fast;
> And men and women who guard their chastity;
> And men and women who remember God much—
> To them God has promised forgiveness and a great reward."
> (*The Qur'an*, 23: 35)

On the other hand, each person has a duty to strive against noxious qualities and habits. Some of these are:

Lying, dishonesty, deceit, untrustworthiness, hypocrisy
Harshness, rancour, niggardliness

Miserliness, envy, hatred
Brashness, shamelessness, self-conceit
Cowardice and opportunism
Laziness.

Bad qualities and habits are like rust on a pure heart. The more rust accumulates, the more insensitive a person's heart will become. The covering of rust
may eventually obscure all good and a person might reach a state where vice
and noxious qualities become not only acceptable to him but beautiful. If there
is still a spark of good left, the door for repentance or *tawbah* (which literally
means returning to your original state) might still be open. The weeds in your
garden must not be allowed to stifle and smother the flowers and the fruit.

In cultivating good qualities, it is important to remember the saying of the
Prophet that the best deeds are those done regularly even if they are small. This
stresses the need to develop good habits, whereby the practice of goodness becomes a matter of course, easy and natural.

Lest you may think that the good life is only to be found on a tight-rope path
of unrelieved consciousness and stress, we refer again to the life pattern of the
Prophet, peace be on him. When he was in private he would worship his Lord
with such intense devotion, standing for long hours in Salaat, that his feet
would become swollen; in matters pertaining to truth and justice, he did not
care about anyone's opinion, seeking only the pleasure of God. But in his living
habits and dealings with people, he was a human being, enjoying good things,
participating in small talk, smiling and joking, yet never departing from the
truth.

Islam does not require of people that their speech should consist entirely of
pious utterances, that their silence should be a meditation, that they should
listen to nothing except the Qur'an or that they should spend all their leisure
time in the mosque.

There is an anecdote related by Hanzalah al-Usaydi, a companion and scribe
of the noble Prophet. Hanzalah said:

"Abu Bakr met me and asked, 'How are you, Hanzalah?' I replied,
'Hanzalah has become a hypocrite.' He said, 'SubhaanAllah! What are you saying?' I replied, 'When we are with Allah's messenger (peace be on him), he
mentions the Fire of Hell and the Garden of Paradise until it is as if we can see
them. But when we leave the Prophet's company and play with our wives and
children or busy ourselves with our properties, we forget much.' Abu Bakr said,
'By God, I experience the same thing.'

He and I then went to visit the Messenger of God (peace be on him) and I
said, 'O Messenger of God, Hanzalah has become a hypocrite.' He asked, 'And
how is that?' I replied, 'Messenger of God, when we are with you, you talk
about Hell-Fire and the Garden of Paradise until it is as if we can see them. Then

we go out and play with our wives and children and deal with our properties, and we forget much.'

The Messenger of God, peace be on him, then said, 'By Him in whose hand is my soul, if you were to continue at the same level at which you were when with me in remembering God, the angels would shake hands with you when you are resting and when you walk about! But, O Hanzalah, there is a time (for this) and a time (for that).' He repeated this phrase three times."

THREE

YOU *and* YOUR LIVELIHOOD

The story is told of a man from among the Muslims of Madinah who came to the Prophet and asked for some nourishment. The Prophet was not one to refuse any request for help. At the same time he did not like to encourage begging or dependence. He therefore asked the man:

"Don't you have anything in your house?"

"Yes," said the man. "A saddle blanket which we wear sometimes and which we spread on the floor sometimes and a container from which we drink water."

"Bring them to me," said the Prophet who then took the items and asked some of his companions, "Who will buy these two articles?"

"I will," said one man, "for one dirham."

Another said, "I will take them for two dirhams."

The Prophet sold the articles for the two dirhams which he handed over to the man and said, "With one dirham, buy food for your family and with the other buy an axe and bring it to me."

The man returned with the axe. The Prophet split a log with it and then instructed the man:

"Go and gather firewood and I do not want to see you for fifteen days."

This the man did and after two weeks had made a profit of ten dirhams. With some of the money he bought food and with some he bought clothes. The Prophet was pleased and said to him:

"This is better than getting a blot on your face on the day of resurrection."

This true story emphasises that as an adult Muslim and in particular when you have a family, you have the obligation to work. You are required to use your initiative and whatever resources you may have to earn a living. If you fail to do so you face the prospect of "getting a blot on your face" or in other words of suffering some form of disgrace through your inactivity and dependence.

The story also points to the most effective method of offering aid and support. If you provide handouts to people who are well, able-bodied and have some resources, however small, you would not in fact be offering effective help to that person. You may help to meet an immediate pressing need but it will only be a one-off, short term remedy. You will in fact be encouraging dependence and the lack of self-respect and esteem in the person you wish to help.

By his simple, practical and far-sighted approach, the noble Prophet showed how people can be made to help themselves and how they can be motivated to seek long-term solutions to meet their basic needs. "Charity is not halaal for the rich or the able-bodied," emphasised the Prophet.

HADITH: ON WORK

To try to earn a lawful livelihood
is an obligation
like the other obligations in Islam

No one has eaten better food
than what he earns
from the toil of his own hands.

It is better for one of you to take a rope
and bring a load of firewood on his back
and sell it
than that he should beg from people
whether they give him anything or refuse him.

Everyone needs a basic minimum to live. You need food sufficient to free you from hunger. You need clothing and shelter sufficient to protect you against exposure to heat, cold or shame. You need security to ensure freedom from fear.

As an adult you need to work to provide these needs for yourself and those who naturally depend on you — like your parents if they are old or your children if they are young. Work — honest work — is an obligation like the other obligations in Islam. Idleness, laziness, begging or waiting for handouts from the state or from charities — all destroy a person's dignity and even his freedom. This does not mean of course that in times of genuine difficulties we are not to seek help and support from others.

Nearly all aspects of earning a livelihood require dealings with others. To preserve a natural and stable social order, all dealings including business and commercial dealings, must be based on the natural virtues of honesty, justice, responsibility and brotherhood. On the other hand any dealing that is characterised by dishonesty, injustice, fraud or deceit whether it is a minor case of giving short measure or a cunning case of exploitation and profiteering destroys the natural good in the individual and breaks the bond of brotherhood and solidarity in society.

Firm ethical values govern economic activity and business relationships in Islam. This is why Al-Ghazali, the famous Muslim scholar, recommended that a Muslim who decides to adopt trade as a profession or to set up a business should first acquire a thorough understanding of the rules of business transactions.

A balanced attitude

Islam recognizes the importance of material well-being. To be deprived of the basic needs of life and to be in a state of dire poverty is to be in a terrible state — so terrible that when the Prophet was asked whether the evils of deprivation equalled the evils of associating others with God, he said yes!

"Poverty," warned the Prophet, "can lead to kufr (rejection of God and ingratitude)."

Beyond merely striving to eliminate poverty, believers are urged to enjoy, and not to deny themselves the good things of this life. These are enjoyed as part of the bounty of God but should not lead to a materialistic outlook and the compelling desire to acquire more and more.

WEALTH AND HAPPINESS

The Prophet, peace be on him, sent a trusted companion of his, Abu 'Ubaydah ibn al-Jarraah, to Bahrain. When the people of Madinah heard that Abu 'Ubaydah was returning with enormous wealth, they flocked to the mosque for the dawn Salaat. The Prophet went to the mosque, prayed and then left. People then gathered around him. He smiled when he saw them and said:

"No doubt you have heard that Abu 'Ubaydah is coming with something from Bahrain!"

"Yes, Messenger of God," they said.

"Be of good cheer. Set your hopes on what will bring you happiness. It is not poverty that I fear for you, but I fear that you will become engrossed with the world as those before you were and that you will pursue it as they pursued it and that it will destroy you as it destroyed them."

In Islam, the urge for material enjoyment is constantly tempered by the need for moderation.

"O you who believe! do not forbid the good things which God made lawful for you, and do not exceed the limits."(5: 87)

"Eat and drink but do not waste, for God does not love those who waste." (7: 31)

Such verses of the Qur'an call for a reasonable and balanced attitude towards wealth and material well-being. Islam is not for life-denial but for life-fulfilment. In this vein, one of the most frequently-repeated supplications of the Prophet and of Muslims is:

"Our Lord and Sustainer, grant us good in this world and good in the Hereafter..."

Wealth—a trust

Naturally, you are not free to do with your wealth as you please. Whatever wealth you have must be regarded as a trust from God and you will be called to account for how you discharged this trust.

"Then (on the day of judgement) you will certainly be questioned about all the favours you enjoyed." (102: 8)

The more you have the more you have to account for. Your worth, according to Islam, is not a function of your wealth. Your wealth is not a sign of your virtue or your excellence. It does not give you nobility or make you part of a privileged class. It is not a means of exploiting others. The possession of wealth is really a test. God says in the Qur'an:

> "It is He Who has made you (His) agents, inheritors of the earth. He has raised you in ranks, some above others, that He may try you in the gifts He has given you. Indeed, your Lord is quick in punishment, yet He is indeed Forgiving, most Merciful." (6: 165)

ECONOMIC ACTIVITY

Earning a livelihood

There are three basic ways of earning a permissible livelihood:
1. profits—from agriculture, industry, trading and investment;
2. wages—for work done;
3. rental income—from leasing, letting or hiring.

These ways of earning a livelihood all require the interaction and cooperation of human beings. No individual owns all the things he needs. Each person has some skill, resource or commodity he can spare while at the same time he needs the skill, resources or commodities of others. Human beings are therefore naturally dependent on one another.

It is the concern of Islam to see that these needs are fulfilled in a way that:

● ensures work and productive effort on the part of individuals;

● there is no injustice or exploitation done to anyone;

● society functions in a smooth manner and that the "general good" and well-being of the society as a whole is preserved.

Economic activity in Islam is therefore governed by what is economically, socially and morally good. Not all profits, wages or rental income are good and meet the above conditions. People are often smitten by greed and may use fraud, deception and other vicious methods to increase their wealth. Economic activity that can be shown to be destructive of man's innate goodness and to be harmful to individuals and society has been declared unlawful or haraam.

Labour and economic risk

Gains from economic activity should be based on two factors: on labour and economic risk. Income from betting or gambling, for example, is therefore unlawful because it is not acquired through work or labour. Such income is called "unearned income". Income from lending money at a guaranteed rate of interest is unlawful partly because it is not earned through labour or economic risk. Income from such activities as usury, gambling, monopolistic trade practices, hoarding and speculation is therefore regarded as unlawful or haraam. All of these practices are not based on productive work and can be shown to create hardship and may even lead to social strain and upheaval.

What is most severely condemned in particular is *riba* which is interest or usury. This involves lending money on condition that you get back not only the sum lent but *an additional guaranteed sum* — without work on your part and without any economic risk. Riba exploits the need of the borrower and may place him in economic hardship. The lender becomes like a parasite feeding on the whims or needs of the borrower. Riba lies at the root of much of the economic and political instability in the world.

The dignity of work

Let us look briefly at some of the ways of earning a livelihood and some of the general principles which affect economic activity.

In the process of securing a livelihood and engaging in economic activity, a person may be either a producer engaged in agriculture or industry; a trader engaged in commerce or a professional person practicing a particular skill.

You may engage in any economic activity as long as it does not involve doing, supporting or promoting anything haraam.

Provided the work you do does not involve what is haraam, you should not feel ashamed of doing any work, however menial, and you should not regard any type of honest and lawful work as contemptible. The work you do does not put you into a higher or lower social class. If you are a landowner or an agricultural producer this does not make you better or worse as a person than an agricultural labourer on your land. If you are a cleaner in a factory, this does not make you better or worse as a person than the owner of the factory. There is dignity in work and labour. In it, there is also Divine blessing and reward as the following account concerning 'Ali, the companion of the Prophet and future head of the Muslim State, clearly shows.

IN WORK, THERE IS BLESSING

One morning, 'Ali ibn Abii Taalib went outside Madinah in search of work so that he could feed his family. He came upon a lady looking for a labourer to carry water from a well to a clay pit. He agreed to carry the water for her in return for some dates. He did so and got about twenty dates. On the way home, he met the Prophet who asked what he was carrying. 'Ali said:

"It is the dates I earned for work I did. My hands are blistered from drawing water from the well with a palm-fibre rope."

The Prophet rubbed 'Ali's face and his hand and in obvious approval said:

"God has blessed this hand."

And he continued:

"O 'Ali, give me a date. I will treat myself with it."

The type of work you do is dependent on your interests and skills, your resources and the needs of your community. The work you do may change depending on changing circumstances and it is advisable to acquire as many skills as possible.

You as an agricultural producer

Agriculture is essential and should be given priority attention in any community. God, according to the Qur'an, has spread out the earth and made it suitable and fertile for cultivation. He sends the "fertilizing winds" to drive the clouds and scatter the seeds and He sends down rain to bring forth vegetation of all kinds. The many verses in which these bounties and favours of God are mentioned all serve to encourage people not only to thank God but to engage in agricultural production.

There are many sayings of the Prophet which commend agricultural production. He has said:

"When a Muslim plants a tree or cultivates a crop, no bird or human being eats from it without its being accounted as a (rewardable) charity for him."

Stressing the importance of irrigation and land reclamation for agricultural purposes, he also said:

"Whoever brings dead land to life, for him is a reward in it, and whatever any creature seeking food eats of it, shall be considered as charity from him."

Agriculture is a vital activity which has benefits in this world and rewards in the Hereafter. People therefore should not easily abandon agricultural production as something menial and degrading and flock to towns to join the ranks of the unemployed as has happened recently in many countries. Even if you live in towns and built-up areas you should seek to plant fruit and other trees wherever possible or grow some of your own vegetables and flowers. This will also help to create a beautiful environment.

In order to achieve the greatest good for individuals and society, there are some basic regulations concerning the use of land, irrigation, the crops you are not allowed to plant and the manner of marketing your produce.

The use of land

A person who owns land should cultivate it himself. If he is unable to do so, he should allow others to cultivate it and may share equitably in the produce. It is not allowed to rent or lease cultivable land for a fixed sum. The reason for this is that a crop might fail and the person renting the land would face hardship in paying the rent. Agricultural land which remains uncultivated may be transferred by the State to those who are willing and able to cultivate it.

In naturally irrigated lands, you should not do anything that would injure the interests of other farmers. In the interests of the common good, you are not allowed to divert running water passing through your land so as to deny a farmer downstream.

Crops you may not cultivate

It is haraam to cultivate a plant, such as hashish, knowing and intending that it will be used by people in such a way as to bring harm to them. Growing tobacco may also be put under this category. Tobacco is used only for smoking which is harmful to health. To plant grapevines, intending that the produce will be used for wine production, should also be considered as forbidden. As far as crops of this sort are concerned, it is not a valid excuse for a Muslim to say that he is growing the crop to sell it to non-Muslims for a Muslim is not permitted to be a party to promoting what is haraam.

Sale of produce

It is not allowed to deal in "futures" selling of crops. You cannot sell a crop before it is actually mature. This is to eliminate speculation and also possible injustice should the crop not materialise. It is not permissible to sell crops before their good condition is clear. The seller has the duty to inform the buyer of any known defect in the produce he is selling. For example, it is forbidden to cover up rotten fruit with good and attractive fruit to give the impression that all the fruit is wholesome.

Animal husbandry

This was another occupation which the Prophet considered very dignified. Although many people do not look upon animal farmers and shepherds with esteem, the Prophet gave dignity to this occupation when he said:

"God did not send a Prophet without his having tended sheep."

"You too, O Messenger of Allah?" asked his companions.

"Yes, I tended sheep for wages for the people of Makkah."

You should observe all the Islamic advice and regulations about the proper care and treatment of animals: to provide for them all that their kind require, not to burden them beyond what they can bear, not to injure them and if you use them for food, to slaughter them in the most calm, kind and efficient manner.

Industrial production

While agriculture is essential and highly encouraged as an occupation, the Prophet saw that it was undesirable that people should confine their economic efforts solely to agriculture and pastoral pursuits. He warned that this would expose a community to various dangers including defeat and disgrace:

"If you deal in usury, calling it by other names, and hang onto the tails of cows, being satisfied with cultivation and ceasing to perform jihaad, God will inflict a disgrace upon you which will not be removed until you return to your religion."

According to this hadith, Muslims need to develop in addition to agriculture, the industries, crafts and skills which are needed to build a strong community.

The Qur'an mentions the opportunities and the needs for various types of industrial production involving the use of iron, copper and other minerals—resources which God has placed at the disposal of man.

"And We provided and revealed the use of iron, in which there is great power and benefits for mankind..."(57: 25)

It speaks, for example, of the value of shipbuilding and the vast expanses of ocean which can be explored in various ways for the benefit of mankind.

In engaging in industrial production and the manufacture of goods, the benefit of mankind and the environment in general and the needs of the Muslim community in particular must be given high priority. Whatever is harmful and is intended for a harmful purpose should not be manufactured or produced.

Whatever is harmful to the beliefs, good morals and manners of a society should also not be produced. The acquiring and even more strongly the making of statues and similar articles are strongly prohibited.

While the manufacture of armaments for the defense of Muslim communities and the repelling of injustice is encouraged, it is possible to regard the production of weapons which cause indiscriminate slaughter of entire populations as unlawful in Islam. This is because their use inevitably involves the killing of innocent non-combatants including children and the aged which is forbidden in Islam. We may therefore consider the manufacture of nuclear weapons as unlawful.

However, Muslims face a major dilemma here in that others have stockpiled such weapons and may be lunatic enough to use them. To deter such people some Muslim scholars have argued that Muslims need to take the responsibility of producing nuclear weapons or continue to face the prospect of being dominated by hostile and evil forces. Those who thus argue for the need to maintain a nuclear deterrent and contribute to a continual nuclear build-up are marching down a dangerous and slippery road. They may find themselves not only working to eliminate hostile and evil forces but contributing to their own suicide and the destruction of mankind and the world.

Such activity as the manufacture of books and magazines and the production of films which corrupt morals in the society is also to be considered unlawful.

Trade

The Qur'an and the Hadith of the Prophet, peace be on him, urge Muslims to engage in trade and commerce, and to undertake journeys for what the Qur'an refers to as "seeking the bounty of God". Those who travel for the purpose of trade are mentioned in the Qur'an side by side with those who fight in His cause:

"Others travel through the land, seeking the bounty of God, and still others fight in the cause of God..." (73: 20)

All trade in Islam is allowed unless it involves injustice, cheating, making exorbitant profits, or the promotion of something which is haraam.

It is haraam to do business in alcoholic drinks, intoxicants, harmful drugs, swine, idols, statues, or anything whose consumption and use Islam has prohibited. Selling or trading in such articles implies promoting them among people and thus encouraging them to do what is haraam. The Prophet, peace be on him, has said:

"When God prohibits a thing, He prohibits (giving and receiving) the price as well."

In many supermarkets and newsagents nowadays, for example, people may sell among other things such items as pork or pork products, tobacco or pornographic magazines which are clearly prohibited in Islam or which are harmful for the health and morals of individuals and society. Any earnings from the sale of such goods are sinful earnings. Honesty and trustworthiness in such business are not counted as virtues.

Professions and Skills

It is obvious that any healthy community or society needs a variety of professions to meet its needs. Professions relating to man's basic needs—food, clothing, shelter, health care, education, defence—are given priority. Bakers, weavers, builders, doctors, nurses, teachers are the sort of professionals and skilled persons any society must have.

If there is a critical shortage of any essential skill or profession, a sensible society will take measures to fill the gaps. In many new Muslim communities in the west for example, there is no shortage of food, clothing or health care. But there is a critical shortage or absence of trained teachers. Muslims should therefore be encouraged to go into the teaching profession. The training and educating of his companions and the selection and deployment of some of them as teachers was one of the primary tasks of the Prophet, peace be upon him. In fact, he said of himself:

"I was sent as a teacher."

In some communities, certain professions and skills predominate over others and there is more prestige attached to them. Medicine, law and civil service jobs often fall in this category. This imbalance is naturally not healthy for any society.

There are of course certain professions which are prohibited in Islam. Any profession that involves a display of the 'awrah of an individual or any sexually exciting or erotic activity is condemned by Islam because of its harmful effects on morals and society. Erotic dancing, suggestive or obscene songs and provocative dramas come under this category. Writing, producing or acting in an erotic drama, for example, will all be regarded as harmful to the honour and good morals of society and are not allowed. Much of the entertainment industry, much of what passes for art and even the way in which certain types of sports (boxing and gymnastics for example) are conducted may be regarded as sinful. If you are inclined to seek a livelihood in entertainment or art, you should make sure that it does not involve any activity or behaviour that is repugnant to the standards of morality and decency which Islam naturally insists upon.

Professions involving the use or propagation of harmful knowledge are not allowed. Under this category will come astrology and the occult arts.

ECONOMIC RELATIONSHIPS

In terms of economic relationships a person may be an employer, an employee, an investor, a consumer, a lender or a debtor.

You as an employer

Your right to conduct economic activity, to own legitimate property and to bequeath it in a legitimate manner must be respected by other individuals and by the state.

You need to be careful about the type of business you run and the dealings you engage in. You may conduct any type of business provided it does not involve anything which is haraam. You are careful about the gains you acquire especially remembering the saying of the Prophet: "An honest and decent businessman will be taken with martyrs and those who love God." You are not allowed to deceive or misrepresent, firm in the knowledge that while a person may attempt to deceive his fellowman, he cannot deceive God. You refrain in your business life from all forms of fraud and deceit. fearing Allah who said, "Woe unto the defrauders."

You need to use your assets with the aim of benefitting people and without creating harm and injustice to individuals and society.

You are not extravagant or wasteful. On the other hand, you are not stingy.

You need to pay Zakaat as required and apply the Islamic inheritance laws.

THE LORD OF 'UMAR KNOWS

When he was the Khaliifah, 'Umar ibn al-Khattaab prohibited anyone selling milk that was mixed with water. While he was making his rounds of the city at night incognito, he heard a lady saying to her daughter:

"Why don't you add water to your milk?"

"How can I do so when the Amiir al-Mu'miniin has prohibited it?"

"The people adulterate their milk. You do so as well and the Amiir al-Mu'miniin will not know."

"If 'Umar would not know, certainly the Lord of 'Umar would know and I would not do such a thing."

You must realise that the wealth and property you acquire are not obtained solely by your capability but by the wish and permission of God. "God enlarges livelihood for whom He wills and reduces it for whom He wills." (13: 26)

You know that what you possess is a trust from God and that everything in the world including man belongs to God who is the real owner. "God is the sovereign of the heaven and the earth and all that is between them..."

You know that the underprivileged in society, "the one who needs to ask and the outcast has a title or share in your wealth" (51: 19).

You need to take care of workers, paying their wages in right amount and punctually and providing them with contentment. You remember what the Prophet said: "There are three kinds of people whom I shall be against: One of them is the man who didn't pay the right wages to his workers after their labours."

You keep workloads of workers to a moderate and reasonable level remembering the warning of the Prophet: "Do not make them responsible more than their capacities."

As an employee

You should attempt to find the most appropriate job and profession to earn your livelihood according to your natural and acquired abilities and skills.

As an employee, you should be inspired by the saying of the noble Prophet that every person is a shepherd and is responsible for his flock or in other words, every person is a steward and is responsible for his trust. You perform your job to the best of your ability remembering the saying of the Prophet: "You will be responsible for what you have done."

You recognize the value of work as opposed to idleness, laziness or begging taking into consideration the saying of the Prophet, "The man who works to support his family is on the way of God and the man who supports his old father and mother is on the way of God as well," and "whoever takes a rest after tiring work to obtain decent gain, rests as forgiven."

"Work, and God, the Prophet and the believers will witness your work." (9: 105)

GO, YOU DO NOT KNOW HIM!

A man came to 'Umar ibn al-Khattaab and spoke in praise of another. 'Umar asked him:

"Are you his nearest neighbour such that you know his goings and his comings?"

"No."

"Have you been his companion on a journey so that you could see evidence of his good character?"

" No."

"Have you had dealings with him involving dinars and dirhams which would indicate the piety of the man?"

"No."

"I think you saw him standing in the mosque muttering the Qur'an and moving his head up and down?"

"Yes."

"Go, for you do not know him..."

And to the man in question, 'Umar said, "Go and bring me someone who knows you."

You are grateful to God for your work and income. You are not envious of others' income nor do you have a hateful attitude towards your employer.

What if you feel your employer is unjust or if you feel you merit or need a better salary and conditions of work? How do you go about changing your situation?

Here is not the place to go into industrial law and relations. However, in line with the Qur'anic injunction to put down contractual agreements in writing, it is recommended that you have from your employer a contract of employment setting down mutual obligations and rights. If you feel that your employer is not fulfilling his agreed obligations, it is your duty as a Muslim to help your employer by pointing out any injustice and advising him to refrain from committing injustice or breach of his Islamic obligations as an employer. You have a duty to cooperate with others to bring an end to injustice and exploitation. You may refer your case to an arbitrator, an imam or a judge and Islam provides for this. In the last resort, you have the option to leave any employment provided you have fulfilled the terms of your contract and take up any other work or enterprise. Your freedom to do so should be respected by all.

You as a consumer

How, why and where should you as a Muslim person spend your wealth? There are four possibilities:

1. You may spend to satisfy needs;
2. If your income is in excess of your needs, you make savings;

3. You may hoard your savings as gold, silver, other jewelry, or other liquid assets;

4. You may invest your savings in production.

As a consumer, your level of spending for consumption is not only determined by your income, but depends on other economic, social and moral requirements.

You are not supposed to spend your income on any things forbidden by the Shari'ah, for example, on alcoholic beverages, gambling, or illegitimate leisure or entertainment.

You must refrain from luxurious and conspicuous consumption:

"Verily, God does not love any of those who, full of self-conceit, act in a boastful manner; (nor) those who are niggardly and bid others to be niggardly, and conceal whatever God has bestowed upon them out of His bounty...

"And (God does not love) those who spend their possessions on others (only) to be seen and praised by men, the while they believe neither in God nor the Last Day..." (4: 36-38)

You should also limit the level of consumption by quantity and keep away from waste:

"O children of Adam! Look to our adornment at every place of worship and eat and drink but be not extravagant and wasteful. Indeed He does not love those who waste." (7: 31)

"Lo, the squanderers are brothers of the Satans, and Satan is ungrateful to his Lord." (17: 27)

Borrowing and debt

You should try to relate your consumption to your income remembering the saying of the Prophet: "May God prevent me from sin and borrowing."

You are not supposed to borrow unless it is necessary. If it is necessary to borrow, you should make a written agreement with sincere intention to repay.

"When you contract a debt for a fixed term, record it in writing." (2: 82)

Pay back in right time for it is unjust to extend the repayment time if you are able to repay a debt in time. To do so is a blameworthy act.

"Whoever borrows with pure intention, God will pay for him; and whoever borrows with the intention of being extravagant and wasteful, God will ruin him."

Nowadays, it is very easy for individuals and nations to fall into debt. The availability and widespread use of credit cards make it very easy for people to run up large shopping bills and debts. Instead of being a facility credit cards have become a source of burden and a millstone for many people. Resulting debts create mental strain and worry and also family and social tension.

"I seek refuge with Thee from poverty. And I seek refuge with Thee from the over-powering of debt and the oppression of men," is part of an oft-repeated supplication of the Prophet.

Regulating the type and level of your consumption has several benefits:
- you do not fall into debt easily;
- you refrain from provoking the jealousy of the poor;
- you will more likely have extra funds either for increasing investment for economic development, or for giving loans, or for giving in charity;
- you therefore help to create greater prosperity and social balance.

These principles concerning the type and level of consumption can also be applied to countries, and make for better international relations.

As investor and creditor

If your income is in excess of your needs, what will you do with the excess?

If you intend to hoard your savings, you will come up against two important Islamic principles: the prohibition of hoarding and the payment of Zakaat on that saving. Therefore, if you keep your wealth idle for a long time, your wealth will progressively decrease with time.

These principles of Islam thus prevent the idleness of saving and stimulate the transformation of the saving into economic life.

"They who hoard up gold and silver and spend it not in the way of God, unto them give tidings, O Muhammad, of a painful doom." (9: 34)

Since you are prohibited from hoarding, you may either invest your savings, give loans, gifts, or set up *waqfs* or charitable endowments.

If you intend to extend loans as an economic activity to earn income and not as social assistance, you will need to bear in mind the important principle of Islam: "Prohibition of gains out of money without having risk of investment." Under this principle, you cannot have a legitimate or pure gain out of your money without yourself working or having shared the risk of investment. Therefore, you cannot lend money to other people or companies or the state or leave it in deposits in a bank on the condition that you are guaranteed a return.

You may however enter into partnerships, or invest your money in businesses or in stock and shares on condition that:

1. you agree to share in the profit or loss of such businesses;
2. these businesses are not involved in any activity prohibited by Islam such as brewing or distilling, speculating in futures' markets such as buying an orange crop before the fruit is mature;
3. you do not sell a commodity that you have not taken possession of.

Lending and Charity

"The likeness of those who spend their wealth in God's way is as the likeness of a grain which grows seven ears , in every ear is a hundred grains. God gives increase manifold to whom He wills." (2: 261)

On the basis of this and many other encouraging advice in the Qur'an and the Sunnah, you are urged to give loans to others in need of help but without economic interest. Such a loan is referred to in the Qur'an as a "goodly loan" or *qard hasan*.

Those who give such loans are expected to deal leniently:

"If the debtor is in straitened circumstances, then let there be postponement to (the time of) ease; and that you remit the debt as charity would be better for you if you did but know." (2: 280)

"He who grants a respite to one in straightened circumstances or remits his debt will be saved by God from the anxieties of the Day of Resurrection," said the noble Prophet.

If you do remit a debt, you should not feel that your wealth or your capital will be lost or diminished. Instead, there will be many benefits:

- you will remove from the borrower the psychological stress and pain of debt;
- you will strengthen social harmony and brotherhood;
- you will have inner satisfaction in being able to help a fellow human being.

Such acts will help to realise the Islamic vision of an enterprising, sharing and caring society. More than this, there is the enduring reward promised by God for all those who do such good.

Waqfs or Continuous Charity

One of the best ways of using excess income is to set up waqfs. These are charitable endowments or trusts which are set up for specific purposes. This involves dedicating a sum of money or the proceeds from a business or rental income from property you own for a specific charitable purpose. There are waqfs for schools, libraries, hospitals, orphanages, mosques and their maintenance, hostels for travellers, the treatment of animals and many other charitable purposes. Once money, land or building is given as waqf. it cannot be taken back. It is an endowment in perpetuity and the rewards from it are continuous, for the noble Prophet has said:

"When a person dies, all his actions come to an end except in respect of three matters which he leaves behind: a continuing charity; knowledge from which benefit could be derived; righteous offspring who pray for him."

The value of work, of seeking a livelihood, the attitude to wealth and its relation to the real purpose of life are all well caught in the fine balance and tension of the saying:

"Work for the world as if you will live forever;

And work for the eternal life as if you will die tomorrow."

If you could attain both the level of work and enjoyment and the level of God-consciousness and sacrifice which this saying summons you to, then you would have achieved fulfilment complete!

FOUR

YOU *and* YOUR FAMILY

You as an individual may be at one and the same time a daughter, a mother, a grandmother, a wife, a sister, an aunt or a niece. If you are a male, you may at one and the same time be a son, a father, a grandfather, a husband, a brother, an uncle or a nephew.

All this may sound very obvious. But many social systems, trends and behaviour patterns in our times care little for whether you are a wife or a husband, whether you are a mother or a father, whether you are a grandmother or a grandfather.

In liberal, "free" societies for example, where the individual is regarded as the basic unit of society, you as an individual may be given the freedom to do what you want, when you want. Because the individual is considered free to live his own life, a woman for example may choose "to live with" one or a succession of men or indeed women. A man may be a father and not know it and his child or children may never know who their father is.

On the other hand, there are systems or social experiments where the individual counts for little and the needs of the commune or the state takes total control. Here the rearing of children becomes a social industry; care, education and the provision of all needs becomes a public affair; and being a parent carries few responsibilities. There may be much material comfort and efficiency in such a system but love and warmth often do not matter. The human being is devalued and natural bonds and needs are stifled or destroyed.

The basic unit of society cannot be the individual or the commune. Both are artificial and produce much personal stress and distress for everyone and in particular for women and children. They also tend to produce societal disorders such as delinquency and crime.

In Islam you are not allowed to be just an individual who is totally free to do whatever you want, whenever you want. Any system which attempts to make the individual the basic unit of society and give him unfettered freedom, does not take into account natural bonds and natural needs.

The most natural unit of society is the family. Many are the laws of Islam which are geared to preserving the institution of the family and the web of relationships within the family. For example, as we shall see, the need to preserve the family, within which the identity and proper upbringing of children is safeguarded, is one of the reasons why adultery and fornication are strictly prohibited and punished severely.

In Islam the family is welded together by three factors:

1. kinship or blood ties which are the strongest natural ties;
2. marital commitments;
3. faith.

Kinship

Kinship or blood ties are the strongest natural ties. There can be no substitute for a mother's love for a child or a child's devotion and gratitude to loving and caring parents. It is because of the strength and importance of these ties that the noble Prophet has said: "He is not of me who severs or breaks the ties of kinship." He also said: "No sin is more swiftly punished than oppression and the breaking of family ties."

Adoption, mutual alliance, or clientage where a weak or persecuted person is taken into a household, do not institute a family in Islam. An orphan or a child in distress has to be given all help and protection but cannot be adopted into a family and take the name of that family and be given such rights as those of inheritance.

Marital commitments

Marital commitments also weld a family together for Islam recognises no more wholesome framework for sexual relations and the rearing of children than marriage. Private consent to sexual intimacy, "common law" associations or "living together", "trial marriages" or "temporary unions" do not institute a family in the Islamic sense.

Faith

The third ingredient in strong family relationships is faith and commitment to Islam. If all members of a family are Muslims, there is likely to be greater harmony and common goals and interests than if family members belong to different faiths.

In some cases, in fact, faith supersedes kinship or marital commitments. A person is required to love and treat his parents with respect and consideration even if they are not Muslims. But he is not required to obey his parents if they ask him to believe in gods other than the One True God or commit any acts which involve the disobedience of God. A person in fact may find himself combatting his own parents or children if they actively seek to oppose or undermine Islam and the interest of the Muslims. There are many well-known, moving and awesome examples of this in Islamic history through the ages — the Prophet Noah's inability to save his disobedient son at the time of the flood; the case of Prophet Abraham and his idolatrous father; the Prophet Lot and his immoral wife; and in the time of Prophet Muhammad, the story of many of his companions who were pitted against a father, a mother, or a son.

Faith can also supersede and break marital ties. A woman who becomes a Muslim is required to divorce her husband if he remains a non-Muslim. Faith also determines who a Muslim woman or man can marry.

Extended family relationships

The Islamic family is not a nuclear family, consisting of only parents and children. It is extended to include grandparents, grandchildren, uncles and aunts and their progeny. These relationships are cemented by various laws, for example, laws of dependence and inheritance.

By preserving extended family relationships, the natural and continuous link between generations is preserved. New generations learn about Islamic culture and habits with ease. Members of the household act as companions and playmates to one another. There is the likelihood of greater warmth and richness in a caring and sharing atmosphere. It should also be easier to deal with many of the difficulties of life. Individualism, egotism and loneliness are thus banished from Islamic family life.

The extended family also provides a ready replacement for various functions. Children can be looked after properly while members of the family, including women, pursue vocational goals or attend to other duties outside the home. Mutual help, harmony and beauty in the household are the aims. Of course, it may not always work out like this, mainly because of individuals' weakness and pettiness and unnatural behaviour which we described in chapter one.

Duties of parents to children

Parents have the obligation to cherish and sustain their children, educate and train them.

Even before a child is conceived, parents' responsibilities begin. It goes back even to the right choice of a spouse. If a man or a woman intends to marry and have children, he or she may choose a spouse for wealth, beauty, lineage or taqwa. The last is the most important quality according to the noble Prophet. Parents' responsibilities therefore begin with the wholesome beliefs, attitudes and good conduct of each partner in a marriage. A couple, even in their most intimate moments, are advised by the Prophet to pray for offspring who are saalih — noble and righteous.

Before and after conception, the mother in particular should ensure that she lives an Islamic life style for her physical and psychological state could affect the foetus yet unborn. She should ensure that she takes no harmful drugs and of course as a Muslim she will steer clear away from forbidden and harmful things like alcohol, smoking or cocaine injections. Altogether, she should ensure that her body is a stable and welcoming environment for her child's first home.

When the child is born, your role as mother is of primary importance, one of the most serious and challenging responsibilities you have.

Especially when your child is under the age of two, for this is the time according to the Qur'an when a child is weaned, you are the person who is naturally meant to wean, comfort and educate the child.

Pay no attention to those who insist that it is society which must look after all children, who seek to abolish the family as a socio-economic unit, and take all women into the field of public activity in the name of the liberation of women.

ON MOTHERHOOD

"Modern civilization has disgraced motherhood in particular. It has preferred the calling of a salesgirl, model, teacher of other people's children, secretary, cleaning woman and so on to that of mother. It has proclaimed motherhood to be slavery and promised to free woman from it.

"Children's homes go together with homes for the aged. They remind us of artificial birth and artificial death... Both are opposed to the family and are the result of the changed role of woman in human life. Their common feature is the elimination of parental relationships: in a nursery children are without parents; in homes for the aged, parents are without children."

(Alija Ali Izethegovic (Yugoslav writer), *Islam Between East and West*, pp.144- 5.)

Of course, if you are the father you too have a great share in the process of *tarbiyyah* of the child. Tarbiyyah means to look after, to nurture, to nourish, to help grow and flourish. Tarbiyyah (from an Arabic root word which means to own, look after and cherish) implies a certain sensitivity towards the child under your care, his emotional and physical needs and capacities. It implies the ability to inspire confidence. It implies the courage to allow and promote creativity and innovation. It implies the ability to trust and not to stifle, to be firm when needed and even to impose sanctions when necessary.

The one who is responsible for tarbiyyah is a *murabbi*.

The primary responsibility for this process of tarbiyyah rests with the parents.

The crucial role of both parents in the formative education and development of a child is stressed in the famous saying of the Prophet, peace be on him:

"Every child is born in a natural state of goodness. It is his parents who make him into a Jew, a Christian or a Magian."

HASN'T A CHILD RIGHTS OVER HIS FATHER?

A man once came to 'Umar ibn Al-Khattaab, the second Khaliifah of Islam, complaining of his son's disobedience to him. 'Umar summoned the boy and spoke of his disobedience to his father and his neglect of his rights. The boy replied:

"O Amiir al-Mu'miniin! Hasn't a child rights over his father?"

"Certainly," replied 'Umar.

"What are they, Amiir al-Mu'miniin?"

"That he should choose his mother, given him a good name, teach him the Book (the Qur'an)."

"O Amiir al-Mu'miniin! My father did nothing of this. My mother was a Magian (fire-worshipper). He gave me the name of Ju'alaan (meaning dung beetle or scarab) and he did not teach me a single letter of the Qur'an."

Turning to the father, 'Umar said:

"You have come to me to complain about the disobedience of you son. You have failed in your duty to him before he has failed in his duty to you; you have done wrong to him before he has wronged you."

Of course in the web of relationships fostered by Islam, not only parents, but grandparents, uncles and aunts, sisters and brothers, neighbours and teachers — all have an important role in the tarbiyyah of new generations.

As a grandparent, through your wisdom gained through experience, you can provide and derive great enjoyment from children and give much needed relief to parents under stress. We are reminded of the example of the Prophet in his care for his daughter Fatimah and his love for her children, Hasan and Husayn.

DO YOU KISS YOUR CHILDREN?

A man named Al-Aqra ibn Habis visited the Prophet and was surprised to see him kiss his grandsons, Hasan and Husayn.

"Do you kiss your children?" he asked, adding that he had ten children and never kissed one of them.

"(That shows) you have no mercy and tenderness at all. Those who do not show mercy to others will not have God's mercy shown on them," commented the noble Prophet.

It is a matter of sadness that many children are denied the benefits of not having a grandparent to cherish and dote on them, to take them on journeys back in time and spin yarns for them. We say again that the trend towards nuclear families is a trend for the impoverishment of children.

Tarbiyyah or Education of Children

In the tarbiyyah of children, you should remember that children often learn from example. The proper conduct and example of parents are crucial in the upbringing of children. Parents who expect their children to be disciplined and to work hard must themselves be disciplined and work hard. Parents who expect their children to be truthful must not be in the habit of telling lies. Also, it is important to remember that the treatment given to children in the early years of their life can have far-reaching effects on their mental and emotional state later on in life.

In the tarbiyyah of children, you should try to remember that:

● Children should be happy and cheerful, and have a zest for life and living. They should be able to feel something of the carefree joy and excitement of growing up, especially before they are mukallaf. They should not be battered and terrorised.

● They should be trained to grow up with the attitudes and habits, the *adab* or etiquette or Islam: "Be generous, kind and noble to your children and make their habits and manners good and beautiful (*Akrimuu awlaadakum was ahsinuu adabahum*)," said the noble Prophet. Among the virtues and habits they should develop are:

- the habit of being honest and truthful;

- the habit of being gentle and polite — for according to the noble Prophet, "Gentleness adorns everything" — without being timid, afraid and cowed down;

- the habit of being helpful and considerate without being loutish in their behaviour to others;

- the habit of being clean and neat and tidy, of looking after their personal hygiene and appearance.

Children need to develop the *adab* or the etiquette of Islam: when and how to greet; how to speak, sit, eat, and how to perform natural functions like personal toilet in the clean and efficient manner as taught by the noble Prophet; to do everything in the manner, time and place that is appropriate for it, for example: to be reverent in Salaat, attentive in class, robust and full of zest in play.

Children need to develop physical fitness and skills, to be strong and courageous. The Prophet recommended that children be taught horse-riding, swimming and archery. One Muslim ruler once suggested that his child be taught swimming before reading and writing on the grounds that someone else may read and write for him but no one can swim for him! From the noble Prophet's recommendations, we see that children need to lead an active outdoor life and be proficient in some of the martial arts. They should have the stamina for demanding play and demanding work. This implies at least that they should be adequately fed.

Children need to develop a thirst for knowledge, beneficial knowledge — through listening, observation, reading, interacting with others. It is recommended that children be taught from an early age to recite and read the Qur'an and develop a love for it. At an early age, they have the capacity to memorize it and it is common for many children and youths to memorize the whole or large parts of the Qur'an. From the age of seven, the Prophet recommended that children should get in the habit of performing Salaat and by the age of ten they should be required to do so regularly.

Children need to develop skills and to be creative and inventive. They should be trained from an early age to take on responsibilities, to organise and take initiative rather than be timid and submissive. They should be able to spend their time usefully and profitably. They need to develop the skills that would fit them for contemporary living and for the particular society in which they live. This may involve anything — from the skills of running an efficient and creative home to the skills that would enable them to earn a living and help in the process of tarbiyyah when their turn comes. Give a person a fish and you feed just one person; teach a person to fish and he can then feed hundreds, says an apt Chinese proverb.

Above all, correct tarbiyyah should ensure that children develop a love for Islam, a love for God and His Prophet and that they develop a feeling of pride in being Muslim and a willingness to strive for the good of others. They need to realise the benefits of Islam, the foundations on which it is based and their need for Islam. They need to value Islam and live by Islamic values.

Sexual morality and sex education

Because of the grave dangers that children and others are now more and more exposed to from an early age, it is important to pay attention to this aspect of education.

Appropriate sex education at the appropriate time and in a manner appropriate to Islamic ideals is not only desirable but necessary. It is especially necessary because of the destructive trends in the world today.

Sex education is taught within the framework of religious obligations. A mother or female teacher would naturally be the best person to teach a daughter and the father or male teacher a son.

Children are to be taught what is permissible (halaal) and what is forbidden (haraam) with reasons and consequences. No immoral or dissolute person is therefore allowed to teach.

All teaching is to be imparted within the limits of modesty and chastity and no encouragement should be given to lewdness and experimentation.

Sex education is imparted in stages according to the natural physical and emotional development of children. The ages given below for each stage is approximate and may vary slightly from child to child.

1.   The age between seven and ten called the age of discretion *(sinn at-tamyiiz)* at which training is given, for example in the etiquette of asking permission to enter rooms and in the etiquette of "looking" at others. Significantly, a child is recommended to begin performing Salaat from the age of seven. This requires the proper etiquette of maintaining personal hygiene, including the washing of the private parts after going to toilet. The context in which private

parts are discussed allows the subject to be mentioned openly and naturally and without any unhealthy secretiveness or courseness.

2.   The age between ten and fourteen known as the age of puberty *(sinn al-muraahaqah)* in which the child is prepared for the next stage but trained to keep away from all sexual passions. A child is trained to perform Salaat regularly from the age of ten. One of the purposes of regular Salaat, according to the Qur'an, is that it keeps one away from all that is "shameful and bad".

3.   The age normally between thirteen and sixteen known as the age of maturity *(sinn al-buluugh)* at which the child now turned adult is taught the etiquette of sexual behaviour in preparation for marriage. A person is taught to practice chastity and self-restraint until marriage or if for whatever reason he or she is unable to marry.

At the first stage, as soon as the awareness of the opposite sex become apparent, children are taught to seek permission before entering rooms and that they are not allowed to look at the private parts of another, including someone of the same sex. It is not natural or necessary, for example, that they be taught details of copulation at this stage.

At the age of discretion, children need to be prepared for the stage of puberty so that when physical changes occur they would know how to react, how to clean themselves, how to prepare for the obligatory Prayer and other related matters.

At the age of puberty, when males produce semen and females start their monthly reproductive cycles, everyone becomes mukallaf and all the obligations of adulthood devolve on them — the duty to have ghusl when necessary and desirable, to make Salaat, to fast, to preserve their chastity, and to keep their "awrah covered (see box). They need to be taught explicitly what is halaal and what is haraam.

'AWRAH

•   The 'awrah of a male is the part of the body from the navel to the knee. The 'awrah of a female is the whole body with the exception of the face, hands, and feet.

•   It is not allowed for a man to show his 'awrah to anyone except his wife.

•   A woman may not show her 'awrah to anyone except her husband. However, among Muslim males whom she cannot marry (such as her father, brother, son, uncle, or nephews) her body from the chest down to her knees excluding the arms may not be shown.

Among Muslim females, a Muslim woman may not show any part of the body from the navel to the knee. Accordingly, a Muslim woman may not look at the thighs of her adult daughter, sister, mother or friend while bathing or otherwise.   Among non-Muslim females, a Muslim woman may not show any part of her 'awrah.

(Source: 'Abdullah Naasih 'Ulwaan, *Education and the Training of Children in Islam (Tarbiyyatu-l Awlaad fi-l Islaam)*, Dar as-Salaam, Aleppo, 1981).

At the state of preparation for marriage, persons need to know the rights and obligations of husband and wife to each other. These include the etiquette of sexual contact and behaviour and the need for spouses to have physical and emotional satisfaction in marriage.

Both the Qur'an and the Sunnah are explicit on matters of sex and sex education. The object is to create an open, balanced and responsible attitude based on knowledge. Islam is opposed to treating sex as a completely taboo subject which gives rise to feelings of guilt. It is also opposed to treating it in a completely casual and immoral manner without the due regard to modesty and respect that something as intimate and personal as sexual life demands.

Children's duties to parents

While parents are naturally disposed to love their children, children are often disposed to disregard their parents. It is for this reason, and because of the enormous debt that an individual owes to his parents, that the Qur'an has made it compulsory on the child to treat his parents with all goodness and mercy. On the other hand, it has not placed a similar compulsory obligation on parents. God says in the Qur'an:

> "We have enjoined on man goodness towards both his parents. His mother bore him by bearing strain upon strain, and his utter dependence on her lasted two years. Hence, O Man, be grateful to Me and to your parents (and remember that) with Me is all journeys' end." (31: 14)
>
> "And your Lord has commanded that you worship none but Him and that you be kind to parents. If either or both of them reach old age with you, do not say to them (so much as) 'Uff!' nor chide them but address them in terms of honour, and out of kindness lower to them your wing of humility and say, 'My Lord and Sustainer, have mercy on them both as they nurtured, cherished and sustained me in childhood." (17: 23-24)

It is thus a compulsory duty (fard 'ayn) on every adult Muslim to show goodness and mercy and act righteously to his parents throughout their lives. This applies even to parents who are not Muslims. Excluded from this are parents who promote *shirk* or ask their children to associate anything or being in worship with God, or ask them to commit any act which involves the disobedience of God. Only in such cases must children disobey their parents.

The duty of a child, however old he or she may be, to parents are:

- to show love and gratitude to them;
- to speak to them with kindness and respect;
- to strive to do everything that would please them and make them happy;
- to offer good advice and guidance to parents when it is needed especially if they are not Muslim;
- to avoid any angry or exasperated expression or reaction to what parents

THE STORY OF ALQAMAH

"Shall I not tell you," asked the noble Prophet, "of the gravest of the major sins? It is to associate others with God and to disobey parents."

There was a young man at the time of the Prophet, Alqamah by name. He devoted himself to worship, performing Salaat, fasting and giving charity. He became seriously ill and his wife, in great distress, went to the Prophet and said:

"My husband is critically ill and I want to tell you of his condition, O Messenger of God."

The Prophet summoned three of his trusted companions — Bilaal, Suhayb and 'Ammaar — and told them:

"Go to Alqamah and let him recite the Shahaadah."

They went and found him in a critical state and tried to make him say the Shahaadah — "Laa ilaaha illa Allah" — but the words would not come from his tongue. They reported this to the Prophet who then asked:

"Is any of his parents alive?" and was told that his mother was, but that she was very old. The Prophet sent someone to ask her to come to him if she could; if however she was not able, he himself would go to her. Her immediate response, showing how much she respected the Prophet, was:

"By my life, I am the one who should go to him." Slowly, with her walking stick, she proceeded to the Prophet. She greeted him and he returned the greeting of peace and said to her:

"Tell me the truth... How has your son Alqamah been?"

"Messenger of God," she said, "he performs much Salaat, fasts and gives a great deal in charity."

"And how are you (to him)?"

"Messenger of God, I am angry with him."

"Why?"

"O Messenger of God, he preferred his wife against me and disobeyed me."

Thereupon the Prophet said, "The anger of Alqamah's mother has certainly prevented Alqamah's tongue from uttering the Shahaadah." He then asked Bilaal to gather a huge bundle of firewood.

"Messenger of God, what will you do?" asked Alqamah's mother.

"I will burn him in the fire right in front of you."

"O Messenger of God! My son! My heart cannot bear that he should be burnt before my eyes."

"Mother of Alqamah! God's (punishment) is more severe and long lasting. If you really want God to forgive him, then show that you are pleased with him. By Him in whose hand is my soul, Alqamah will not benefit from his Prayer, his fasting and his charity so long as you remain angry with him."

"O Messenger of God! I call God to witness and the angels and those Muslims who are present here with me, that I am pleased with my son Alqamah."

Thereafter Alqamah's tongue was released and he repeated the words of the Shahaadah — 'I testify that there is no deity but God and I testify that Muhammad is the Messenger of God.' That very day he passed away. The Prophet himself performed the Janaazah (Funeral) Prayer and reminded the Muslims of the gravity of the sin of making a mother angry and the rewards of keeping her satisfaction and pleasure.

might say or do and which they do not agree or find favour with;

● to refrain, according to a saying of the Prophet, from condemning your own parents by denouncing the parents of others for they in turn might denounce your parents;

● to refrain from disobeying them for this was regarded by the Prophet as one of the major sins in Islam together with the sin of *shirk*;

● to look after their needs especially when they become old and cannot properly look after themselves. This involves not showing any signs of displeasure or distaste when they are sick or incontinent. Instead, repeat often the beautiful Qur'anic prayer:

"My Lord and Sustainer! Be kind and have mercy on them as they cherished, nurtured and sustained me in childhood."

● to continue to pray for them and ask God to forgive them even after they have died for the noble Prophet has said that when a person dies all his actions come to an end except three: a continuous charity, knowledge from which people benefit, and a righteous child who prays for him;

● to fulfil, after their death, any contracts they might have left and to maintain contact with and be kind to their friends.

One of the benefits of being good and kind to parents is that goodness and kindness is passed on from one generation to another according to the saying of the noble Prophet:

"Be good and kind to your parents and your children will be good and kind to you."

In particular, a person is required to be good and kind to his mother and show gratitude to her for the trials and agonies she experienced in giving birth to him; for nurturing and providing for his needs in helpless childhood especially; and for being his first school in life. This is why the noble Prophet emphasized repeatedly that a mother has the first claim on a person's care, closeness and companionship.

Someone asked God's messenger, peace be on him, to whom he should should show kindness and he replied. "Your mother." He asked who came next and he replied, "Your mother." He asked again who came next and he again replied, "Your mother." He asked who came next and he replied, "Your father, then your relatives in order of relationship."

A man came to the Prophet, peace be on him, and said: "Messenger of God, I desire to go on a military expedition and I have come to consult you." The noble Prophet asked him if he had a mother and when he replied that he had, he said:

"Stay with her, for Paradise is at her feet."

Marital Ties

We have seen how the family in Islam is welded together by ties of kinship. It is also held together and extended by marital ties and permitted relationships which are the most natural and beneficial for individuals and society.

For many people, and indeed for many social systems and religions that are not based on firm foundations, it is often difficult to determine what is natural and beneficial for both individuals and society. To decide what is morally right and good has become a major dilemma for many individuals and societies.

So far as the interaction between society, morality and sex is concerned, there are four choices apparently open to any society:

1.   an entirely homosexual society;

2.   an entirely promiscuous society;

3.   a society in which no sexual relations exist except between husband and wife;

4.   a laissez-faire society in which all the above forms are tolerated.

Which of these four choices can be said to promote the welfare of individuals and society? In answering this question, it should be reasonable and natural to say that only those relationships that help to promote people's welfare ought to be commended and described as moral. Also, whatever can be shown to have dangerous anti-social consequences cannot be considered morally right or good.

A society of homosexuals only will mean the death of mankind since it severs sexual behaviour from its reproductive function. Homosexuals advocate a view of human relationships that is at odds with the natural order and stability of human society. We do not need to go into the perverse nature and the bad consequences of homosexuality which is described in the Qur'an as an "abomination" and those who indulge in it as "committing excesses".

An entirely promiscuous society is thought by some to be the best. In such a society, it is imagined that everyone will have complete freedom to choose whoever he likes at whatever time he prefers. With such freedom will come the deepest enjoyment as well as the reproduction of the species.

The reality will be different and there will be frightful difficulties. People will become obsessed with sex. Strange as it may seem, sexual deprivation will be a major problem. Incest and deviant behaviour will be common as it is in many societies that are promiscuous. Sexually transmitted diseases will spread.

The effects of all this on human values and behaviour are incalculable. Overall, it will have a degrading effect on sex itself and on human relationships. Sex will not be seen in the context of a whole, loving relationship, but will become an end in itself and in the process destroy respect, love, care and responsibility in human relationships.

Some of these effects can already be seen in several societies.

Many criminal tendencies both among the young and among the old are discovered to have their origins in broken homes and unstable families. The most efficient social services cannot cope with the legions of parentless children which a promiscuous society produces. And there is the terrible cost in terms of personal pain and agony of children naturally wanting to know who is their father or indeed who is their mother? In many countries of the world today, more than half the population is illegitimate. If present trends continue, the figures will keep on rising.

Some might say: Well, no one has ever seriously advocated a completely homosexual society or a completely promiscuous society. All we want is a society where every individual or group of individuals shall have the freedom to lead the kind of sexual life they prefer. In such a mixed society, married people, will live side by side with promiscuous individuals and homosexuals. Each will respect the ideas and choices of the others and tolerate their behaviour. We must be tolerant for tolerance is a great virtue.

But this will not do either.

If we can see clearly and if we then admit that the consequences of homosexuality and promiscuity are harmful, it is not reasonable or natural to tolerate the factors responsible for them. Tolerating homosexuality and promiscuity means encouraging them and pushing more and more people to practice them. Marital relationships will be affected. Married people may even be regarded as odd or "eccentric" in such a society and may even not be tolerated as the example of Lot's people shows:

"And remember Lot when he said to his people, 'Will you commit abominations such as none in all the world has ever done before you?

"Verily, with lust you approach men instead of women. Indeed, you are a people given to excesses!

"But his people's only answer was this: 'Expel them from your land! They are folk who make themselves out to be pure.' "(27: 56)

By elimination then, the society with the most good and the least evil is a society based on the family and marital relationships. Married people in such a society will not tolerate but do their best to eradicate the causes of homosexuality, promiscuity and sexual laisser faire. This will be the rational society with the best hope of happiness. In such a society:

● sex is enjoyed within marriage without being given undue prominence over other needs and values;

● sex does not become the purpose of life but an important ingredient which helps to make it more happy and enjoyable;

● children are born and well-looked after.

The best way of achieving these aims is:

1. to have a healthy attitude towards sex;
2. to exhort people to marry and to marry for the proper reasons;
3. to show them how best to preserve and enjoy their married life;
4. to make it possible for them to terminate an unsuccessful marriage;

5.   to lessen the factors which may tempt them to look for sexual satisfaction outside marriage;

6.   to severely punish those who seek sexual gratification in non-marital avenues, whether pre-marital or extra-marital avenues.

1.   A healthy attitude

The human species is biologically a pair-forming species. This may be shown by observation and is also mentioned in the Qur'an as one of the signs of God's wisdom, love and care.

"And among God's wonders is this: He creates for you mates out of your own kind so that you might incline towards them, and He engenders love and tenderness between you. In this, behold, there are signs indeed for people who think."

The need for sexual relations is natural for adults. If this need is naturally fulfilled within marriage, it does not carry any feelings of immorality, guilt and sin. In fact, just as adultery, fornication and homosexuality are punishable offenses, satisfying sexual needs within marriage merits reward. The Prophet once remarked that a man is to be rewarded for performing the sexual act with his wife, and when some of his surprised listeners wondered how could a person be rewarded for satisfying his own desire, the noble Prophet said:

"Do you not see that it he were to satisfy it in a prohibited manner he would be committing a sin? So if he satisfies it in a lawful manner, he will be recompensed."

A Muslim husband and wife who come to perform the sexual act, do not do so with guilty consciences or the feeling that they are about to do something that degrades them or remove them further from God. They come with the feeling of doing something which God approves and for which He gives a good reward. Following the example of the Prophet, they perform it in the name of God.

2.   Encouraging people to marry

There is no celibacy or monasticism in Islam. The noble Prophet has said:

"Marriage is part of my Sunnah (example) and whoever disdains my sunnah is not one of me."

The Prophet exhorted young people to marry and advised all concerned to make marriage easy for those who want to marry. The Prophet himself took a keen interest in encouraging his companions to marry and giving them practical help in setting up a home as the story of Rabii'ah ibn Ka'b shows (see box).

The noble Prophet encouraged people to marry a partner for the sake of good character, piety and religiosity instead of just wealth, noble stock or beauty.

The practice of dating and courting, of pre-marital relations, of "trial unions and marriages" are firmly prohibited. In fact, it is not allowed for a man and

---

DON'T YOU WANT TO GET MARRIED?

"I was a young man and poor. I had neither family, nor wealth, nor place of abode. I used to shelter in the Suffah (a raised platform) of the mosque with other poor Muslims like myself. People used to call us the "guests of Islam".

I had the good fortune of being in the Prophet's service and being his companion in this world. (Once) the Prophet called me and asked:

'Don't you want to get married, Rabii'ah?'

'I do not want anything to distract me from your service,' I replied. 'Moreover, I don't have anything to give as *mahr* (dowry) to a wife nor any place where I can accommodate a wife.' "

Rabii'ah went on to tell how the Prophet sent him to a couple with the request to marry their daughter to him, how he instructed a man of his clan to collect a nuwat's weight in gold for him)Rabii'ah) to give as dowry and purchase a sheep for the *waliimah* (wedding celebration), and how he also asked his wife 'Aa'ishah to give some barley for the walimah which she did saying, "By God, we do not have any other food."

Rabii'ah was obviously thrilled by these arrangements and said: "So we had bread and meat for the waliimah."

After the wedding, the Prophet also gave him a piece of land to set up home.

---

woman who are not within the prohibited degrees of marriage, to be alone together or to have any physical contact. A man may not sit alone with his female cousin for example if they are not married.

Both parties in a marriage must give their free and willing consent to the marriage. Parents may recommend a suitable marriage partner for their child of marriageable age but no parent or guardian has any right to force a daughter or a son to marry anyone.

3. *Showing how to enjoy and preserve married life*

The marriage relationship is summed up in the metaphor of the Qur'an:

"They (wives) are your garments and you (husbands) are their garments." (2: 187)

Marriage, like a garment, is meant to be a comfort, a protection, and a security. It beautifies and warms personalities. It enfolds, covers and conceals what is private from the eyes of the world.

For a happy marriage, everything ultimately depends on the free will, the intentions and attitudes of the individual husband and wife.

In the Islamic marriage sermon, there is no mention of marriage itself but there is the repeated emphasis on taqwa or God-consciousness from which all duties and rights spring.

Husbands as well as wives have duties as well as rights but the best of them are those who perform their duties without insisting on their rights.

Duties of a husband

As a husband, you are to remember that the way you treat your wife is a test of

---

ISLAMIC MARRIAGE SERMON

"In the name of God, most Gracious, most Merciful.
    O Mankind! Be conscious of Your Lord and Sustainer
Who created you from a single soul and from it created its mate and from them
both has spread abroad a multitude of men and women.
And remain conscious of God in Whom you claim (your rights) of one an-
other, and of the ties of kinship.
Indeed, God is ever watchful over you." (4: 1)

    "O you who have attained to faith! Be conscious of God with all the con-
sciousness that is due to Him, and do not allow death to overtake you before
you have surrendered yourselves unto Him." (3: 102)

    "O you who believe! Remain conscious of God and (always) speak with a
will to bring out (only) what is just and true (whereupon) He will rectify your
conduct and will forgive you your sins.
And (know that) whoever pays heed to God and His apostle has already
attained a mighty triumph." (33: 70-71)

---

your moral worth for the noble Prophet said: "The best of you are those who
are best to their wives."

You have a duty to support your wife and provide her with adequate food,
clothing, a matrimonial home and essential education.

You should, following the example of the Prophet, help your wife with
household work.

You should resolve not to hate your wife because if a husband "dislikes one
of his wife's characteristics he would be pleased with another (of her qualities)".

When you intend to have sexual intercourse with your wife, the noble Prophet advised that you should court her and approach her in a gentle manner,
not in a rough way as animals do. And when you have satisfied yourself, you
should wait until she is also satisfied.

You have the overall duty of providing for and managing your household.
This is emphasized in the saying of the noble Prophet:

"Each one of you is a shepherd and is responsible for his flock...A man is a
ruler in his family, and he will be questioned about those under his care. A
woman is a ruler in the house of her husband and she will be questioned about
those under her care..."

Duties and rights of a wife

As a wife, you have a duty to obey your husband in whatever does not involve
disobedience to God for the noble Prophet has said, "If a woman performs the
five daily Salaat, fasts in the month of Ramadaan, preserves her chastity and
obeys her husband, say to her: Enter Paradise through whichever of its gates she
pleases." There is one thing in particular in which a wife should strive not to

disobey her husband, and that is when he invites her to come to bed.

You have the right to express your views and make suggestions on all matters but the best role you can play in keeping the marital tie intact and strong is to recognize your husband as the person responsible for the running of the family. This is the general rule. You however have responsibility for those under your care, according to the hadith quoted above.

You have the right to your own individuality, to retain your own name, and to own, inherit and use property as you wish. You have the right and the duty to pursue education and vocational goals that would develop your talents, protect the interests of your family and strengthen the Muslim community.

4. Safeguarding marriage and family

The marital system is the only choice that is open to a rational society. It is only natural for such a society to protect marriage and family relationships from harmful influences. It is an insane society which insists on the strength of the marital bond but goes on to encourage or even remain indifferent to factors which endanger or rent it asunder. You cannot be consistent if you say that it is better for people to confine their sexual relations to marriage but at the same time advocate or tolerate such things as the publication of obscene literature and the exhibition of pictures of naked bodies, the wearing of immodest clothes, the making, screening and viewing of films which make public what should be private, the indiscriminate mingling of men and women, discotheques, beauty contests and other aspects of the sex industry now one of the biggest in the world. If it becomes normal for people to tolerate or indulge in such activities, it would be difficult and indeed impossible to keep family ties properly intact. It would be difficult to safeguard the love, warmth and trust on which happy marriage relationships are based. Your attitude to such activities should be shaped by the principles governing what is haraam such as whatever leads to the forbidden is also forbidden.

If you always keep in mind the great value that Islam puts on married life, you will appreciate the wisdom of restrictions on the free association of men and women, the type of clothes they wear and on certain forms of their artistic expression. You will also appreciate particular rules such as that which requires a man not to enjoy the sight of a woman who is not his wife, but to cast down his eyes if he happens to glance at her by chance. A woman is asked to behave in the same way towards a man who is not her husband. This is not because there is something dirty or ugly in people but because the look is often the first step to grosser offenses. The Qur'an asks the Prophet to "Say to the believers, that they cast down their eyes and guard their private parts. That is purer for them."

In all such matters, you need to preserve and develop the essential natural quality of *hayaa'* which implies modesty and chastity, and a sense of shyness, shame and propriety. Hayaa' is a characteristic of both men and women.

DRESS: SYMBOL OF THE CIVILIZING POWER OF ISLAM

Dress serves three functions:
- to protect the body from the weather, from heat and cold, wind and rain;
- to adorn and beautify the human personality;
- to help to safeguard the modesty and decency of a person and safeguard the moral ideals of a society. Dress therefore has a moral function.

Appropriate dress both for men and women is naturally important for a society where sexual relations is confined to marriage.

To make it easy for people to live within the bounds of morality, they are required to wear clothes that conceal and not reveal or accentuate their bodily charms and thus reduce or eliminate temptations.

Islam, being a universal religion, has not prescribed any particular form, fashion or style of dress. However, it sets certain requirements of dress whatever the climate or region. These requirements apply to both men and women.
1. Dress should cover a person's 'awrah.
A man's 'awrah extends from the navel to the knee;
A woman's 'awrah is the whole body with the exception of the face, hands and feet.
2. Dress should not be transparent.
3. Dress should be loose-fitting .
4. Dress outside the home should not worn for the sake of showiness, whether it is glamorous garments that make for pride or excite admiration, envy or lust, or whether is is rough garments that are meant to draw attention to poverty or alleged piety. Men are not allowed to wear silk or gold and women should not wear perfume outside the home.

Proper dress is one of the outer symbols of the civilizing mission and power of Islam.

5. *Punishment for premarital or extramarital sexual acts*

A person who is married and commits adultery and who either confesses, or whose act is proven by pregnancy, or who does so in a manner that four persons witness and testify to his detestable act pays for it with his life. The punishment for false accusations of adultery is also severe.

A married person committing sodomy is also to be punished by death.

A person who is not married and commits fornication is publicly flogged with a hundred lashes and exiled or imprisoned for a year. An unmarried person committing sodomy will be treated in a similar fashion.

The reasons for these severe punishments are: to preserve marital ties and family life and the stability of society; to safeguard the interests of children and future generations of mankind and protect honour and chastity.

6. *Terminating an unsuccessful marriage*

No one can pretend that all marriages are always happy and blissful. However hard you may try, unforeseen difficulties may make married life intolerable. Islam prescribes every precaution to prevent the break-up of a marriage. It recommends counselling and mediation by relatives, friends or a judge to help resolve differences and problems. But when married life does not fulfil its purpose and becomes unbearable, the marriage bond is severed as a last resort.

If a man decides to divorce his wife, there is opportunity for reconsideration. After the first pronouncement of divorce, a man may not have intercourse with his wife for three months. The pronouncement of divorce must not be made when the wife is in her monthly periods.

A woman may obtain a divorce from her husband either by mutual agreement or by petitioning a judge. She may seek divorce in case of cruelty, intense dislike, non-fulfilment of the terms of the marriage contract, insanity, impotence, desertion without giving reason or providing maintenance, and other similar causes. (See the Qur'an, 4: 20; 4:128; 4: 130).

For the health and stability of mankind, family units and family relationships must be protected and safeguarded from all the ravages of our time. The natural and consistent way in which Islam cements and regulates these relationships offers the only hope for an afflicted humanity.

Islamic values in the home: design for Islamic living

We have dealt at length with the natural need to control sexual relationships and safeguard the institution of the family inasmuch as the pressures on and threats against this precious and delicate institution are now so numerous and

---

CONCERNING ADULTERY

"Do not come near to adultery for it is a shameful deed and an evil, opening the road (to other evils). (*The Qur'an*, (17: 32)

"There is no sin after shirk (associating others with god) more gross in the sight of God than a drop of semen which a man places in the womb which is not lawful for him." *(Hadith)*

'Abdullah ibn Mas'uud reported: "I asked the Messenger, may God bless him and grant him peace: 'Messenger of God, which is the biggest sin?'
He replied: 'To set up rivals with God by worshipping others though He alone has created you.'
'What next?' I asked.
'To kill your child lest it should share your food.'
'What next?' I asked.
'To commit illegal sexual intercourse with the wife of your neighbour,' he replied."

"The *zina* (adultery and fornication) of legs is walking (towards an unlawful person with bad intention); the adultery of the hands is touching and patting, and the adultery of the eyes is casting passionate glances at persons unlawful (for you)." *(Hadith)*

REFORMING INDIVIDUALS—THE PROPHET'S METHOD

A young man went to the Prophet and asked:

"Messenger of God, give me permission to commit adultery."

The companions of the Prophet shouted at the youth. The Prophet restrained them and told the young man to come close to him. The young man came and sat before the Prophet who asked him:

"Do you like adultery to be committed with your mother?"

"No! May God make me your ransom!"

"In the same way, no one would like it for their mothers. Would you like it for your daughter?"

"No! May God make me your ransom!"

"In the same way, people would not like it for their daughters. Would you like it for your sister?"

In this way, the Prophet continued, mentioning the youth's maternal and paternal aunts. Each time, the youth answered "No!" and the Prophet replied,

"In the same way, people would not like it."

Finally, the Prophet placed his hand on the youth's chest and said: "O Lord, purify his heart, forgive his sins, and preserve his chastity."

Thereafter, there was nothing more odious and detestable to the youth than adultery.

---

great. Over and above this, there is of course the need to enrich family life by positive attitudes, values and practices.

The Islamic values of faith, love, compassion, cleanliness and beauty all need to be nurtured in the home. Briefly, the ideal Muslim home would need to be:

• simple and not ostentatious for the Prophet said: "Eat, drink, give sadaqah and wear good clothes as long as these things do not involve excess and arrogance."

• spacious, to allow privacy for parents and separate beds for children from the age of ten, for the noble Prophet has advised: "Separate (your children's) beds when they are ten years of age." This is obviously to prevent such disgusting crimes and sinful behaviour as incest.

• clean, for the noble Prophet has said that "Cleanliness is part of Faith" and also "Purity is half of Faith."

• beautiful and free from such things as statues or revolting pieces of art for he noble Prophet has said "God is Beautiful and loves beauty."

The ideal Muslim home is:

• a place where there are the basic necessities of food and clothing (see the Qur'an, 2: 233; 2: 235-6), where meals are eaten together and where there is hospitality and generosity;

• a place where the greeting of Peace (Salaam) is heard at dawn and at night and at times of going and coming;

● a place where love, tenderness and mercy is the norm for the Qur'an says ''And we have made between you love and tenderness.''

● a cheerful place, for ''Smiling is charity'';

● a place where the recitation of the Qur'an is heard daily and where knowledge is imparted and pursued;

● a place where Salaat is performed and everyone, young and old, has a sense of time and place — time, in particular, related to the times of Salaat, and place — determined by the direction of the Qiblah.

This is the basic minimum.

Treatment of relatives

The Muslim family is, as mentioned earlier, not just a nuclear family of husband, wife and children but is extended to include relatives as well.

As a Muslim, you are required to maintain a close and caring relationship with relatives. According to a saying of the Prophet, you are required to visit relatives, inquire about their circumstances, spend on them and give them sadaqah if they are poor.

WHAT A LOVELY PROPERTY!

Abu Talhah was one of the wealthiest men in Madinah. He had orchards and groves of datepalms. His favourite possession was an orchard called Bayr Haa. It was in the direction of the Prophet's mosque. The Prophet often went to this orchard and drank of its cool, fresh water.

Anas, a companion of the Prophet, said that when the verse of the Qur'an was revealed: ''You will not attain to righteousness until you spend in charity out of what you love'', Abu Talhah came to the Prophet, peace be on him, and said:

''Messenger of God! God Almighty has revealed to you (and he recited the verse). In fact the most beloved of my possessions is Bayr Haa. It is now a sadaqah for the sake of God Almighty. I desire the righteousness that would come from (giving) it... Do with it, Messenger of God, whatever God shows you.''

''What a lovely property that is! How fruitful and profitable it is! I have heard what you said. I think that you should give it to your relatives,'' said the noble Prophet.

''I shall do so, Messenger of God,'' replied Abu Talhah and he divided it up among his relatives and his cousins.

From the above we can see that the institution of the family is maintained by feelings of love and tenderness, by the Islamic laws of morality and decency and by practical measures of mutual assistance and support.

Strong, stable and healthy family units provide the foundation for strong, stable and healthy communities and societies.

FIVE

YOU *and* YOUR NEIGHBOURHOOD

The story is told of a man who saw a green and beautiful valley. It was calm and peaceful. How wonderful it would be to live in this valley all alone, he said to himself. I can spend my time reflecting on nature and worshipping God, doing no harm and having no harm done to me. The man went to the Prophet and told him what he had seen and what he wanted to do. But the wise Prophet did not allow him to do as he wished.

NATURALLY SOCIAL

While the human being is in need of quiet moments, of time to reflect alone, of privacy and solitude, he is by nature a social being. To live in society and interact with others is a natural or inborn characteristic of human beings. The human being was not forced into being social nor did he simply learn by experience that he cannot live in total isolation and solitude. Neither did he just use his reason to decide that it was better if he cooperated and shared with others.

One of the reasons for saying that social life is natural is suggested in the noble verse of the Qur'an:

"It is We who portion out among them their livelihood in the life of this world, and We raise some of them above others (from the standpoints of possibilities and capacities) in degrees, so that some might obtain labour of others." (43: 2)

This suggests that people are not created alike in their possibilities and capabilities. If people were all alike, there would be no need to obtain any service or help from others. God has created people with different physical, spiritual, intellectual and emotional capacities. He has made some superior in some ways and others superior in other ways. He has thus made all need each other and naturally inclined to interact with one another. This is thus the basis of the social or interconnected life of human beings.

People therefore naturally need one another for their mutual benefit. This is why withdrawal from society is not allowed in Islam. No one may just disappear into his green and luscious valley, forget about others and do as he likes.

Since man was created in a naturally good state, the purpose of community or society is to promote and work for all that is good. Also because some people go against their natural state and commit acts of crime or evil deeds, the purpose of community or society is also to discourage or fight against all that is bad or evil. The need for such interaction and cooperation is expressed in a beautiful parable related by the noble Prophet:

> "The case of those who observe the limits set by God and those who are careless about them is like passengers on a ship who cast lots to determine who should occupy the upper deck and who should be on the lower deck and disposed of themselves accordingly. Those who were on the lower deck passed through those of the upper deck whenever they had to fetch water. So they said to the occupants of the upper deck: If we were to bore a hole through part, we would not then have to trouble you. Now, if the occupants of the upper deck were to leave the others to carry out their design they would all perish together; but if they were to stop them from carrying it out they would all be saved."

This parable shows that it is foolish to allow everyone to do whatever he wants to do and whenever he wants to do it. To be liberal in the sense of being tolerant of every type of behaviour can be disastrous. People need to work together for the common good.

The basis of cooperation

The basis of interaction and cooperation has been laid down by the Qur'an itself:

"Cooperate with one another on the basis of righteousness and God-consciousness, and do not cooperate with one another on the basis of sin and transgression."

(Transgression (Arabic: 'udwaan) here means going beyond the limits of permissible behaviour set by God.)

The Qur'an in fact suggests that individuals can only prosper if they, altogether, acquire knowledge and faith, if they do good deeds *and* if they collectively encourage and promote truth and steadfastness. If they don't, they will find themselves in a state of loss and ruin. This is stated in the brief surah of just three verses called *"Al-Asr"* or Time.

"Consider Time!
Man is indeed in a state of loss
Except those who attain to faith

and do good works
and enjoin upon one another to uphold the truth
and enjoin upon one another to be steadfast.''
(The Qur'an, 103: 1-3)

This surah sums up the Islamic view of human history. It sets out the conditions which save a community from loss and ruin. At the same time it tells what peoples and communities must do to be strong and prosperous. Foremost among these is not wealth, or power or the strength of numbers although all these are important as means to an end. It is above all, the combined and total commitment to truth and justice and the determination to remain steadfast that save a community from ruin and guarantee its strength and prosperity.

A sense of belonging to a community or group is natural to the needs of man and a vital part of a person's identity. In the last section we have shown that man needs the care, warmth and support of the family which is the basic unit of Islamic society.

Beyond the family, people need the goodwill, support and fellowship of friends, neighhbours and the wider community and society. People need to create the environment, the facilities and the network of relationships that promote and enhance the good and combat and discourage the bad. People need to identify with and feel part of a group or community that work towards these goals.

In the rest of this chapter, we shall look, in some more detail, at man's natural need for good company and friendship. We shall also look at the need for caring neighbours and a healthy and stable neighbourhood and environment.

FRIENDS

For various moral, psychological and social reasons, people need good company and close friendship. The type of friends you have often indicate the type of person you are. Show me your friends and I will tell you what you are, says the well-known proverb.

The noble Prophet pointed to the value of good company when he said that it is better to be alone than in the company of the wicked, and it is better to be in the company of the good than to be alone.

Good company can be a great source of help and support in leading a virtuous life while bad company can lead to sin and ruin. This is clear in the advice given in the Qur'an:

"And keep yourself content with those who call on their Lord morning and evening, seeking His countenance, and let not your eyes pass beyond them to those who seek the pomp and glitter of this life; nor obey any whose heart we have permitted to neglect Our remembrance, who follows his own desires, whose case has gone beyond all bounds." (18: 28)

The Prophet has given similar advice in choosing companions and forming friendships. He was asked:

"What is the person that can be the best friend?"

"He who helps you when you remember God, and he who reminds you when you forget Him." he replied.

Then he, peace be on him, was asked:

"And which friend is the worst?"

"He who does not help you when you remember God and does not remind you of God when you forget," he replied.

Then he was asked: "Who is the best among people?"

He replied: "He who when you look at him, you remember God."

These are the principles that should guide your friendships and govern your feelings towards all those around you. It can be very difficult to live up to these principles when you have people of the same age urging you on to be "with it", and to seek forbidden fun and enjoyment in "the pomp and glitter of this life". Such friends could make you forget your cherished values and principles and rob you of a dear and important piece of your life, forever.

Ideally, you should try to influence your friends to identify with what is good and beautiful. Should you fail to so influence them and a choice has to be made between friends and principles, then principles must come first. You cannot afford to fall into disobedience and ruin for the sake of friendship and popularity.

Besides helping one another to move along the path of virtue and strengthening one another's character, true friends help each other in a number of practical ways.

To stress the importance of friendship and brotherhood in providing for daily needs and in the building up of Muslim society, the Prophet initiated a unique arrangement on his arrival in Madinah. He paired off each Muslim Muhaajir from Makkah with an Ansar from Madinah in *mu'aakhaah* or brotherhood. Each was to support the other with shelter, material help, education, companionship and advice. These relationships grew into strong bonds of friendship and brotherhood. They helped to create a vigorous and a caring society. We can thus see that the entire existence of the Muslim community, described in the Qur'an as the "best community" — *khayru-l ummah* — depends on the right sort of company, sincere friendship and brotherhood.

True friendship is nurtured on love, sincerity and generosity. Friendship is in loving rather than in being loved. The noble Prophet advised, and in fact warned, that "You will not truly believe unless you love one another." And as a master of interactive communication, he went on to ask:

"Shall I tell you something whereby you will love one another?"

"Multiply the greeting of peace among yourselves," was his answer.

He advised that you should love for your brother what you love for your self. To strengthen these feelings of affection, the noble Prophet recommended

---

A FRIEND WEEPING FOR HIS FRIEND

When Zayd ibn Haarithah, the servant of Muhammad, was killed at the battle of Mu'tah, the Prophet peace be on him, said:

"Zayd strove in the path of God sincerely as he should. Today he has met his Lord and he is serene."

Thereafter, Zayd's daughter found the Prophet weeping over the corpse of her father and said:

"What do I see?"

The noble Prophet, with tears in his eyes, said:

"A friend weeping for his friend."

Through such actions and sentiments, the Prophet, peace be upon him, showed his gentleness and true human friendship and brotherhood.

---

that "If a person loves his brother, he should tell him so." Love can even be expressed by a smile and "Smiling in the face of your brother Muslim is an act of charity" on your part.

A true friend provides emotional support as well as practical help. A friend will visit another when he is sick, will seek to relieve him of debt or any other type of difficulty if he can. He will even given preference to his friend's needs over his own even if as a result he faces hardship himself. This quality of giving preference to others (Arabic: *iithaar*) is highly praised in the Qur'an in as much as it shows a real absence of greed, covetousness or ostentation in a doer of good.

In the real world, friendships are not always blissful and trouble-free. Disagreements and arguments do arise which sometimes put a strain on even the most well-intentioned persons. If such situations arise, there are procedures in Islam which make reconciliation easy. For example, the noble Prophet has instructed that it is not permissible for a believer to keep away from a believer for more than three days. After the lapse of this period, he should go and meet him and greet him with the greeting of peace. If he returns the greeting, they will be sharers in the merit of reconciliation. If he does not return the greeting, he will be guilty.

Gifts and visits

The giving of gifts and the exchanging of visits are two ways recommended by the Prophet of strengthening friendships and relationships in general.

He himself set the example by being liberal and generous in giving. He gave food and items of practical use like household utensils. He recommended the giving of perfume for "it is light" and fills the air with fragrance.

On visiting, he instructed both hosts and guests on how they should behave so that visiting becomes a source of mutual pleasure and not a burden and a cause for embarrassment. For example, the noble Prophet advised:

"He who believes in God and the Last Day should honour his guest according to his right."

"What is his right, Messenger of God?" he was asked.

"A day and a night, and hospitality for three days. That which might be beyond this is charity," he replied.

On another occasion, he said:

"It is not permissible for a Muslim to stay so long with his brother as to involve him in sin."

"Messenger of God, how would he involve him in sin?" he was asked.

"By prolonging his stay so that the host has nothing left with which to exercise hospitality," he answered.

MAN SHALL BE WITH WHOM HE LOVES

The Prophet, peace be on him, used to say in his supplications:
"O Lord, grant me Your love,
And the love of those whom You love,
And the love of those who would bring me close to Your love.
And make Your love dearer to me than cool water."
Whereupon, a nomad asked him:
"When will be last Hour be?"
"What preparations are you making for it?" asked the Prophet.
"By God, I am not preparing for it Prayer or Fasting or any great action, but I do love God and His messenger."
The Prophet, peace be on him, smiled and said:
"Man shall be with whom he loves."

NEIGHBOURS AND NEIGHBOURHOODS

"Do you know what the rights of neighbours are?" asked the noble Prophet. And he went on to give a list:

"Help him if he asks your help.
Give him relief if he seeks your relief.
Lend him if he needs a loan.
Show him concern if he is distressed.
Nurse him when he is ill.
Attend his funeral if he dies.
Congratulate him if he meets any good.
Sympathise with him if any calamity befall him.
Do not block his air by raising your building high without his permission.
Harass him not.
Give him a share when you buy fruits, and if you do not give him, bring what you buy quietly and let not your children take them out to excite the jealousy of his children."

This hadith shows that you must at least know who your neighbours are. In big cities nowadays, there are many people who live in blocks of flats or on the same street who do not know one another. Moreover, in Islamic terminology, a neighbour is not just the person who lives next-door to you or in your own neighbourhood. A fellow student, your colleague at work or a fellow-traveller on a journey are all regarded as your neighbour. In terms of preferential treatment, the neighbour who lives closest to you has priority.

There is no distinction between a Muslim and a non-Muslim so far as the human needs and rights of neighbours are concerned.

You are not only required to have goodwill to your neighbour but should offer practical care and help when he is sick or in need. Nobody can be a believer, said the Prophet, if his neighbours pass the night hungry while he has his stomach full.

You also need to give emotional support by sharing in his joys and sorrows. Naturally, you also need to refrain from causing any harm or injury, any verbal or physical harassment or emotional stress. Nobody can be a true believer unless his neighbours feel secure from his his hands and tongue, warned the noble Prophet.

You also need to be extremely sensitive to your neighbours' feelings, for example by not causing embarrassment by indulging in conspicuous consumption. The advice about taking your purchases quietly to your house shows how sensitive you must be to the feelings and economic situation of others. There should be no boasting or flagrant display of wealth. There should be no such thing as "keeping up with the Jones's".

The advice of giving help to neighbours and others in society of course is not addressed to the rich or the strong alone; it extends to the poor and the weak and indeed to everyone. This is further shown by the Prophet's definition of charity or *sadaqah*. He, may God bless him and grant him peace, is reported to have said:

"There is no person who does not have the obligation of doing charity every day that the sun rises."

Whereupon he was asked:

"Messenger of God, wherefrom would we get something to give in charity (so often)?"

To which he replied:

"Indeed the gates to goodness are many: glorifying God, praising Him, magnifying Him, saying 'There is no god but Allah', enjoining the good and forbidding the wrong, removing any source of harm from the road, listening to the aggrieved, guiding the blind, showing the seeker his need, striving as far as your two legs could carry you and with deep concern to give succour to him who asks, carrying with the strength of your arms the burdens of the weak. All these are acts of charity which are an obligation on you."

And he added:

"And your smiling in the face of your brother is a charity, your removing of stones and thorns from people's paths is charity and your guiding a man gone astray in the world is charity for you."

From this saying, we can see two main concerns of the Prophet, peace be on him: to awaken the springs of goodness in the human heart; and to strengthen the society with the bond of love, affection and brotherhood.

The wisdom of the Prophet lies in expanding the scope of doing good so that it becomes within the reach of every individual. For example, not everyone can afford to say, "Take this penny or this pound." "Take this dime or take this dollar." Not everyone has the strength to say, "Take this helping hand." But everyone, rich or poor, weak or strong, can say, "Take this smile. This is my sadaqah to you." And when the smile is returned, the bond of goodness in society is strengthened.

Material and economic help is often crucial in relieving people's distress. But to limit charity to tangible things like money and clothes and food is to divide people into receivers on the one hand and givers on the other. This may give rise to humiliation on the one hand and pride and conceit on the other. The Prophet by emphasising that "Smiling is charity" has shown that feeling and sensitivity form the core of human relations. And this should be how callousness, hatred and envy are removed and a caring, tender and beautiful neighbourhood and society is created.

THE MILKER OF THE SHEEP IS HERE, MOTHER!

During the time of the Prophet, Abuu Bakr as-Siddiiq, would go to the homes of the old, the orphans, the weak and the needy in his neighbourhood to help them in whatever way he could. He milked the goats of some, kneaded flour and helped bake bread for others. For all this he was known as the most kind and merciful of people.

After the death of the Prophet, when Abuu Bakr became the Khaliifah and the head of the Muslim state, some of these people feared that they had lost the gentle care and the services of Abuu Bakr. He heard a widow saying:

"Today, our sheep will not be milked."

"By my life," said Abuu Bakr, "I will milk it for you."

As soon as he could, he went to the widow's house and knocked at the door. A little girl opened the door and as soon as she saw him, she shouted:

"The milker of the sheep is here, mother!"

Supervising Neighbourhoods

No one of course can pretend that everyone in a neighbourhood will act with such care and tenderness to everyone else. Even within a family, and so too even in the closest-knit communities and neighbourhoods acts motivated by greed or hatred are committed. There is evil and crime. There is malicious gossip and backbiting. There is envy and jealousy. There is suspicion and spying. This is why Islam does not stop at appealing to each individual to be good. Nor does it stop at only commanding or promoting good on a collective basis. It requires the individual and the community to combat evil. But this is not done in any arbitrary manner. It is not done with vengeance and vindictiveness.

In combatting evil, there are three things which are essential: knowledge, gentleness and patience. Knowledge must come before command and prohibition, gentleness accompanies it, and patience follows, although all three really go hand in hand. As the Prophet, peace be upon him, said: "Gentleness beautifies everything; harshness disfigures." If one is not forbearing and patient one will do more harm than good.

Individual initiative

With this is mind, you can understand and act on the frequent order in the Qur'an "to enjoin the good and prohibit the bad". There are many sayings of the Prophet in this regard too:

"Whoever sees something bad, let him change it with his hand; if he is not able then he should do so with his tongue; if he is not able, then he should hate it in his heart and this last shows the weakest faith."

"Help your brother whether he is a wrong-doer or is wronged," advised the Prophet.

"Messenger of God, I may help him if he is wronged but how can I be expected to help a wrong-doer?" asked a surprised companion.

"You must prevent him from wrong-doing — that will be your help to him," said the noble Prophet.

There is a place for individual initiative in dealing with petty instances of bad behaviour and conduct. In seeking to prevent a person from such conduct, your first duty is to offer gentle advice, to point out using reason the consequences of a particular wrong-doing, and to try to bring about a change for the better in the person concerned. In this process, a soft and gentle approach is required for, just as you are not allowed to enter a house without first knocking and asking permission, so you cannot get access into a person's heart by barging in and using violent means.

The aim of correcting should not be to create embarrassment and it should not be done in a manner as to alienate a person. Correction must involve imparting knowledge and the reason and wisdom behind a ruling.

Change to be meaningful and permanent often needs to be gradual. It may involve changing years of habit and ways of thinking and doing things. This is why patience is so important in bringing about change and reform.

Public supervision

Other more reprehensible trends, petty offences and other crimes in a neighbourhood or society cannot merely be left to individual initiatives. When for example, the problem of drug-trafficking and drug-taking is as organised as it has become in many neighbourhoods and communities, it needs collective action and the sanctions of the law to deal with such a problem.

In organised Muslim neighbourhoods and society, there is the institution of the *hisbah* or public supervision which is there to see that individual and public conduct of people conform to the moral and legal injunctions of Islam. The person who is responsible for the hishah is the *muhtasib*.

The muhtasib has three main sets of functions:

1.   to see that the community as a whole had proper facilities for the performance of worship, like the maintenance of mosques and arranging the daily and other congregational Salaat. He would see to it that no one wilfully stays away from the compulsory Prayer;

2.   to see that justice was maintained in the neighbourhood or community, to ensure that public law and order was maintained, to protect people from dishonesty and malpractices like bad workmanship, faulty measures, fraud, extortion, hoarding of essential supplies and so on.

3.   to supervise various municipal services like hygiene conditions, removal of garbage, water supply, architectural design of buildings and the local environment as a whole.

There are the institutional means for a neighbourhood or a community to watch over its affairs and for immediate action to be taken. If a person was found guilty, sanctions were applied on the spot without any recourse to any lengthy judicial procedures. A sanction may either be a fine, or a decision to impose a total social boycott on a person so that noone speaks to him, buys from or sells anything to him, or visits him.

Matters of a serious nature must necessarily be referred to judicial authorities in a community. Respect for the moral and legal code of Islam and the equality of all before the law are essential for the security and well-being of a society.

ENVIRONMENTAL CONCERNS

A vital part of the well-being of any community is the concern for the environment in which the community lives and has its being. The main concern of environmental design is to facilitate ibaadah and generate behaviour that is in accordance with the Shari'ah. People should therefore aim at creating an environment that is clean, beautiful and peaceful: clean because the Qur'an says that "God loves those who keep themselves pure and clean" and the noble Prophet said that "Purity is half of the faith"; beautiful according to the saying of the Prophet that "God is beautiful and loves beauty"; and peaceful because Islam itself aims at total peace.

Accordingly, a high standard of cleanliness need to be maintained by all individuals, and in homes, streets, parks, shops, markets, and other public places in neighbourhoods and communities. This is the responsibility to begin with of everyone who lives in a locality. Concern for the environment begins with the individual. If an individual does not maintain clean personal habits, there is no way he would be concerned with proper garbage disposal, clean streets and beautiful surroundings. Local government authorities have their jobs to do in this regard but they cannot do an effective job unless individuals desire and work for clean homes and neighbourhoods.

An environment based on Islamic principles would be one in which public health and hygiene is stressed, where measures are taken to ensure, for example, that water is not polluted and that there are adequate facilities for waste disposal.

An Islamic environment will also be clean so far as its morals and its economic dealings are concerned. Its economic sector will know no liquor shops, drinking houses or pubs and will be a totally "dry" area. No use or trafficking in drugs will be allowed; it will have no gambling houses or "twilight" zones where forms of "entertainment" and other practices contrary to the Shari'ah are conducted. It is thus an environment in which public morality and decency is observed. "A community in the midst of which sins are committed and which could be but are not corrected by the community is most likely to be encompassed in its entirety by the punishment of God," said the noble Prophet. This is a prescription for initiatives like "Neighbourhood Watch" schemes to monitor, control and eliminate crime and socially harmful trends and practices.

On the positive side, an Islamic environment is one that is filled with the greeting of peace: "A rider should greet a pedestrian, a pedestrian should greet one who is sitting, a small group should greet a large group and a younger one should greet an older one..," said the noble Prophet. If this simple advice is followed in letter and in spirit, it would serve to eliminate or at least reduce all sorts of loutish behaviour, muggings, "aggro" and other forms of tension in contemporary society.

THE OBLIGATIONS OF THE STREET

The noble Prophet, peace be on him, came upon a group of people on the street and admonished them:

"Refrain from sitting in the streets."

"Messenger of God," they pleaded, "we cannot help sitting in the streets because there is no other place where we can sit and discuss matters."

"In that case," advised the wise Prophet, "fulfil the obligations of the street: restraining of looks, removal of obstruction, reciprocating greetings, enjoining good and forbidding evil."

One of the principles of the Shari'ah, based on a saying of the Prophet, that is applicable to the environment is: *Laa darar wa laa diraar*—there shall be no injury nor perpetuation or reciprocation of injury. This applies to land and water use, the construction of building and walls, rubbish disposal and so on.

You are not allowed for example to construct a wall so high that your neighbour will be deprived of sunlight and air. You are not allowed to leave a house empty knowing that there are homeless people in the neighbourhood. You are not allowed to leave cultivable land uncultivated if there are unemployed people in the community willing to cultivate the land on the basis of sharecropping. You are not allowed to divert or pollute pure water to deprive or harm human beings or animals. You are encouraged to plant trees and fruit trees in particular and this would undoubtedly help to create a greener and more beautiful environment.

The Built Environment

So far as the built environment is concerned, the Islamic environment will have planning standards and an architecture:

- that are in harmony with the surroundings;
- that make for beauty yet discourages waste and conspicuous consumption;
- that make for privacy of the home and family and the protection of modesty;
- that facilitate worship ('ibaadah) and will not detract from the remembrance of God.

Geometrical designs, arches, arabesque decorations may be considered Islamic in that they are beautiful and do not contravene the Shari'ah. However, in themselves they do not make Islamic architecture. A house with beautiful geometrical designs and arches but which is firmly sealed so that it can be cooled by noisy air-condition units does not serve the function of an Islamic dwelling. It is difficult in such a dwelling to hear the *adhaan* or the call to Prayer. Such dwellings often contribute to the slow social and spiritual death of neighbourhood communities. On the other hand, a traditional *mashrabiyyah* or lattice-work window is not only beautiful but serves to let in light and the sound of the adhaan. Moreover, it keeps out the prying gaze and thus helps to maintain privacy. Such features of a building help to serve the function of Islamic architecture. Buildings which serve no Islamic purpose like mausoleums and statues, no matter how beautifully they may be constructed or decorated cannot be called Islamic. Islamic architecture is determined primarily by function or use and not by form. The form of a building must serve and enhance its function.

An Islamic neighbourhood will have adequate facilities for healthy recreation.

COMMUNITY MOSQUES

The main physical feature of any Islamic neighbourhood or community is the masjid or mosque. Wherever Muslims have settled, they have sought to have a masjid which means literally "a place of prostration". The noble Prophet has said that the whole earth is a masjid meaning that man must have the natural freedom to perform Salaat and worship wherever in the world he is when the time of Prayer comes. However, a masjid in the form of a building or a site is necessary to provide the vital focus for any community, giving it shape and direction.

Ideally, there should be a place of worship within earshot of the adhaan and within walking distance of the homes it primarily serves. In this way, it becomes easy for daily life to revolve around the mosque and the times of Prayer. When the activities of a neighbourhood or a community are centred around the mosque, there is likely to be a sense of peace and security, as well as unity of purpose and direction. There is something natural about this as it orients man constantly to the Source of his being and the main purpose of his creation.

Strong neighbourhood communities contribute to the health and stability of the wider community and society. To this, we now turn in the next chapter.

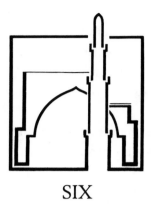

SIX

YOU *and the* WIDER COMMUNITY

Human interaction, as was shown in the last chapter, is naturally necessary because people are endowed with different abilities and capacities. God has made people to need one another and depend on one another, to live in community and society.

People may feel a sense of community with others of the same race and who speak the same language. They may regard themselves as a tribe or a nation. Their sense of community or nationhood is further strengtened if they live in or lay claim to a particular land. In this case racialism and linguistic nationalism is strengthened by territorial nationalism. People take pride in their groups or nations. Some go so far as to say: "My people or my nation, right or wrong!" and may stick with their tribal, racist or nationalistic group under all circumstances.

You may in fact find it easier and more practical to work with others who speak the same language or dialect, who come from the same locality and are accustomed to the same type of food. But such things — language, place of birth, cuisine — are not sufficient to give any group the goals or motivation for living an ethical life. The goals such a group sets are usually chauvinistic goals: your supreme struggles are for protecting or expanding your language, your race, or your own economic power, perhaps at the expense of others.

Of course there is no good reason why you should not want to protect your language or your economic interests. It is natural to want to do so. But these goals do not promote your main concern as a human being, to live a life of virtue that would be in keeping with and strengthen the naturally good state in which you were created and also to help other human beings to live such a life.

As a Muslim, you may maintain an affinity with others who speak the same language, who come from the same clan or tribe and who belong to the same geographical area. However, your primary and overriding identification is with the society or community that is welded together by faith and ethics. You identify with this community because it acknowledges man's true relationship with his Creator and because it promotes all that is good and beneficial and discourages all that is ugly and harmful for man. Such a community or society works for the common good not only of its own members but for the common good of mankind as a whole. In no way are you allowed to say, "My community right or wrong!"

A word commonly used for community in Islam is *jamaa'ah*. A jamaa'ah might be a small group of three persons, a congregation in a mosque, or the Muslim citizens of a state.

The Muslim community or jamaa'ah is guided by firm principles of what is right and what is wrong based on the Qur'an and Sunnah of the Prophet. These are the sources for the moral and legal code of Islam — the Shari'ah. The Shari'ah describes what is the nature and purpose of the best communities. It sets out the conditions that are necessary for strong and stable communities. It establishes principles or supreme values which help to guide the community through changing times and conditions. It provides a range of institutions which anchor the community. It defines the roles of various people in the community including leaders, scholars, businesspeople, and others. It is an organised community with people having clearly defined obligations and inalienable rights and freedoms. We will discuss each of these in turn.

Purpose of community

The purposes of the Muslim community are essentially two:
1. To establish the system of Islam (the Diin) for the service of God;
2. To protect the interests of people.

The first purpose—establishing the faith or system of Islam—implies among other things: inviting people to all that is beneficial, commanding all that is good and just, and forbidding evil and oppression according to the provisions of the Shari'ah.

Specifically, this involves such duties as "establishing" Salaat in the community, collecting and distributing Zakaat and looking after the needy in society, applying the provisions of the Shari'ah to settle disputes or to punish crime so as to preserve the limits set by God, defending the community and so on.

The second purpose — protecting the interests of the people — is linked to the preservation of one of the five essentials: true religion or diin, life, intellect or reason, honour, and property. There are definite norms and guidelines in the Shari'ah to determine how these values are to be protected. The protection of these values are not left to the arbitrary political or judicial powers in a state or the whims and opinions of the masses. This may happen in secular states which also profess to work to realise "the public interest".

Let us look at some specific examples to show how some of these values are protected.

1.   Any community which has sufficient resources but where people face poverty, starvation and eventual loss of life will not be fulfilling its purpose to protect life and will be considered blameworthy.

2.   In order to preserve the interests of people in so far as "honour" is concerned, there are fixed and severe penalties in Islam for such crimes as rape. In a secular state, a judge in an arbitrary manner may be and is often lenient in sentencing a person who has committed this barbaric act. He may merely impose a prison sentence of a few months or years after which the criminal is then let loose in society, free to commit the same act. "Honour" in such a system will always be exposed to violation and women in particular will always feel vulnerable.

3.   In order to protect reason, honour, and indeed life, any Muslim community will be required, for example, to impose an absolute ban on the manufacture and trafficking in alcohol. No community which allows this could be said to be Muslim and carrying out its purposes.

Nature of the Muslim community

Everyone in a Muslim community, regardless of the colour of his skin, the language he speaks, or the place of his birth has a duty to work for the realisation of the purposes of the community. This is not only because of narrow self-interest and need but stems from the moral duty to strive to be "the best community — commanding the good, forbidding evil and believing in God", as described by the Qur'an.

The Muslim community has been described by the noble Prophet as having mutual support and compassion and acting like "a single body — when one part of which is afflicted, the other parts feel pain and fever". The Qur'an also describes the community of believers as forming "a solid well-knit structure".

Thus, if you as an individual in an Islamic society feel indifferent to your community or society, if you do not feel concern and pain when it is hurt, you should regard yourself as a selfish sinner; your morals are in trouble, your conscience is in disorder and your faith is undernourished. You may not even be justified in claiming to be part of this community for the noble Prophet has said: "Whoever does not concern himself with the affairs of Muslims is not one of them."

PRINCIPLES OR SUPREME VALUES

The Islamic community is committed to and governed by a number of prime values. Some of these are:

- submission to God alone
- freedom governed by responsibility and discipline
- justice and kindness
- equality strengthened by brotherhood
- shuura or mutual consultation.

These values are realised in a community through the use of knowledge and power resources. An ignorant or a weak society cannot hope to be free and to implement justice, for example.

We have already discussed the importance of Tawhiid or submission to God alone. Of the other values mentioned above, justice and shuura are the key ones. In a sense both freedom and equality are part of justice. Freedom of movement, freedom to work and earn an honest living, freedom of peaceful association and expression are all guaranteed by the practice of justice. So too is equality of opportunities and equality before the law for all members of a community. Here we shall just take a closer look at the supreme values of justice and shuura which must characterise any Muslim community or society.

FREE SPEECH AND RESTRAINT

While making his usual rounds of the city at night, the Caliph 'Umar ibn 'Abd al-'Aziiz accompanied by a policeman, entered a mosque. In the darkness, they came upon a man asleep and crossed over him. The man awoke, raised his head and shouted:

"You, are you mad?"

"No," replied 'Umar.

The policemen was about to beat the man when 'Umar said:

"Don't. He only asked me, 'Are you mad?' and I answered, 'No.' "

Justice

Justice is perhaps the most important of the supreme values of Islam. In fact, it can be said that the main purpose of revelation and the task of Prophets has been to establish justice.

Thus, one of the early scholars of Islam has said that "When the signs of Justice appear and its face is shown in any way, that is where the Law of God and His religion are found".

Justice is the first principle of social life. It can be shown to govern all relations in life: between ruler and ruled, rich and poor, husband and wife, parents and children. Even in the ordering of an individual's personal habits, justice must be done to the respective requirements of body, mind and spirit. As we have seen, it is unjust, for example, to neglect your body and its needs in search of spiritual development.

In all Islamic institutions, justice can be seen to be operating: in the lines of congregational Salaat where no one has precedence over another by virtue of power, wealth or rank; in the equality of all before the law such that noone, whether ruler or criminal turned "prosecution witness", can claim immunity; in the family where no preference should be shown by a parent to one child over others and so on.

In all your dealings, you are required to stand firmly for justice even if it be against yourself and your kith and kin, for love too can lead to injustice.

The fear of committing injustice may even prevent the doing of an act that is otherwise permissible. In fact one of the derived principles of the Shari'ah is that all permissible things are permissible provided that no damage or harm results to others from their practice and that in the event that such damage or harm is suspected or confirmed, the permissible shall be prohibited to avert such damage or harm.

THE QUR'AN: ON JUSTICE

"God enjoins justice and kindness, and giving to kinsfolk, and forbids indecency and abomination and wickedness." (*(An-Nahl*, 16: 90)

"God orders that you return trusts to their owners and that if you judge between people, you judge justly." (*An-Nisaa'*, 4: 58)

"And do not let hatred of any people dissuade you from dealing justly. Deal justly, for that is closer to God-consciousness." (*Al-Maa'idah*, 5: 9)

"O you who believe! Be firm in justice as witnesses for God, even in cases against yourselves, your parents or your kin." (*An-Nisaa'*, 4: 135)

"And if you give your word, you must be just, even though it be against your kin, and fulfil the covenant of God. For that is what He has commanded you that you may remember." (*Al-An'aam*, 6: 152)

"We have sent Our Messengers will all evidence of truth, and through them We bestowed revelation from on high and (thus gave you) the Balance (to judge between right and wrong) so that people may be firm in justice; and We bestowed (on you) from on high (the ability to make use of) iron, in which there is awesome power as well as many benefits for mankind. And (all this was given to you) so that God shall know who would stand up for the cause of God and His Apostles..." (*Al-Hadiid*, 57: 25) (Here there is sanction for the use of force of arms or power to uphold justice in the cause of God and in the rights of His creatures.)

"The indictment shall be upon those who oppress people, and those who commit injustice and wrong-doing on earth shall be severely punished." (*Ash-Shuura*, 42: 42)

"And those who commit oppression shall know what kind of destiny they shall meet." (*Ash-Shu'araa*, 26: 227)

HADITH: ON JUSTICE

"If anyone walks with an oppressor to strengthen him, knowing that he is an oppressor, he has gone forth from Islam."

"*Asabiyyah* (partisanship, chauvinism, nationalism) means helping your people in unjust causes."

"He is not one of us who proclaims the cause of 'asabiyyah.
He is not one of us who fights for the cause of 'asabiyyah.
He is not one of us who dies in the cause of 'asabiyyah."

Shuura

The collective affairs of all Muslim communities need to be run on the basis of shuura or mutual consultation. The Qur'an in a verse revealed at Makkah described the Muslims as "those who answer the call of their Lord and establish

Prayer and who conduct their affairs by mutual consultation (shuura), and who spend of what We have bestowed upon them".

Whether Muslims are involved in the running of a small community group, the administration of a mosque, the management of a school or a business corporation, or the governance of the affairs of state, they are obliged to practice shuura.

There are two conditions to be observed in the exercise of shuura:
The first is that shuura is not applicable to questions on which an injunction exists in the Qur'an or in the Sunnah, both of which constitute binding legislation. Matters in this category are outside the scope of shuura, except when its purpose is only to interpret the injunction or to enforce it. For example, the fixed rate of two and a half percent Zakaat on wealth cannot be referred to or changed by any group of scholars consulting together. They may however need to exercise shuura to work out what is the level below which no Zakaat is payable in a particular community. The amount may vary from one community to another, depending on such factors as cost of living indexes.

The second is that when a question is referred to shuura, the advisors cannot reach a decision contradicting an injuction of the Qur'an or the Sunnah. For example, no advisors to a government seeking to raise production levels in factories can decide that time off will not be given to workers to perform the compulsory Friday Congregational Prayer or that Muslim workers should not fast in the month of Ramadaan. No educational ministry or institution, in the name of education reform, is allowed to pass a law forbidding women students from observing Islamic dress requirements.

Matters to be brought before a shuura are normally of a delicate and important nature requiring knowledge and deliberation to reach decisions on them. An example of such a matter which we have just mentioned is how should Muslims calculate the minimum level of income below which no Zakaat is payable.

As for daily administrative matters which do not require policy or strategic decisions, and especially when there is need for quick action, no shuura is necessary.

Shuura is not merely advisory. The decision reached after mutual consultation by a majority of advisers is binding on the ruler or leader of the Muslim community or state. The principle of shuura was strictly followed by the Prophet himself and by his companions.

Provided that proper processes of consultation are observed and seen to be observed, the people in a community should all regard the decision of a shuura as binding on them. It may happen that a minority may not agree fully with a decision taken but in this case they should accept the decision of the majority provided that this does not involve any disobedience to the Shari'ah. In the time of the Prophet, for example, the majority decided that the Muslims should leave Madinah to confront the enemy forces at Uhud outside the city. The Prophet himself felt that they should defend themselves from within the city but he followed the majority decision.

The Islamic rules on shuura are so flexible as to allow any Muslim community to choose the best means to suit its requirements according to the circumstances of time and place. One community may decide to choose its leader or executive by direct election. Another may choose to do so through indirect elections by nominated representatives. The principles of shuura, like the principles concerning dress in Islam, are general and allow for variety in the detailed forms.

Shuura promotes unity and the striving for unified goals in a society. It is an indispensable condition for promoting the common good, to ensuring a sense of responsibility, participation and commitment in members of a society.

The practice of shuura should serve to prevent the emergence of despotic, authoritarian and arbitrary styles of leadership in a community. It also serves to prevent alienation, the growth of factions and conflict in a community.

The principles and practice of justice and shuura are best suited to dealing with dissension and discord that may arise within a community — between individuals, members of a family or conflicting groups or interests. There are processes for counselling, arbitration and even for applying sanctions against stubborn and unruly elements. The forty-ninth surah of the Qur'an, Surah al-Hujuraat, is an important one to study and apply in order to promote harmonious social relationships. The judicial institutions of Islam are equipped both for conducting arbitration and for applying sanctions and punishment. The proper discharge of these functions are important for the natural and stable growth of societies. The alternative is anarchy or oppression.

COMMUNITY INSTITUTIONS AND PEOPLE

For natural and stable growth, each community needs to have not only the values which we have briefly described above, but also the appropriate institutions, resources and skills.

Political institutions

Each community needs to agree on the best ways of choosing leaders and appointing responsible persons for running its affairs. Institutions and structures for this may vary from place to place. They must be developed in such a way as to ensure that the best and most capable persons are appointed to positions of responsibility instead of those who actively seek influence and power for their own ends.

Institutions must work on the principles of shuura and justice, unity and brotherhood. Cliques, factions and parties that promote division in the community are to be discouraged. However, the existence of groups in communities looking after special interests and needs — such as education, housing, sport, emergency relief, medical research, animal welfare — may not be divisive but work towards the overall good of society.

In forming rules and procedures for community organisations and institutions, from the smallest committee to the most complex organs of state, there need to be checks and balances that control the arbitrary use of power, that ensure respect for the rule of law, and a free flow of information except in defined cases where security is at risk. There need to be provisions that ensure that the rights of all are respected and that defined obligations are discharged.

Leadership in a Muslim community

In any properly organised group or community, leadership is important and necessary. The noble Prophet has advised that even if there are as few as three persons going on a journey, they should appoint one as their leader.

A Muslim leader should be:

• God-conscious *(muttaqi)* and having a respect for and commitment to uphold the moral and legal code of Islam, the Shari'ah;

• knowledgeable in the Shari'ah, especially its main concerns, its values and principles to be able to deal with issues as they arise on the basis of sound knowledge. In addition he should have competent and specialist advisers also rooted in knowledge of the Shari'ah;

• having appropriate mental and physical ability such as courage, sagacity and strength in addition to personal qualities that would inspire trust and confidence in people;

• responsive to the needs of people.

MY LORD WILL QUESTION ME

'Umar ibn 'Abd al-Aziiz returned home sad and downcast after attending the funeral of his predecessor, the Khalifah Sulayman ibn 'Abd al-Malik.

"Why do I see you looking downcast?" asked his attendant.

"Anyone in my position will be downcast," said 'Umar. "There is no one in this Ummah but I desire to give him his right without his writing to me or demanding it from me."

Feeling conscious of his great responsibility, he was moved to tears. His wife found him crying and asked him why he was.

"I have been appointed to look after the affairs of this Ummah. I have been thinking about the poor and the hungry, the sick and the lost, the hardworking one without any clothes, the despairing orphan, the lonely widow, the one who has been wronged, the stranger and the captive, the old and those with families and little money, and such people throughout the land and in the far corners of the state. I knew that on the day of Judgement my Lord will question me about them..."

Muslims have faced many problems as a result of the political leadership of their societies. Often these had their roots in alien, hereditary or nepotistic practices which have no sanction in Islam. Often, political leadership has been at odds with the learned scholars of the community. This led to injustice and oppression. The ideal situation is for leaders to be scholars and for scholars to be leaders and actively involved in political processes.

I WILL GATHER THE FIREWOOD

It is related that while on a journey, the Prophet ordered his companions to prepare a sheep for food.

One man said, "I will perform *dhabh* on it, Messenger of God."

Another said, "I will skin it."

Another said, "I will cook it."

And the Prophet said: "I will gather the firewood."

To this they all said, "Messenger of God, you don't need to work; we will do whatever is to be done."

"I know that you will do for me whatever is to be done," said the Prophet, "but I do not like to be set apart from you. God does not like to see His servant aloof from his companions."

I AM ONLY A MAN FROM AMONG YOU

Abu Hurayrah went to the market with the Prophet to buy some clothes. The seller stood up and kissed the hand of the Prophet, peace be on him. The Prophet withdrew his hand and stopped the man from kissing his hand saying,

"This is the practice of the Persians with their kings. I am not a king. I am only a man from among you."

The garments were purchased and Abu Hurayrah wanted to carry them for the Prophet. The Prophet did not allow him and said: "The owner of something has more right to carry it."

MAKE YOURSELF AT EASE

A man came to the Prophet to speak to him but felt timid and overawed. the Prophet said to him:

"Don't be afraid. Make yourself at ease. I am just the son of a woman who ate dried meat in Makkah (i.e I am just a simple ordinary person)."

DO NOT STAND...

One day the Prophet peace be on him was walking and he came upon a group of people. They were about to stand before him out of reverence and respect. He stopped them and said:

"Do not stand as the Persians stand, some in glorification of others."

HERE IS MY BACK

When the Prophet, peace be on him, felt that he was going to die after his mission was complete and God had completed His favours on him, he went on the mimbar and addressed the people:

"O people, if there is anyone whose back I have beaten, then here is my back; let him retaliate against me. If there is anyone whose honour I have wronged, then here is my dignity and honour; let him retaliate against me. If there is anyone whose wealth I have taken, then here is my wealth; let him take from it and fear no enmity or grudge, for this is not my style."

Members in a Muslim community

Human resources are arguably the most valuable in any community and society. Any community needs to be concerned to protect these resources, ensure their health, strength, dignity and general well-being, obligations and rights.

Any Muslim community should seek to ensure that the physical and intellectual capability of all its members should flourish to the best of their ability. Capability should be built up in depth. There should be equal opportunities for growth. Elitism is not a feature of Muslim communities whereby only a selected few are given the facilities and opportunities for intellectual leadership or a selected few are given the the responsibility for political or military management.

In the time of the Prophet, every able-bodied man was expected to be fit and ready to defend the interests of the community. There were no expensive standing armies as such. At the approach of any danger, the noble Prophet could call upon individuals with the required skills or mobilize the whole community to face threats of a more dire nature. Because defence now requires a wide range of scientific, technical and other skills, strong Muslim communities would need to have a continuous programme of defence training and alertness.

There was also knowledge in depth such that everyone strove to understand and more importantly put into practice what he or she had learnt. People did not leave knowlege to a priestly class or a group of professional 'ulamaa'.

The ethic of work and striving was also firmly embedded in this society but it was also a caring and compassionate society in which the needy, widows and orphans were well looked after.

It was a society where people were free to do anything that was lawful without any restrictions. There was no crippling bureaucracy, no stifling legal restrictions. There was freedom to speak the truth, freedom of access to the head of the community, freedom to roam the earth in search of knowledge or livelihood. People were not kept under surveillance, they were not faced with the anxiety of carrying an identity card wherever they went, their lives were not pried into, they were not suspected and hounded. They could meet and associate freely for mutual self-help and for peaceful purposes.

These are some of the ideals and practices that should be upheld and cherished in any Muslim community so that people are able to grow and develop naturally and support one another for the greater good.

The Mosque—of pivotal importance

The mosque is a symbol of the aims and purposes of Muslims' collective life. One of the main functions of any Muslim community is to "establish Salaat". As such, the mosque which is primarily a place of congregational Prayer proclaims man's abiding relationship with God. It is also a symbol of feelings of brotherhood, equality and compassion that must exist among believers in God.

One of the first acts of the noble Prophet on reaching Madinah was to build a masjid or mosque. Apart from congregational Prayer, this mosque served as school, reception centre for visitors, travellers and the needy, mobilization point for armies, treasury for the collection and distribution of Zakaat, a court of law for the settling of disputes and the passing of sentences, and even an arena for the display of skills and martial arts. This masjid was the dynamic, throbbing heart and nerve-centre of the community.

The mosque brings people together for the best purposes. It works against individualism and selfishness. While, for example, it is permissible to perform the daily Salaat individually, it is more meritorious to perform it in congregation. Any two or more worshippers constitute a group for Salaat purposes. When Salaat is being offered in congregation, one cannot opt out and perform it individually.

One Salaat a week—the mid-day Salaat of Friday—has to be performed in congregation. The khutbah or sermon is an essential part of the Jum'ah Salaat and is for the purpose of reminding Muslims of their duties, discussing problems and issues that affect the community, facilitating the flow of information and encouraging united action. The khutbah is normally divided into four parts: praising God; asking His blessings on the noble Prophet; admonition, advice and directives to the community; and supplications to God.

Where the khutbah has become formalised and ritualised and totally in a language many people cannot understand, it is important and necessary that it should be enlivened and made relevant to the needs of the particular Muslim community. It should be an effective means of communication and serve to mobilize Muslim human and other resources. This also applies to the khutbahs of the Eid Salaats which must also be performed in congregation. The manner of celebrating these Eids also emphasises the ethical and humanitarian concerns of Islam.

Every congregational Salaat must be led by an Imaam (leader) whose movements the congregation follows without exception. The group must stand behind the imaam in straight rows, foot to foot and shoulder to shoulder without discrimination between the worshippers. The mosque, through congregational

Salaat, is thus a constant reminder to Muslims to uphold unity, equality, brotherhood and concern for others. The content of the Salaat, the ideas presented to the mind through the required recitations, strengthen the self in its determination to will and do the good, to avoid evil, to fill the world with value.

The community has a duty to uphold and establish Salaat. Salaat is a vital pillar of the Islamic system. Who ever upholds it, upholds the system. Whoever abandons it, destroys the system.

It is therefore important that mosques should once more become the living hearts of communities. They should be places not only of Prayer, but of guidance, education, support and solidarity. The notion that mosques should be schools and even universties has served to sanctify the pursuit and goals of knowledge in Muslim societies. In many places now, there are clinics, day centres for children, dormitories and facilities for youth training which are an integral part of mosque complexes. Such trends may serve to reduce the growing secularisation of societies. They should be encourged so that mosques may once again be springboards for community action and involvement. It is important that the design and the equipment of mosques should reflect and be suited to these multi-functional use instead of being merely much admired and lofty samples of monumental architecture.

ECONOMIC INSTITUTIONS

The Muslim community is a practical and caring community. It recognises the value of material well-being and the fact that people naturally stand in need of one another. The major instrument for ensuring a caring and healthy community is the institution of Zakaat.

Zakaat and Social Welfare

For as long as humans are humans, who have differing capacities and motivations for economic action, there will be some who are poor. Indeed the majority of humankind are now afflicted by poverty.

Every human being carries the Divine *amaanah* or trust to transform the elements of nature into sources of nutrition and comfort, of wisdom and beauty, efficiency and enjoyment for himself and others.

Built into this amaanah or trust is the requirement on those who have been blessed with wealth and means, to spend out of their substance on those in deprivation and misery. Islam teaches people that the poor and the deprived have a "title" or a "right" in the wealth of the rich (70: 24-25) and constantly exhorts the rich to meet that obligation. In this sense, the rich stand in need of the poor. If they do not fulfil this "right" of the poor, they will be called to account.

While voluntary sadaqah or charity is encouraged and its scope extended so that even the poor can offer sadaqah (in the shape of a smile for example), Islam has established the institution of Zakaat to make concern for the poor a permanent and compulsory duty.

Zakaat consists of an annual contribution of two and a half percent of one's income or "appropriated wealth" to public welfare. The rate of zakaat on other types of wealth such as agricultural produce and jewelry is more. It is incumbent on minors and adults, males and females, living or dead. After debts, zakaat is deducted from the inheritance of any deceased Muslim.

"Appropriated wealth" excludes debts and liabilities, household effects (except jewelry) required for living; and land, buildings, and capital materials used in or for production. Zakaat is due on current year's income as well as on the accumulated incomes of the past and on all stocks in trade.

Islamic law empowers the Islamic state or community to collect the zakaat, and keep a distinct account of it, separate from the public funds of the state treasury.

Zakaat funds must be spent on the eight categories specified in the Qur'an, namely, the poor and the destitute, the wayfarer, the bankrupt, the needy converts, the captives, the collectors of zakaat, and in the cause of God. The last category allows zakaat funds to be used for the general welfare of the community — for education of the people, for public works, and for defense of Islam and the Muslim community.

Benefits of zakaat

1. Being a religious duty, it offers the donor the inner satisfaction of a duty accomplished. The funds on which zakaat has been paid bring satisfaction and reward in this world and the next; funds on which no zakaat has been paid will bring suffering and punishment in this world and the hereafter. The very word zakaat means "sweetening" and it implies that those funds on which no zakaat has been paid are "bitter". The word zakaat also means purifying.

2. Zakaat makes for social welfare and solidarity and eliminates class and economic barriers, class animosity and hatreds; it eliminates arrogance on the part of the giver and humiliation on the part of the receiver.

3. The need to pay Zakaat acts as a stimulus to investment of income in productive enterprise, for capital that is allowed to remain idle would would progressively diminish in zakaat levies. Invested in production, it adds to society's wealth and could help in job creation. Zakaat also has the basic meaning "to grow": wealth grows with spending and investment.

4. Zakaat is a great promoter of wealth circulation throughout society, which is one of the main features of any healthy economy. The Qur'an condemns the accumulation and circulation of wealth in the hands of the rich only.

Other economic institutions

Zakaat is only the minimum contribution to social welfare in a community. There are other economic institutions that a society would need to develop to preserve its strength and integrity.

A Muslim community needs to have its own institutions for banking and finance, for thrift and insurance, its own investment and consumer priorities that would be in conformity with the moral and legal code of Islam. This requires new thinking and new initiatives. This is within the reach of any community beginning with small-scale projects and starting from the bottom up.

Muslim communities and societies need to have economic policies that would meet the basic needs of the people, change consumer tastes and levels so that people can live within their means especially considering the saying of the Prophet that "the little but sufficient is better than the abundant but alluring". Muslim communities need to be wary of the debt trap through which the energies and resources of a people are mortgaged to international banking institutions. The level of debt from loans and interest remains one of the major sources of impoverishment of many societies.

Educational Institutions

Education institutions in many existing Muslim communities often produce timid and imitative people who are not able to contribute to the welfare and strength of society.

Muslims of today need educational institutions that would produce courageous, enterprising, and creative men and women who aim at *ihsaan* or excellence in all things, and who are able to cotribute to the welfare and strength of society. Muslim communities need an education and an outlook that will not make them accept humiliation and oppression. This was the type of education and training that the Sahabah received in the "continuous education school" of the noble Prophet. The focus of this education was not fine buildings and expensive equipment but the human mind, heart and body.

Collective Obligations

While the individual Muslim has the duty to acquire such knowledge as to enable him or her to perform personal obligations such as knowledge of Salaat and the rules of fasting, the community has the collective obligation to ensure that it has the knowledge and skills to meet its essential needs and supplies.

The Islamic community needs for example to promote the industry of certain individuals in farming, weaving and building for people cannot go without food to eat, clothes to wear and dwellings to live in. It is amazing how this simple rule is neglected by many societies who have abandoned agriculture for large-scale industrial development. This has resulted in dependency on outside sources for food. In crisis situations, this has led to starvation, suffering and death and the ransoming of large populations to outside forces.

The study of the Shari'ah is a collective duty since knowledge of it is a prerequisite for enjoining the good and forbidding the bad which is the purpose of the Islamic society or state.

Jihaad is a collective duty, and each community needs to train and equip itself to defend itself against aggression and to protect the freedom of mankind.

The concept of fard kifayah thus imposes on the community the need to assess its essential needs, plan for the fulfilment of these needs through training of individuals and the allocation of resources to encourage agriculture, industries and institutions to cater for these needs.

These are some of the aspects of community formation and concerns in an Islamic system. It would be seen that the Islamic system does not encourage selfish and destructive individualism. Neither does it stand for rigid collectivisation and control from above. It is a society of the middle way where individual freedoms are enjoyed within a guided and disciplined, caring and creative society.

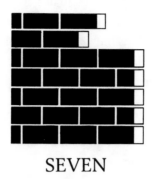

SEVEN

YOU *and the* UNIVERSAL UMMAH

People who share a particular worldview, group themselves together and refer to themselves as "We". For many people, the main factor which brings them together them is the colour of their skin or their race. For racists, their special "we" hinges on, for instance, being white or black, Jewish or Arab, Malay or Chinese. For others, this special "we" hinges on class or occupation. Marxists for example would see themselves mainly as workers pitted against exploiting capitalists. For some others, their identity comes mainly from devotion to an individual. For Christians for example it is the love of Christ which brings them together.

Defining the Muslim "We"

For Muslims, their special "We" does not hinge on any racial, class, occupational, regional or linguistic identity. The reason for this is that such identities do not provide any guide to what is good and true on the one one hand and what is false and reprehensible on the other.

The adherents of Islam are not marked out as Arabs, Turks, Persians, Semites, Berbers, Kurds, Malays, Hui Chinese, Mandingos, poor, rich, oppressed, whites, blacks, Asians, Easterners, Westerners or Muhammadans. None of these can truly define this "we" of the Muslims who belong to the ummah or the universal community of believers. It is therefore absurd to label Muslims as an "ethnic community" as is often done in places like Britain.

What then is the Muslim people? It is a people that is surrendered to God. Their real identity is based on faith in God. This bond of faith is the most important basis for binding people together in harmony and for achieving the highest values for which man was created.

Because of the overriding demands of this faith, there can be no such thing as a Marxist Muslim or a Baathist Muslim. The ummah cannot accept within its fold any person who professes an ideology or beliefs which go against the basic teachings of Islam. However, you need to be very careful in labelling anyone a Kaafir or an unbeliever and putting him outside the pale of Islam. You cannot label as an unbeliever any Muslim who professes the Shahaadah, acts accordingly, and performs the obligatory duties of Islam, unless he clearly professes the word of unbelief, refuses to acknowledge a fundamental principle of Islam, or commits an evident act of unbelief such as rejecting the verses of the Qur'an.

The irreducible elements in Islam have served to keep Muslim history on course despite many intellectual and military challenges in the past and at present. These elements have also given Muslim civilization and culture unity and stability.

Unity and Variety

At the same time, there is an extraordinary richness and variety in Muslim cultures made possible by the fact that Islam's moral and legal code assumed that everything is allowed unless it is prohibited, and not vice versa. Local customs therefore which do not contradict any principle or law of Islam have been incorporated with ease in the cultures of Muslim peoples.

In this way Islam has discouraged what is obnoxious and preserved much of what is good in human cultures. It has not sought to impose a total and dull uniformity. While it established Islamic institutions like Salaat and promoted the use of Arabic, it did not seek to obliterate local languages, dress, cuisine, artistic expression or vernacular architecture. There was nothing of the brashness and destructiveness that have gone hand in hand with the sweeping spread of European culture. One British nineteenth century writer noted for example that "the history of European settlements in America, Africa, and Australia presents everywhere the same general feature—a wide and sweeping destruction of native races by the uncontrolled violence of individuals if not of colonial authorities".

Unity and variety are thus two characteristics of the Muslim ummah. Because of the essential unity, it is possible for a Muslim to travel to any part of the world and feel instantly at home among local Muslims, despite differences in dress, language, or economic conditions. He would exchange the same greetings of peace, *"As-salaamu alaykum"*, he would perform the Salaat in congregation with ease, and he would normally feel something of the welcoming warmth that is accorded to a brother in faith. Despite the picture of desolation and ruin which the ummah generally presents, there is still much of warmth and beauty, openness and generosity of soul in Muslim communities the world over.

As a Muslim, you belong to this ummah by virtue of your faith in God and in particular by your profession of the Shahaadah. Of course, for practical purposes Islam requires and in some cases allows bonds in addition to faith—such as family and kinship ties, clans and tribal bonds and patriotic attachments—so long as these do not conflict with or damage the overriding requirements of faith. These requirements could separate a man from his father, son, wife or clan or make him leave the land of his birth in search of justice and freedom to practice his faith.

"WHAT ARE THESE PEOPLE DOING HERE?"

A man once visited the prophet's mosque in Madinah. There he saw a group of people sitting and discussing their faith together. Among them were Salmaan (who came from Persia), Suhayb who grew up in the Eastern Roman Empire and was regarded as a Greek, and Bilaal who was an African. The man then said:

"If the (Madinan) tribes of Aws of Khazraj support Muhammad, they are his people (that is, Arabs like him). But what are these people doing here?"

The Prophet became very angry when this was reported to him. Straightaway, he went to the mosque and summoned people to a congregational Salaat. He then addressed them saying:

"O people, know that the Lord and Sustainer is One. Your ancestor is one. Your faith is one. The Arabism of anyone of you is not from your mother or father. It is no more than a tongue (language). Whoever speaks Arabic is an Arab."

Bilaal, Suhayb and Salmaan were not only regarded as non-Arabs but were former slaves who suffered injustice and oppression. They were close and beloved companions of the Prophet. For the strength of their faith and their steadfastness, these have had a special place in the the hearts of Muslims through the ages. It is therefore neither race, status nor wealth which gives members of the Muslim ummah their identity. It is the consciousness of being human and affirming the oneness of God that is the basis of the unity of the ummah.

The colour of your skin or the language you speak does not confer any worth or advantage on you as a human being in the sight of God. Yet, people order their world and conduct their social, political and economic affairs on the basis of skin colour and language. On this basis, they regard themselves as superior to others with a different skin colour and often brutalise, oppress or shun them altogether. Racism or racial consciousness is thus one of the major sources of evil and danger in the modern world.

The variety of skin colours and languages among humans is not meant to give rise to meanness and brutality. It is meant to show something wonderful, subtle and sublime in God's handiwork:

"And among God's signs are the creation of the heavens and the earth, and the variations in your languages and your colours; truly in that are signs for those who know." (30: 22)

"Mankind! We created you from a single pair of a male and a female, and made you into nations and tribes, that you may know one another. Indeed, the noblest among you in the sight of God is the one who is more deeply conscious of God." (49: 13)

The institutions of Islam serve to strengthen the fact of human unity and in particular the unity of the believers. We have already seen that the congregational Prayer serves to strengthen the feeling of equality and brotherhood among believers. What demonstrates above all the unity of the universal Islamic community or ummah is the institution of Hajj.

HAJJ—THE GREATEST GATHERING OF MANKIND

Hajj is the pilgrimage to the "House of God" in Makkah which is compulsory on every adult Muslim in any part of the world who has the means to undertake the journey. Hajj is the fifth pillar of Islam and brings together yearly what may justly be described as the greatest gathering of mankind.

Hajj is, above all, a journey of individual self-renewal inspired by piety and devotion to God.

In this quest, the individual is strengthened by the knowledge that thousands of human beings from all over the world regardless of their worldly status, language or race, are in pursuit of the same goal – the pleasure of their Creator.

Many of the rites of the Hajj go back to the Prophet Ibrahiim (Abraham) and there is a sense of history, of going along the same straight way that has been the way of the prophets of God and those who followed them. There is also a natural feeling of cosmic identity on the part of the pilgrim as he goes anticlockwise around the cube-like structure of the Ka'bah clothed in the simple garments of the state of Ihraam, or as he stands soul-shaken on the plain of Arafat from noon till the sun sinks below the horizon.

Some of the powerful emotions experienced during this great act of worship are described in the four accounts below:

IMPRESSIONS OF HAJJ

1. Ahmad Kamal of the Soviet Union

"Makkah is not a place. It is the Beginning, the Present, and the Forever, and whoever enters Makkah feels this and is shaken.

Most pilgrims come here gratefully to discharge a duty owed to God. But ever since the beginning men have come to the Ka'bah to seek refuge with God, bodily refuge from harm at a foe's hand, or sanctuary where the confused heart can find way and the wounded soul be healed. Today, again, there are pilgrims for whom Makkah and the holy places are a haven after savage trials and relentless persecution – pilgrims escaped from Muslim lands under foreign, atheistic rule,. Countless devout Muslims trapped in nations now Soviet, forbidden by the Communists to worship God or perform the Pilgrimage, have perished attempting to cross closed frontiers and come here. A few thousands, survivors, have made Jeddah and Makkah their house of exile, taking some solace from their nearness to the holy places.

Before, – and again one day, God willing – pilgrims came from Albania and Bosnia and Hertzgovina, from Poland and the Caucasus and Crimea, from Turkistan and Kazan and Siberia, from China and from all the other lands where today, Pilgrimage is banned. Some of these peoples, like the Crimeans, have been annihilated and never will be seen in Makkah again, the others dwell in slavery...

And now the eyes of the pilgrim will behold the Ka'bah. Master the emotions. This is an hour for awareness and conscious reverence. This is one of the great experiences of life...

The soul-shaken pilgrim entering the Sanctuary of Makkah and for the first time beholding the Ka'bah knows a humility and an exaltation which are but a prologue for Arafat. Here, by the mountain, the pilgrim will pass what should be spiritually and intellectually, the noblest hours of life. The tents of the Faithful will cover the undulating valley as far as the eye can see. This immense congregation with the sacred mountain at its centre is the heart of Islam. This is the day of true brotherhood...

We are promised that in these hours by Arafat, God will send down His forgiveness and mercy to those who are deserving and they will feel His presence.

This is the day of brotherhood and heartbreak — heartbreak that we have not yet learned to cling to this solidarity where we dwell and labour in valleys and on mountains far from Arafat.

This is the day of promise: the guarantee of what Islam shall be when Muslims everywhere achieve the oneness today known only at Arafat."

(From *The Sacred Journey* by Ahmad Kamal, London, 1964)

2. Michel Jansen — USA

"I have deep roots in America. Some of my father's forbears migrated to the Virginia Colony in 1609, and on my mother's side are ancestors who fought with Washington and Lincoln and a great grandfather who was a Pony Express rider.   Until I was sixteen, I myself had had an upbringing generally regarded as typically American, Midwestern, middle class and Protestant. I grew up in Bay City, Michigan, belonged to the Episcopal Church, went to Sunday School and sang in the church choir.

At sixteen however, I discovered the Qur'an. These words (of the first chapter), simple, and direct, so impressed me that I immediately set out to memorize them. Indeed they drew me into Islam, an example perhaps of Prophet Muhammad's assertion that everyone is born a Muslim and made a Jew or a Christian by his parents.

From that time forward I charted my life in the direction of Mecca...

Before I had embarked on the Pilgrimage, its rituals seemed to me just so many curious exercises. But as I participated in the event of the Pilgrimage, the meaning of these rites unfolded, my understanding of Islam was deepened and I learned more fully what it meant to be a Muslim. Indeed, this is why God had commanded Muhammad to issue the call for the pilgrimage: "That they (the pilgrims) may witness things that are of benefit to them..." (*The Qur'an*, 22: 28)

(For example, towards the end of the Hajj when the time of making the Sacrifice came), I began to feel uneasy. Since I have not completely outgrown the tender-heartedness I had known as a child, I had balked at the idea of the Sacrifice long before being confronted with it and now the time had come to do it. What was I to do? As a girl I had cared for lost dogs or stray cats, adopting any fledgling that had fallen from its nest, splinting a bird's broken leg with matchstick and feeding injured butterflies on sugar syrup. But a companion had been adamant. "You must do the Sacrifice."

Back at our building in Mina I turned to the Qur'an. I found that the Sacrifice has many meanings: it commemorates Abraham's offering of his son's life and God's rejection of this sacrifice in exchange for Abraham's submission to God's will; it marks the end of idolatry among Arabs; it is an offering of thanksgiving to the God of Creation Who has been so benevolent to mankind; and it teaches the well-to-do to share their blessings to "eat thereof (the Sacrifice) and feed the beggar and the suppliant". (22: 36)

As I pondered what I had read, a great weight was lifted from my conscience. I suddenly saw that the Sacrifice *upholds* the sacredness of life, that it, in fact, constitutes a pledge by the pilgrim that he will slay for sustenance only. And where I had felt reluctance before, I now felt eagerness to fulfil *all* the requirements of my pilgrimage.

(From *Aramco World Magazine*, Nov-Dec 1974)

3. Malcolm X — USA

"There were then of thousands of pilgrims, from all over the world. They were of all colors, from blue-eyed blonds to black-skinned Africans. But we were all participating in the same ritual, displaying a spirit of unity and brotherhood that my experiences in America had led me to believe never could exist between the white and the non-white.

You may be shocked by these words coming from me. But on this pilgrimage, what I have seen, and experienced, has forced me to re-arrange much of my thought patterns previously held, and to toss aside some of my previous conclusions. This was not too difficult for me. Despite my firm convictions, I have been always a man who tries to face facts, and to accept the reality of life as new experience and new knowledge unfolds it. I have always kept an open mind, which is necessary to the flexibility that must go hand in hand with every form of intelligent search for truth.

During the past eleven days here in the Muslim world, I have eaten from the same plate, drunk from the same glass and slept in the same bed (or on the same rug) - while praying to the same God with fellow Muslims, whose eyes were the bluest of the blue, whose hair was the blondest of blond, and whose skin was the whitest of white. And in the words and in the actions and in the deeds of the 'white' Muslims, I felt the same sincerity that I felt among the black African Muslims of Nigeria, Sudan and Ghana.

We were *truly* all the same—brothers.

All praise is due to Allah, the Lord of all the worlds."

(From the *Autobiography of Malcolm X*, New York, 1964).

4. Muhammad Asad — Austria

"...hidden from my eyes in the midst of this lifeless wilderness of valleys and hills, lies the plain of Arafat, on which all the pilgrims who come to Mecca assemble on one day of the year as a reminder of that Last Assembly, when man will have to answer to his Creator for all he has done in life. How often have I stood there myself, bareheaded, in the white pilgrim garb, among a multitude of white-garbed, bareheaded pilgrims from three continents, our faces turned toward the Jabal ar-Rahma—the Mount of Mercy—which rises out of the vast plain: standing and waiting through the noon, through the afternoon, reflecting upon that inescapable Day, 'when you will be exposed to view, and no secret of yours will remain concealed'...

As I stand on the hillcrest and gaze down toward the invisible Plain of Arafat, the moonlit blueness of the landscape before me, so dead a moment ago, suddenly comes to life with the currents of all the human lives that have passed through it and is filled with the eerie voices of the millions of men nd women who have walked or ridden between Mecca and Arafat in over thirteen hundred pilgrimages for over thirteen hundred years...I hear the sounds of their passed-away days,the wings of faith which have drawn them together to this land of rocks and sand and seeming deadness beat again with the warmth of life over the arc of centuries, and the mighty wingbeat draws me into its orbit and draws my own passed-away days into the present, and once again I am riding over the plain...

We ride on, rushing, flying over the plain, and to me it seems that we are flying with the wind, abandoned to a happiness that knows neither end nor limit...and the wind shouts a wild paean of joy into my ears. ''Never again, never again, never again will you be a stranger!''

My brethren on the right and my brethren on the left, all of them unknown to me but none a stranger; in the tumultuous joy of our chase, we are one body in pursuit of one goal. Wide is the world before us, and in our hearts glimmers a spark of the flame that burned in the hearts of the Prophet's Companions. They know, my brethren on the right and my brethren on the left, that they have fallen short of what was expected of them, and that in the flight of centuries their hearts have grown small and yet, the promise of fulfilment has not been taken from them...from us...

Someone in the surging host abandons his tribal cry for a cry of faith: 'We are brethren of him who gives himself up to God!'- and another joins in 'ALLAHU AKBAR' — 'God is the Greatest — God alone is Great!' ''

(From *The Road to Mecca*, 1st ed., 1954)

Hajj, like perhaps no other occasion, has the capacity to lay bare the fancies and vanities of man. The *talbiyyah* or the special refrain announcing man's willingness and eagerness to acknowledge and obey God resounds throughout the Hajj environment:

Here I am, O Lord, here I am!
Here I am; no partner hast Thou; here I am!
Surely to Thee is all Praise, all goodness and all Sovereignty;
No partner hast Thou!

The simplicity, beauty and power of this refrain create the mood in which the pilgrimage is performed. However, the atmosphere and environment in which the Hajj is performed can be and has been marred by the intrusion and dominance of many alien and incongruous planning concepts and technologies and by the behaviour of pilgrims who often show little trace of the *adab* of Islam.

There is in fact a warning in the Qur'an to those who might be tempted to mar or ruin the desired mood of the Hajj by selfish or wicked conduct. The Qur'an instructs:

"Whoever undertakes the pilgrimage...shall, while on pilgrimage, abstain from lewd speech, from all wicked conduct, and from quarrelling; and whatever good you may do, God is aware of it. And make provision for yourselves—but, verily, the best of all provisions is God-consciousness: remain then conscious of Me, O you who are endowed with insight." (2: 197)

The mood of Hajj can also be marred or ruined by the environment and the physical conditions under which Hajj is performed. Noise from earth-shattering technology and hi-tech urban planning styles as well as the un-hygienic practices of many pilgrims have transformed the hajj environment for the worse. Simple and more natural solutions in keeping with the natural physical environment of the Hajj will be best suited to maintaining the spirit and the atmosphere of contemplation, devotion and intense personal rectification which is the object of the Hajj.

Natural laws affecting the rise, decline and fall of societies

It is the duty of all those who belong to the Ummah to work for, preserve and enhance the unity, strength and integrity of the Ummah. The Muslim ummah, like any other society, thrives or suffers, rises or falls, moves forward or declines according to conditions and laws. These conditions or laws apply to other societies also. The Qur'an mentions four factors which contribute to the rise and decline of societies.

Justice and injustice

The first is justice and injustice. If a society is just it will thrive. If it is unjust, no matter how powerful it appears to be, it will perish. The story is told in the Qur'an for example of the Pharaoh of Egypt who had a lust for power and control. He regarded himself as the supreme lord and he treated his subjects as his slaves. He ruled through dividing people and setting them against one another. He persecuted the Israelites in his country, killed their sons, and seized their women to serve him and his henchmen. For such acts, he is described as "one of the corrupters". Such acts of social oppression and injustice destroy societies and civilizations. Sadly, many parts of the Muslim ummah today are afflicted by such oppression and injustice even by rulers who lay claim to being Muslim.

Unity and disunity

The second factor in the rise and decline of societies is unity and disunity. Muslims are commanded to come together on the basis of faith, through holding fast to God's firm rope. For Muslims, the condition of unity must be faith and a commitment to truth and other laws and values of the Shari'ah. Unity could never be for the perpetuation of an injustice or the propagation of falsehood.

AT HAJJ:

THE FAREWELL SERMON OF THE NOBLE PROPHET

"All praise is for God. We praise Him. We seek His help and pardon and we turn to Him. We take refuge with God from the evils of ourselves and the bad consequences of our actions. There is none to lead him astray whom God guides aright and there is none to guide him aright whom He misguides. I bear witness that there is no deity but God alone without any partner. I bear witness that Muhammad is His servant and His messenger.

I admonish you, servants of God, to be conscious of God and I urge you to obey Him...

O people, listen to me as I deliver a message to you for I do not know whether I shall ever get an opportunity to meet you after this year in this place (the Valley of Arafat, 9 Dhu-l Hijjah, 10 AH).

O people, indeed your lives, your properties and your honour are sacred and inviolable to you till you appear before your Lord, like the sacredness of this day of yours, in this month of yours, in this city of yours. You will certainly meet your Lord and He will ask you about your actions. Have I conveyed the message? O Lord, be witness!

So he who has any trust to discharge, he should restore it to the person who deposited it with him.

Be aware, no one committing a crime is responsible for it but himself. Neither is a son responsible for the crime of his father nor is a father responsible for the crime of his son.

O people, listen to my words and understand them. You must know that the Muslim is the brother of a Muslim and the Muslims are one brotherhood. Nothing of his brother is lawful for a Muslim except what he himself allows. So you should not do injustice to or oppress yourselves. O Lord, have I conveyed the message?

Behold, everything of Ignorance is put down under my feet. The blood revenges of the (pre-Qur'anic) days of Ignorance are remitted...

O people, verily the Satan is disappointed from being ever worshipped in this land of yours. But he is satisfied to be obeyed in actions of yours you think very trifling. So be cautious of him in your religion.

Verily, I have left among you something clear which if you hold fast to, you will never go astray after that — the Book of God and the Example (Sunnah) of His messenger...

(The speech was continued the following day at Mina).
"O people! Be conscious of God. And even if a mangled Abyssinian slave becomes your leader hearken to him and obey him as long as he establishes and institutes the Book of God.

Do listen to me. Worship your Lord and Sustainer. Perform your five daily Salaat. Fast your month (of Ramadaan). Make pilgrimage to your House (the Ka'bah in Makkah). Pay the Zakaat on your property willingly and obey whatever I command you. Then will you enter the Paradise of your Lord and Sustainer.

Verily, you will meet your Lord and Sustainer and He will ask you about your actions. Do not go astray after me so that some of you strike the necks of others. Have I conveyed the message?..."

(And the speech was continued on the 11th or 12th of Dhu-l Hijjah)

"O people, verily your Lord and Sustainer is One and your ancestor is one. All of you descend from Adam and Adam was made of earth. There is no superiority for an Arab over a non-Arab nor for a non-Arab over an Arab; neither for a white man over a black man nor a black man over a white man except the superiority gained through God-consciousness (taqwa). Indeed the noblest among you is the one who is most deeply conscious of God...

"Have I conveyed the message?"

"Yes, O Messenger of God," his Companions all replied.

We are to shun disunity and discord. Discord saps confidence and results in a decline or loss of power: "And do not wrangle with one another, lest you lose heart and your power decline." (8: 46). Working for unity often calls for tact and wisdom, as well as firmness and strength.

Enjoining good and forbidding evil

The third factor in the rise and decline of societies is whether people enjoin good and forbid evil or not. The Qur'an speaks much and often of the need to enjoin good and forbid evil. Failure to do so will result in ruin. The fate of some unbelievers among the Israelites was disgrace and ruin because of their failure to restrain one another from reprehensible acts: "Nor did they forbid one another the evils they committed; evil indeed were the things they did." (5: 59) Conversely, the essential qualities of a successful and superior ummah is enjoining the good and forbidding the bad and believing in God.

Morality and debauchery

The fourth factor in the decline of societies is debauchery and moral corruption. Two words used in the Qur'an for this are *zulm* and *fasaad*. All debauchery, all departure from the right road of humanity, is zulm. Zulm as used in the Qur'an refers to injustice to others as well as debauchery and immoral acts. It applies to the encroachments of a person or group on the rights of another person or group. It also applies the injustice an individual perpetrates upon himself or the injustice a group perpetrates upon itself.

Judged by these criteria, the present-day Muslim ummah is in an advanced state of decline and ruin.

In so far as justice is concerned, the Muslim ummah is by and large ruled by oppressive regimes that serve foreign interests and values. These regimes have amassed a vast array of sophisticated technology and training for controlling their citizens. One result is that many very basic human rights and freedoms are denied to people such as the freedom of peaceful association. There is no place where the Shari'ah is adhered to in its totality and people who call for the implementation of the Shari'ah are looked upon as dangerous fundamentalists.

So far as unity is concerned, the ummah is divided into a vast number of nationalistic units with each nation jealously guarding its own borders and narrow interests. The idea that there should be free movement of people and resources for the general good of the ummah remains a dream. There have been attempts to have some form of cooperation among these countries but these attempts need to be anchored more firmly on the basis of Islamic values.

The concept of enjoining the good and forbidding the evil has largely been ignored and overtaken by the introduction of policies of "development and progress" which bring with them alien values, habits and goals which have led to injustices on a vast scale.

The Muslim world thus presents a picture of bleakness and desolation ravaged by war and civil strife, illiteracy and disease, hunger and starvation, dirt and squalor in many places, opulence and waste in others, bureaucracy and corruption everywhere. These are some of the painful realities.

Yet, the ideals persist and will always beckon, offering the chance of sanity and hope for betterment. But betterment does not come with merely hoping.

INDIVIDUAL DUTY TO THE UMMAH

Each Muslim who knows what Islam stands for has a duty to work for the unity, strength and integrity of the Muslim ummah. Many people know and realise this. But the problems facing the ummah often seem too big and complex, and world structures and systems so infinitely intricate and powerful as to induce helplessness or a preoccupation with minor issues and problems.

The agenda for Muslim unity and strength has a long list of items. At the lowest level it requires individual awareness and effort and at the level of the ummah it requires vision and sincerity, and formidable intellectual and organisational skill.

As an individual, you can work for Muslim unity and strength in many ways:
* by acquiring and propagating knowledge and comprehension of Islam in all its concerns;
* by reforming yourself in order to achieve correct belief, a sound body, good character, cultured thought, an honest livelihood, well-organised use of time and resources;
* by developing an attitude of care and concern for others, avoiding all forms and expressions of dislike, condescension and discrimination against others, whether Muslims or non-Muslims, because of the colour of their skin, their type of hair, the language they speak or their accents;
* by having a strong feeling of brotherhood with other believers for true brotherhood is the companion of faith and division is the companion of unbelief. Unity produces strength but there can be no unity without love. The lowest degree of love is purity of intentions and unspitefulness of the heart; the highest degree of love is complete selflessness: "And those saved from the covetousness of their own souls are the ones that achieve prosperity." (59: 9)

- by belonging to and working with a group or organised community to promote the interests of Muslims and of humanity;

- by seeking as an individual or a group to instruct and guide society to righteousness by encouraging virtue, enjoining all that is good, helping people, trying to win public opinion to the side of Islam, and observing the Islamic principles in all walks of life. This is part of the duty of *Da'wah* or inviting others to Islam;

- by seeking to influence and change governmental policies and programmes so that they are in line with Islamic principles and serve the interests not only of citizens in the state but of all members of the ummah and indeed of humanity. This requires not slogans and demonstrations in the first instance but well-thought out and developed alternative policies and strategies in the range of matters that an Islamic government is obliged to deal with: spreading education, protecting public health, overseeing public utilities, developing the resources of the land, providing opportunities for people to work, guarding the public treasury, strengthening the morals of the people, maintaining peace and order, providing security, implementing the Islamic moral and legal code, and spreading the call of Islam.

If a government sincerely and efficiently carries out these purposes, it has a right to your loyalty and support. If a government neglects its duties and falls short of its responsibilities, you have the duty first of all to advise and guide. If a government persists in wrong-doing and transgression of the Shari'ah, you have a duty to work for its replacement for ''There is no obedience due to a creature that involves the disobedience to the Creator.''

- by working for cooperation and unity of Muslim peoples, communities and institutions throughout the world, facilitating the flow of information, investment and resources, appropriate technologies, and people in a sort of Pax Islamica so that hunger and starvation, disease and illiteracy, war and strife are all removed from Muslim lands;

- working to ensure that an invigorated ummah once again take on the moral lead of a humanity that has transgressed and rebelled against God.

These are mammoth tasks. They require clear objectives, detailed planning, sound administrative sense, vision, knowledge, commitment, patience, striving, sacrifice.

INSTITUTIONS FOR COHESION AND STRENGTH

Da'wah

Islam provides the institutions, the framework and the guidelines for realising the cohesion and strength of the ummah. We have mentioned Da'wah in this context as the first instrument to bring back or call people to Islam.

Da'wah literally means invitation. It does not mean coercion or force. It means calling people to Islam "with wisdom and kindly exhortation". Even when the Prophet Moses was asked by God to meet Pharaoh, he was told to speak to him in "gentle words" and hold out the hope of reform to him.

Da'wah is normally taken to mean preaching Islam to non-Muslims. But da'wah in fact applies to Muslims as well. Da'wah to Muslims is a call for reform (*islaah*) and renewal (*tajdiid*). It applies to your own family and relatives, or even the congregation in a mosque. Here da'wah takes the form of reminding, clarifying and elucidating the teachings of Islam. It does not require you to be angry and engage in dispute and confrontation. It requires wisdom and gentleness.

Da'wah does not only mean preaching. It means helping to look after people's needs and caring for them. You cannot call people to believe in God when they are starving and dying. Your first duty then is to provide food. You cannot call people to Salaat if they do not have clean water to wash and clean clothes in which to pray. You cannot ask people to study the Qur'an and the Sunnah if they do not know how to read. Your first duty then is to teach them to read. You cannot ask people to undertake jihaad when they are sick and debilitated by disease. Your first duty is to provide medical care and attention.

Da'wah then involves the provision of basic necessities of food, clothing, shelter, education and health care. There are millions who belong to the Muslim ummah who do not have or are denied these basic needs. These needs should be provided from resources within the ummah. The fact that they are often provided by others exposes the ummah to humiliation, loss and infiltration.

Jihaad

This leads to consideration of another important instrument for protecting the interests of the Ummah and of mankind—Jihaad.

Jihaad basically means striving and refers to the unceasing effort an individual must make towards self-improvement and self-purification. It also refers to the duty on Muslims, at both the individual and collective level, to struggle against all forms of evil, corruption, injustice, tyranny and oppression whether this injustice is committed against Muslims or non-Muslims.

Jihaad is to promote justice. This cannot be done without strength and power. Notions of equity without power to enforce it has no practical value.

A Muslim, according to the well-known saying of the Prophet, has the duty to try to put down an evil with his hand, that is, with physical force. If he cannot do so, he must combat it with his tongue by campaigning against it. If he cannot do so, then he should at least hate it in his heart — this last represents the weakest manifestation of faith.

Muslims are not permitted to allow themselves or others to become or remain the passive victims of others' injustice or aggression. It is not natural that people should accept humiliation and so:

"Permission (to fight) is given to those against whom war is wrongfully waged, and verily God has indeed the power to succour them: those who have been driven from their homelands against all right for no other reason than their saying, "Our Lord and Sustainer is God.

For, if God had not enabled people to defend themselves against one another, (all) monasteries and churches and synagogues and mosques — in all of which God's name is abundantly extolled — would surely have been destroyed.

And God will most certainly succcour him who succours His cause, for verily God is most Powerful, Almighty, (well aware of) those who (even) if We firmly establish them on earth, remain constant in Prayer, and give in charity, and enjoin the doing of what is right and forbid the doing of what is wrong. And with God rests the final outcome of all events." (22: 39-41)

The above verses imply that the defence of religious freedom is the foremost just cause for which arms may and indeed must be taken up, otherwise according to another verse "corruption would surely overwhelm the earth".

Linked with advice of the noble Prophet quoted above, we can see that the Muslim is thus not only required to give assistance to the victim of tyranny but to stop the one who is committing it in order to bring about the rule of righteousness, freedom and justice for all people.

Islam itself signifies peace and the relationship between the Islamic state with other peaceful states is devoted to the exchange of knowledge and the furtherance of mutual benefits.

With aggressive powers, the duty of the Islamic state is:

1. To repel hostility by all peaceful means if possible: "And if they incline towards peace, incline also to it." (8: 61)

2. If peaceful means do not succeed, war becomes obligatory: "If anyone makes war on you, make war upon him in like manner." (2: 194)

3. The State may conclude peace only after aggression has been repelled: "And fight them until oppression ceases and all religion is for God alone. But if they desist then let there be no enmity except against the wrongdoers." (2: 193)

War is thus justified only as a means of upholding the right and repulsing the wrong and not the sake of greed or false pride. This is the meaning of Jihaad "in the way of God".

Islam has specific laws for the conduct of war. Fore example, these were the instruction of Abuu Bakr, the first Khalifah after the Prophet, to a Muslim army:

"Do not be harsh on them; do not kill children, old men or women; do not cut down or burn palm trees, do not destroy fruit trees, do not slay a sheep or camel except for food. If you see people who have taken refuge in monasteries, let them be safe in their place of refuge."

In these instructions, we see the spirit of Islam which abhors aggression, destruction and bloodshed and enjoins justice, mercy and tolerance.

Islam demands for the sake of self-defence and the ensuring of peace that the Muslim ummah and those societies which make up the ummah must be strong enough so that no aggressor would ever be tempted to attack and that they should never be taken unaware by treacherous moves.

All Muslims, including scholars and people in positions of responsibility and leadership in the Muslim world, are faced with the great and awesome challenge of promoting and protecting the unity, strength and integrity of the ummah and of assuming, for the benefit of mankind, the moral leadership of the world.

EIGHT

FACE *to* FAITHS

From what we have said so far, there are a number of statements about God, the universe and man which ought to be considered as valid:

- The Creator of the universe and of man is One; the Creator or God is One.
- Mankind as a species is one.
- The basic nature (*fitrah*) of all human beings is the same.
- The guidance given by God to man has always been the same. True religion, in the sense of God's guidance to man, therefore, can only be one.
- One of God's gifts to man, in addition to a basically good nature and guidance to preserve this nature, is freedom of choice. Man may use this freedom of choice to live according to the guidance of God and so preserve his good natural state. He may also use this freedom of choice, under various influences and for various motives, to deviate from this guidance either slightly or to a great extent; or he may choose to reject this guidance altogether and so bring harm to himself.
- Man also has the opportunity to abandon his errant or misguided ways and return to true guidance, to the callings of his inherently good nature and so achieve harmony with himself, with the rest of creation and with his Creator. From this harmony comes true happiness and satisfaction.

FRAMEWORK FOR UNDERSTANDING

The above statements provide us with a framework for understanding human society and history. They should help us to deal with such questions as:

How do we explain the fact that there exist so many different religions or worldviews?

If many of these religions claim to lead man to the same goal, how do we account for both the similarities and differences between one religion and another?

Can any one religion lay exclusive claim to the truth?

The above statements could also provide us with guidelines to determine the type of attitudes and relationships we have with people of other faiths and worldviews.

The origin of religions

In the first chapter, we discussed briefly the widely held notion that the religion or worldview of early man was "primitive". According to this notion, man's religion began in animism (the worship of stones, trees, the sun and other objects) and evolved through beliefs and practices like ancestor worship and polytheism. Then only it moved on or progressed to a higher monotheism or belief in one God as man became more developed and progressive. This notion is part of the linear view of history — that human beings move in a continuous line from being primitive to being more and more developed and progressive.

This notion of the origins of religion does not fit in with the Islamic view of the nature of the first man who was endowed with knowledge and guidance by a wise and just Creator. According to the Islamic view, first there was belief in One God and only later this belief came to be overlaid by animistic, polytheistic and other elements. Man either became forgetful, or using his freedom of choice he deliberately deviated from the straight path of guidance.

There is evidence for this Islamic view in many regions and cultures of the world. The idea of a Supreme God, the Creator, prevails in many tribal religions of Africa and among people as far apart as the inhabitants of Tierra del Fuego and the Arctic. Strikingly, they have very sound ideas about creation and a Supreme Ruler whom they do not represent through images.

Zoroastrianism, named after Zarathustra whose time and place are a riddle (500 or 2500 BCE), has many ideas and doctrines which are familiar to other faiths. Zarathustra is said to have first encountered an angel as an emissary from God, called people to have faith in Him alone and Judgement after death and left behind scriptures. Even in Hinduism, so extensively polytheistic, one can find the idea of One God under all the layers of *shirk*. In Hinduism, many of the "attributes" of God were apparently transformed into images and there is a suggestion that Rama and Krishna were messengers of God who were turned into gods incarnate in the same way that Jesus was in Christianity.

How did the true religion of God come to be overlaid by polytheistic ideas and other elements?

For various motives such as power or prestige or economic gain people created objects of worship or set up themselves as supreme beings to be revered and obeyed. Other people out of fear or feelings of group solidarity also worshipped these objects, sometimes in addition to the One God. Some also regarded their leaders as divine or as having Divine powers.

Eventually all it took was the passing of a generation for such attitudes and habits to be accepted as normal and right simply because "we found our fathers and our forefathers'' engaged in such worship and such practices. This was the state for example in which the young Abraham found his people.

Periodically God sent guides or prophets to every people to bring them back on course to the Straight Path of acknowledging and worshipping the One and Only God. Some people followed the prophets and reformed their ways. Many people, through habit, devotion to their ancestors or their version of what their ancestors did, or through economic or political vested interests or plain stubbornness, stuck to their old misguided ways. Some even went further and persecuted the prophets and their followers.

All true prophets maintained that they were not seeking power, fame or wealth or any favours for themselves but that they had the genuine interests of the people at heart. Some people, realising their need, accepted the leadership of the prophet sent to them, but when their need was fulfilled, they turned their backs on the prophet's instructions. This was the case with the Israelites and their need for the leadership of Prophet Moses to deliver them from the Pharaoh of Egypt. After leaving Egypt, some of them forsook God and turned to the worship of a calf they had made with their own hands. Many other peoples, before and since, have adopted these strange practices of idol worship and polytheistic practices even after accepting and following Divine guidance.

After the departure of a prophet, often ironically out of devotion to that prophet, some people would add to or alter his message. They would attribute capabilities and powers to the prophet such as he himself never claimed. This is in keeping with people's propensity to exaggerate or embellish a story more and more with each telling. This is evidently what has happened in the case of Jesus. It is suggested that this was also the case with Rama and Krishna in the Hindu tradition.

In this way a new religion is formed. It may contain some of the original truths taught by the prophet side by side with new-fangled myths and legends and practices. Lacking any firm point of reference, this new religion keeps on changing from one place to another and from one epoch to another. This has been the case with Christianity.

In time, using their reason, some people find themselves in all honesty, being unable to accept the fantastic claims that are made of a religion or they see that these religions are unable to provide adequate or satisfying answers to the many aspects of life and human relationships. They reject this religion and because this is the only religion they know, they think that all religion is the same and so they reject religion as such altogether and the belief in God altogether. This is how atheism, humanism and secularism have arisen in the West and under its influence spread to different parts of the world.

True religion is essentially one

From the beginning of mankind, true religion or guidance from God has always been one. People have strayed from or corrupted this guidance. True prophets have sought to renew and purify this guidance. But the various peoples to whom these prophets were sent often created their own "mixture" or religion both from what is true and from their own ingredients, additions and corruptions. To the extent that they took from what is true, we have similarities in the various "mixtures" or new-fangled religions. To the extent that they added their own corruptions, we have differences in these mixtures or religions.

The one true religion has always taught belief in and obedience to the One God and this is what Islam literally is. According to the Qur'an, true religions (in the plural) do not exist; true religion (in the singular) exists. All the Prophets summoned us to one religion, to one primary course and goal.

"God has ordained for you that religion which He commended to Noah, and that which We inspire in you (O Prophet Muhammad), and that which We commended to Abraham, Moses and Jesus; uphold the religion and do not grow divided on it." (42: 13)

True religion or Islam has always been essentially one thing in all times and all places. A statement like "Islam was the last of the revealed religions" is therefore erroneous. All true Prophets were Muslims which literally means those who submit to the One God. Their message was essentially the same—Islam: to call men to worship and submit to One God. Adam was a Muslim, Abraham was a Muslim, Moses was a Muslim, Jesus was a Muslim. Zarathustra, if he was a true Prophet, was a Muslim. Rama, if he was a true Prophet, was a Muslim.

This reasoning, that true religion is one, is based on the worldview that sees man as a single species with the same natural needs. It is only when people deviated from true religion and set up their own factions and sects that the unity of mankind was split asunder, each one exulting in its own sect, faction or "religion". What then should be the relationship between the upholders of the true religion and the followers of other religions and ideologies? There are three main positions which can be adopted.

The first is based on the fact that God created man with a free will, with the freedom to choose correct guidance or not. If God had wanted, he could have made all human beings, like angels, submit to His will. This freedom of choice, although it carries its own responsibilities and burdens for the individual, must be respected. No one can be compelled to believe or disbelieve. The Qur'an clearly states, "There is no compulsion in religion" even as it emphasizes that Truth and right guidance provided in Islam has been made distinct from error.

Tolerance and protection

The initial position of a Muslim to other faiths is thus one of tolerance. More than this, the protection of freedom of belief and worship for followers of other religions has been made a sacred duty of Muslims. Remarkably this duty was fixed at the same time when the duty of Jihaad was ordained:

"Permission (to fight) is given to those against whom war is being wrongfully waged, and verily, God has indeed the power to succour them: those who have been driven from their homelands against all right for no other reason than their saying, 'Our Lord and Sustainer is God!'

"For, if God had not enabled people to defend themselves against one another, monasteries and churches and synagogues and mosques — in which God's name is abundantly extolled — would surely have been destroyed." (22: 39-40)

The above verses gives precedence to the *sawaami'* (monasteries), the *biya'* (churches) and the *salawaat* (synagogues) over the mosques in order to underline their inviolability and the duty of the Muslims to safeguard them against any desecration or abuse, and protect freedom of belief.

Indeed, Islam requires that protection be given to people who do not believe in revealed religion at all, provided they refrain from molesting the believers. The Qur'an declares:

"And if any of the idolaters seek your protection (O Muhammad), grant him protection so that he may hear the Word of God, and afterwards convey him to a place of safety; for they are people who do not know the truth." (9: 6)

The second position is based on the knowledge that even after he has erred or gone astray man has the chance and the capacity to return to his good nature and the Straight Path. Man often needs to be helped in this process by being reminded of his nature and his purpose in life. This process of reminding or inviting others to truth and justice is what we have referred to in the last chapter as Da'wah. As a result of Da'wah, people may choose to return to their naturally good state and become Muslim in which case they accept all the obligations and rights of Muslims and are welcomed wholeheartedly into the community of believers. Alternatively, they may choose to remain in their religion. In this case their right to do so is respected. They are guaranteed freedom of worship and autonomy in their institutions. They have the right to manage their own affairs and the obligation to live in peace and co-existence with others.

A third position arises when people have not only strayed but actively rebel and commit evil and injustice despite calls on them to give up their evil ways. Such people, whether they belong to a religion or not, cannot be left alone but need to be combatted in the interests of security and to protect such values as life, honour and so on.

With this background, it may be useful to take a more detailed look at some existing religions and worldviews.

"THE PEOPLE OF THE SCRIPTURE"

> "Say: (O Prophet): 'O People of the Scripture! Let us come together on a fair and noble principle common to both of us: never to worship or serve any but God, never to associate any being with Him, and never to take one another as Lords besides God.' " (3: 64)

The "People of the Scripture" or *Ahl al-Kitaab* denotes those people to whom God conveyed His guidance through a Divine scripture or revelation to one of His Prophets before Muhammad. The term Ahl al-Kitaab may therefore be rendered as "followers of earlier revelation"and is taken to refer primarily to Jews and Christians.

Jews

In the Qur'an, Jews are referred to as Yahuud and Banii Israa'iil or Children of Israel. The scripture or Divine guidance addressed to them was the Tawraat which was revealed to Moses, may God's peace and blessings be on him. However, this Tawraat is not to be understood as the Torah of the Old Testament in its present form. Although the books comprising the Torah may have originally been based on the Divine message, they were re-formed and continually re-written by scribes and priests over a period of time.

From the standpoint of Islam there can be no doubt that Abraham, Isaac, Ismail, Jacob, Joseph, Moses, David, Solomon — may peace and blessings be on them — were all prophets whom God had sent forth with a Divine message. These prophets are all mentioned in the Qur'an. Their message was always one and the same in essential content and consisted above all of the recognition of God, of His unity and transcendence, of the Day of Judgement, of the purposiveness of history, and of man's responsibility to manage his life and his resources as God has directed.

Many Jews still identify with the essentials of this Message and thus there is much similarity between them and Muslims. There is an uncompromising stress on the Oneness of God and there are may similarities in values, morals and living habits. This strand of Judaism has been referred to as the universalist strand.

There is another strand of Judaism, which may be called tribal or ethnocentric, which stresses that God is the "God of Israel", of Abraham, Isaac, Jacob and of their descendants and that God's purpose is to vindicate, defend and avenge "His own people". Accordingly, this strand looks on the Covenant as the "Promise" by which God has bound Himself to favour His people and to continue to favour them regardless of their moral performance.

Accordingly, it is not impressed by the Day of Judgement or the Hereafter. It interprets the Day of Judgement as the Day on which it will be vindicated, and revenged, against its earthly enemies, rather than the Day on which God reckons with all men their moral and immoral works and passes a judgement of reward or punishment to each on the basis of his or her own works. This view interprets the covenant in material and racist terms. It has led to political Zionism.

The Qur'an does recognise that God has favoured the Jews (2: 47, 122). This favour, however, depends on the fulfilment of a covenant between them and God, their part of which is to serve God and do good works. The covenant grants to the Jews the rewards of children, land, prosperity and happiness, and requires of them to worship God alone and to practice charity, justice and righteousness (5: 12). The covenant equally stipulates that if the Jews fail to keep their part of the covenant, God will inflict upon them His punishment. Defeat, dispersion, suffering and unhappiness would be their lot (3: 112; 17: 2-8). Islam knows nothing of a "Promise", the doctrine that God is bound to favour a people regardless of their beliefs and actions. This is true for any people. God's covenant does not extend to the evildoers and the perpetrators of injustice.

At the time of the Prophet Muhammad, peace be on him, and under the Constitution of Madinah which was signed by the Jews, Jewish religion, culture, institutions and property were not only tolerated but guaranteed. As far as the Torah or Jewish law is concerned, Islam recognised the Jewish observance of it as not only legitimate but as desirable and obligatory on Jews for the continuation of group life under the constitution. The Jews were required to set up their own law courts, to judge themselves by the precepts of the Torah and the executive power of the state was placed at the disposal of the rabbinic court. Islam thus recognised Judaism as a religion de jure which no other religion or political system ever did.

By contrast, in the history of the Christian West, the Jewishness of a person was often seen as an abomination to be met either with proselytisation or conversion, or persecution.

Seen in this perspective, the problem of Israel which has embittered Muslim-Jewish relations in the twentieth century is not essentially a "religious" problem. Muslims bear no responsibility for creating this problem. Yet they are affected by it and suffer from it. For Muslims, the problem of Israel is essentially a moral issue in which truth, justice and freedom from oppression are at stake.

Christians

Many are the important elements that are common to Islam and Christianity. Muslims and Christians share many similar beliefs, values, moral injunctions and principles of behaviour. The Virgin Mary and her son Jesus, may peace be upon them both, are mentioned often in the Qur'an. In fact, there is a chapter of the Qur'an named after her called Maryam. The major difference between the two faiths concern the nature and role of Jesus, peace be on him.

Jesus, referred to in the Qur'an as 'Isa ibn Maryam — Jesus the son of Mary

> 'Verily, in the sight of God, the nature of Jesus is as the nature of Adam, whom He created out of clay and then said unto him, "Be" and he is. This is the truth from your Lord and Sustainer; be not then among the doubters...
>
> "Say, O followers of earlier revelation! Come unto that tenet which we and you hold in common; that we shall worship none but God, and that we shall not ascribe divinity to anyone beside Him, and that we shall not take human beings for our lords beside God." (3: 59, 64)

— is one of the greatest of the prophets of God whom Muslim hold in very deep love and respect.

The Qur'an confirms that Jesus was born of a virgin mother (Mary) through the same Power that brought Adam into being without a father and that with God's permission he wrought many miraculous deeds. He was given the power to speak as a babe, to heal the sick, to raise the dead, and to reach the hearts of men with the guidance he brought from God. Finally, when he was in danger of being killed by some of his own people, He was "raised up" by God. The Qur'an states that he was not killed nor was he crucified.

The Qur'an states emphatically in passage after passage that Jesus is not God's son, that he never claimed to be God's son or of Divine nature but rather charged his followers to worship God alone. It also states that the notion of the Most High God having a son is so totally degrading to and far removed from His exaltedness and transcendence that it actually constitutes an awesome piece of blasphemy.

> "And some assert: 'The Most Gracious has taken unto Himself a son.' Indeed (by this assertion) you utter something monstrous, at which the heavens might well-nigh be rent into fragments, and the earth be split asunder, and the mountains fall down in ruins! That men should ascribe a son to the Most Gracious, although it is inconceivable that the Most Gracious should take unto Himself a son! Not one of all the beings that are in the heavens or on earth appears before the Most Gracious other than as a servant." (19: 88 -93).

Islam obviously rejects the Christian doctrine of the Trinity — that there are three Gods in One and One in three! This is so utterly unreasonable and "monstrous" a doctrine that its utterance "might rent the heavens into fragments, split the earth asunder and bring down the mountains in ruins"!

Islam also does not accept the notion that Jesus died on the cross, and that he died to save humanity's sin. It does not accept the notion of Original Sin whereby Adam's original disobedience of God has been inherited by all his descendants. In other words, it does not accept that all human beings on earth are sinful because of Adam's disobedience of God. Adam repented and was forgiven by God.

Islam therefore affirms that every human being comes into the world innocent and sinless. A new-born babe does not bear the burden of a sin committed by an ancestor. This would be a negation of God's attribute of justice and compassion.

To further claim that the taint of this sin is certain to put every human being into Hell for all eternity unless the Deity sacrifices Himself for His creatures is also a denial of the justice and good will of the Creator towards His creation. No one can be saved except by the mercy and grace of God and by His acknowledging and surrendering himself to the Creator and His guidance. A person can turn to His Creator in obedience and repentance without the need for an intermediary or intercessor.

"And remain conscious of a Day when no human being shall in the least avail another, nor will compensation be accepted from any of them, nor will intercession be of any use to them, and none shall be succoured." (2: 123)

Other Religions

Although the practices of many religions also belong properly to the history of unbelief rather than belief, the attitude of Islam to the followers of such religions is one of tolerance and guaranteeing of freedom of worship.

The Zoroastrians of Persia were recognised as an autonomous community within the Islamic State and were accorded the same privileges and duties as the Jews.

When Muslims went to India, they came into contact with Buddhism and Hinduism. How should Buddhists and Hindus be treated was the question the Muslim commander directed to the head of the Islamic state. They appeared to worship idols and their doctrines were at the farthest remove from Islam.

The judgement of the Muslim scholars was that so long as Hindus and Buddhists did not fight the Islamic state and as long as they paid the military exemption tax, they must be free to worship their gods as they please, to maintain their temples and to determine their lives by the precepts of their faith. Thus the same status as that of the Jews and the Christians were to be accorded to them.

It was such firm principles and policies that allowed non-Muslims to protect their identity under an Islamic state and which explain the continuing presence of non-Muslim communities in the Muslim world.

This system of granting autonomy to religious communities is known as the *Millat* system (millat meaning religious community) or the *Dhimmi* system (dhimmi meaning covenant of peace or protected status). The system is the only one that can preserve freedom of worship, respect for the laws, customs and culture of different communities, and co-existence of communities. Modern concepts of nationalism and statehood have destroyed the culture and autonomy of many communities in favour of a common citizenship and the subjection of all citizens to common laws.

About the rights of religious communities protected by the Islamic state, the Prophet Muhammad, peace be on him, has warned: "Whoever oppresses any dhimmi (non-Muslim who has made a covenant of peace with the Islamic state) I shall be his prosecutor on the Day of Judgement."

This is the norm under Islamic law. It cannot be denied that there were evil rulers in the Muslim world and where these existed both non-Muslims and Muslims suffered.

Secular ideologies

Perhaps the major challenge facing man today is the dominance of secular, materialistic ideologies which have not only set their own goals but which have attempted to shape religion according to its own worldview and purposes. In fact a secularised view of religion is what is consciously or unconsciously accepted by many followers of religion, including nominal Muslims.

There is however no common ground between secularism and Islam. Secularism rejects belief in God, belief in the Revelation and belief in the Hereafter. The fundamental assumption of secularism is that material well-being is the present world is the essential means to human happiness. Material well-being is not a means but an end in itself. Economic growth and efficiency is the main preoccupation of secular ideologies. Increasing wealth and the pursuit of leisure and pleasure are the main goals of secular man.

Secularism makes religion "an individual personal matter, a thing of the conscience, a matter of private faith" which has little to do with man's social, economic or political life.

The extreme form of secularism is historical materialism especially as propounded by the Marxists who proclaim with Marx that "Communist man must believe that the entirety of history is the creation and work of man ... He must further be convinced that he possesses tangible proof that he created himself, and that he can pursue the course of this creation." (Marx, *Critique of Hegel's Philosophy of Law*). He also wrote: "The religion of the workers consists in denying God and in attempting to revive the divinity of man." And Lenin concluded, "Now we must go to the limit: to a definite and final elimination of religion." This is an expression of extreme hatred, fanaticism and intolerance. Muslims are thus left with no choice but to defend religion from such unremitting hostility.

PROMOTING UNDERSTANDING

Dialogue/Trialogue

In our times, there are several attempts to promote understanding and even cooperation among various faiths. There exist various forums for Muslim-Christian dialogue. Where Jews are included, these forums are referred to as "Trialogue of the Abrahamic Faiths". Other inter-religious or inter-faith forums exist which include adherents of other religions such as Hinduism and Buddhism.

These attempts at bringing together adherents of various religions are sometimes based on the idea that what people should stress is faith and a common belief in God as a necessary bulwark against the pervasive godlessness and secularism that have gripped the world. These attempts may be useful in that in place of ignorance of others' beliefs, some understanding would be sown. This may help to remove suspicion and even strife.

These attempts are questionable however when they aim at bringing religions together in common acts of worship and ecumenical services. Baldly stated, ecumenism often gives rise to confusion and hotch-potch especially, when, from an Islamic standpoint much of what passes for religion and religious practices belong not to the the history and practice of religion but to the practice of paganism. Islam cannot be regarded as just one other religion among religions. Truth must be distinct from falsehood.

Some forms of dialogue can in fact lead to secularism and limiting the scope of the moral and legal code of Islam. Some Christians in predominantly Muslim lands have promoted with great skill and much success the doctrine of common citizenship, common aspirations, and a common nationalism among adherents of different religions. In the process, the moral and legal code of Islam — the Shari'ah — has been reduced to a few matters of personal status. In the process, the only winner is secularism under which religion becomes a personal matter. This is one of the sources of tension in Muslim-Christian relations. There is naturally a feeling of injustice on the part of Muslims that they are not allowed to live their lives completely according to the Shari'ah in these secularised states.

DA'WAH

The real obligation that Muslims have to people of other faiths is to invite them to Islam and the worship of One God free from all human associations. This is the obligation of Da'wah. Da'wah literally means inviting and welcoming. There can of course be no hint of arrogance and aggression in giving someone an invitation, any coercion or force for the Qur'an has specifically laid down: "Let there be no compulsion in religion" even as it goes on to insist that "Truth has been made distinct from falsehood". Da'wah must then be practiced with due attention to the Qur'anic advice, "Call to the way of your Lord and Sustainer with wisdom and with fair counselling."

Focus and priorities

The task of da'wah is a delicate one. The best da'wah is through your personal example, to mirror in your daily life and habits the natural values of truth, goodness, beauty and justice, and shun all the negative values and habits condemned by Islam.

Your neighbourhoods and communities also need to reflect the values of Islam. Many Muslim communities now are not a good advertisement for Islam. Your communities need to be clean, caring and compassionate, peaceful and safe, hard-working and disciplined, open and welcoming. It is important that people who come to Islam should find a secure haven and a welcoming home in Muslim communities where they can feel naturally at ease.

You need to have a good understanding of the worldviews of people and communities you come in contact with. You need to understand their life-styles, their needs and their problems. You need to see the dominant trends in these communities. Then only will you be able not only to offer Islamic alternatives to specific problems but also the kind of direction a community needs, to put it back on course, onto the straight way. It is a question of focus and priorities.

By way of example, many people in the West perhaps do not need to be convinced of the pressures that Christian dogma places on reason. The job of putting Christian myths in their place has been done by Christian scholars themselves. To nominal or lapsed Christians in a post-Christian age, you need not spend enormous resources to convince them that Christianity is inadequate as a worldview or that the Bible is not the word of God. Many have already reached this conclusion on their own.

A greater priority in the West and those societies which live under its influence is to make people realise the terrible consequences of secularism and materialism that is a result of the rejection of religion: the arrogance and limited vision of secular man, the constantly changing and chaotic state of his laws and values, the plundering of the earth's' resources, the enormous wastage of human lives drowned in alcohol, disfigured by drugs, flushed out by abortions, wiped out by genocidal economic greed, and so on and on.

In today's world, da'wah should aim at putting back meaning and purpose in people's lives, burnishing their consciences so that the natural values can again shine forth, reviving their powers of reason so that they can once more acknowledge their Creator and Sustainer and their proper place in the scheme of things.

Islam, as we mentioned in chapter one, is both a message and a method for achieving those purposes. It should be remembered that the mission of the noble Prophet, peace be on him, was from the outset a universal mission, for the Qur'an describes him as "a mercy or a blessing for all peoples". Islam is thus the birthright of every human being. No human being may be excluded from the call of Islam.

The spread of Islam: *return to true and natural roles*
A brief look at the spread of Islam since the time of the Prophet will be helpful in showing how Islam dealt with the particular problems of various societies while at the same time bringing them back to their true role as human beings

and into the universal community of believers.

Muhammad, peace be upon him, started by inviting his own family to Islam. His wife, Khadijah, was the first to accept because she knew him to be truthful and trustworthy. He then invited the members of his clan, then the people of Makkah and all Arabia — Arabs and non-Arabs, rich and poor, nobles and slaves, men and women, Jews and Christians and wandering nomads. He sent personal letters to the known potentates of his time inviting them to believe in One God—to the Christian Byzantine Emperor, the Zoroastrian Persian Emperor, the Christian ruler of Egypt and others. His major concern always was that he was true to his trust and that he had conveyed the message, despite harassment, persecution and attempts on his life.

The successors of the Prophet carried on his mission and in a very short space of time in one of history's most rapid and enduring triumphs, the message of Islam spread beyond the Indus, beyond the Oxus into China, and westwards into Africa and Europe.

Islam spread when the Muslims were both politically and militarily strong as in the seventh century and also when they were politically weak as in the thirteenth and fourteenth centuries during the Mongol/Tartar invasions. In this latter case, the invaders ended up by adopting the religion of the conquered. This is unusual and attests to the natural appeal and strength of Islam.

Islam spread because of its simple and intellectually satisfying creed. In the Byzantine controlled lands, Islam offered freedom from imperialist and racist oppression and the cult of priesthoods; in India, the fact of intrinsic human worth, nobility and equality attracted a society steeped in caste division; in Indonesia and Africa, Islam displaced a complex mythology which often pictured the world as alien, frightful, and full of spirits which had to be appeased and a social order which tolerated infanticide and never saw the nakedness of the body or the need to clean it.

In our own day, Islam has an appeal to many in the so-called "developed" world who have become disenchanted with a mysterious and amorphous Christianity on the one hand and the insatiable demands of materialism on the other. Many also come to Islam to find liberation from racism and oppression.

Islam, approached on its own terms and not through the distorting images of the lives of lapsed or disoriented Muslim or of intense and hostile propaganda, will always be a potent summons to the free, rational and natural good state of man regardless of habitat and time.

NINE

YOU *and* GLOBAL ISSUES

Natural human virtues such as truth, goodness, compassion, justice and beauty have been, and are being, widely disregarded and even trampled upon. And so we find millions of people in the world today afflicted by grinding poverty and famine, by oppression and exploitation, by violence and the evil effects of unjust wars. Millions of others are afflicted by ignorance and the pursuit of false ideals, by wastage and ugliness in their own lives and what they have done to God's earth and God's creatures.

THE HUMAN CONDITION

If you look at the human condition, you cannot fail to be moved by the indescribable pain and suffering which many people undergo throughout the world. It is a dead conscience that will not be filled with anguish at the sight of starved and shrivelled bodies, or at the sight of innocent children disfigured and maimed by chemical weapons, or the sight of people who fight for a patch of pavement on which to rest their heads at night.

In anguish and even rage, you may well ask, for example:

What help is there for the millions of people in various parts of the world who face starvation and death as a result of famine, drought, or being driven out as refugees from their own homes?

What help is there for the millions of people who are uprooted from their ancestral homes through political conflict, racial violence, sectarian strife or the economic greed of plundering industrial nations?

What help is there for the health and quality of life of whole communities whose excreta flow in open drains around their shanty dwellings and whose children are infested with tapeworms and other debilitating and life-shortening diseases?

What help is there for the millions of street-children, boys and girls, who roam the megapolises of the world in search of scraps of food by day and shelter from the elements by night?

What help is there for people who toil on plantations engaged in producing cash-crops like sugar, cocoa, coffee, tobacco and cotton for a world market that is controlled by powerful manipulators of the futures markets and the stocks and shares capitals of the world?

What help is there for people who are burdened with debt and high-interest repayments on loans and who are still urged to go on high spending sprees on consumer items they do not really need?

What help is there for people whose rulers have squandered their wealth and pawned their resources to multinational companies, banks or arms dealers who thrive on human conflict and misery and who are subsidized and supported by the industrial giants of the world?

What help is there for these people whose rulers use these weapons of death and destruction not on their real enemies but for terrorizing and subjugating them?

What help is there for men, women and children in towns, villages and valleys who are besieged by a tyrannical government seeking to impose its own ideology and enforce its authority, who face persecution, oppression, torture and even death, and who are constantly hunted by the vigilant eyes of informers who may be their own fellow workers, students, or kith and kin?

What help is there for the millions of unemployed and underemployed both in the industrialised countries and in the impoverished countries of the world?

What help is there for people whose lives are drowned in liquor, who fritter away their days in aimlessness and despair and whose families live in perpetual fear of physical violence and mental torture from their uncontrollably brutal ways?

What help is there for communities living under the stranglehold of drug traffickers, of cocaine and crack, who would kill, rob, maim and impose their rule of fear and insecurity on what were once havens of peace and tranquility?

What help is there for people who are blinded by racism, nationalism or other forms of chauvinism who harass and persecute others solely because of the colour of their skin?

What help is there for the materialists whose main concern is their standard of living and not of life as such, who regard their Creator as either non-existent or irrelevant and unnecessary to their concerns?

What help is there for the sceptics and the disillusioned of the modern world who have grown tired of crass materialism and consumerism and who are groping for a purpose and an identity?

What help is there for the flora and fauna of the finely balanced eco-systems of our global village which is being devastated by man's greed and by highly efficient tools of exploitation and destruction?

And so you can continue asking such questions and adding to the catalogue of falsehood, evil, injustice and ugliness in our world.

SHOULD THESE THINGS CONCERN YOU AND WHY?

Every human conscience that has a spark of life in it ought naturally to be inflamed by the injustice done to and the suffering experienced by other members of the human family and God's creatures as a whole.

At least the sense of concern ought to come from calculations of self-interest. This is so because people depend on one another now more than they ever did in the past. The actions of one person could affect the livelihood and security of thousands of people on the other side of the globe. The world has become more inter-connected. News, goods, and people travel fast and so can disease, economic gain and loss, and destruction from long-range warfare.

More than this, an active concern for the human condition and environment must spring from a sense of trust or *amaanah*. Man lives on this earth, according to Islam, as a trustee. A trustee is someone who does not own things as of right but is responsible for their proper management. Man as a trustee of God, has the duty to see therefore that people live in peace and justice, that they are free from hunger and fear. Man, as a trustee of God, has the duty to ensure that the rights he enjoys to the resources of the earth are not abused. He is not for example to pollute the drinking water of the earth nor is he to slaughter animals except for food or to prevent the spread of disease.

There must therefore be a strong link between faith and an active social conscience just as there is a link between disbelief and hypocrisy on the one hand and callousness and inhumanity on the other. This is well brought out in one of the early surahs of the Qur'an called *Al-Maa'uun* meaning Small Kindnesses or Help:

In the name of God, most Gracious, most Merciful
Have you seen the one who denies the Religion or the Judgement to come?
It is he who repels the orphan with harshness
And does not encourage (or organise) the feeding of the needy.
So woe to the performers of Prayer who are neglectful of their Prayer
Those who want to be seen of men
But refuse even the smallest help.
(*Surah al-Maa'uun*, 107, 1-7)

This surah shows that Islam is no mere set of rituals, nor is it lifeless dogma or some mysterious cult. It is rooted in belief in God and a universal concern for the human condition. Its concern is for mankind as a whole regardless of creed, race or colour. This is in keeping with the Qur'anic description of the role and message of the Prophet as "mercy and a blessing to all creatures".

BASIC HUMAN NEEDS

There are a number of rights that men owe to one another and to the global environment. These rights have always been there but many have become critical in recent times. Man's basic needs start with food, clothing, shelter, and security and go on to include education and intellectual development, spiritual purification and growth. By way of example, we may highlight a few of these basic needs.

Freedom from hunger

It is scandalous that millions of people should live in abject poverty, that millions should starve and die of starvation in a world where there is no shortage of food. Food is stockpiled, dumped, wasted in enormous quantities in some parts of the world to maintain profits and price levels while babes die on their mother's breasts too dry to provide life-giving sustenance.

"Spread peace and distribute food" was the first instruction of the noble Prophet on reaching Madinah after the historic hijrah journey. Throughout his career he sought to ensure that those in need had sustenance even though he and his family had often to go without food. He constantly emphasised the link between belief and caring for people by such statements as:

"He is not a true believer who eats his fill while his neighbour goes hungry." Cutting off supplies of food is not allowed in order to bring people to submission. During the time of the Prophet, a new and ardent Muslim. Thumaamah ibn Uthaal, vowed that "no grain of wheat or any produce" should reach the Quraysh in Makkah "until they follow Muhammad". The boycott was stringently applied by his people. Prices of food rose in Makkah. Hunger began to bite and there was even fear of death among the Quraysh. When this was brought to the attention of the Prophet, he immediately instructed Thumaamah to lift the boycott and resume supplies.

To avoid dependency and starvation, societies should strive to be independent in food production as a primary goal. The practice of giving over land almost exclusively to the production of cash crops like sugar cane, cotton, and worst of all tobacco for the main benefit of foreign multinational companies should be abandoned. The Prophet's encouraged agricultural production and linked it with rewards in the Hereafter. Any person who plants a tree or sows a crop for people, animals and birds to eat of its produce merits reward, according to the noble Prophet.

In emergency cases, there is often the need to mobilise resources and organisational skills on a vast scale to avert disasters of the kind the world now witnesses. The contributions, however small, of individuals is important to help relieve hunger and suffering. Compassion must be translated into practical help.

Freedom from fear

This is another important and basic condition of human life. Fear has become a global problem on a vast scale. People live in fear of eviction from their homes, in fear of oppression and the denial of basic human rights by tyrannical governments, in fear of the ravages of war and sectarian strife, in fear of unemployment and crime.

The techniques and instruments of fear and torture are many and more sophisticated now than ever before. It could even be said that the majority of mankind today suffer from exploitation, oppression and injustice of one form or another.

In a naturally ordered world of submission to God or Islam, people have mutual rights and expectations of one another. In particular they should have clear expectations from a society or state that is governed by the natural values of truth, goodness and justice. For example, people need to take it for granted and feel confident that:

- Human life, body, honour and freedom are sacred and inviolable. No one shall be exposed to injury or death, except under the authority of proper moral and legal system and procedure;
- No person shall be exposed to torture of body, mind or threat of degradation or injury either to himself or to anyone related to him or otherwise held dear by him; nor shall he be made to confess to the commission of a crime, or forced to act or consent to an act which is injurious to his or another person's interests;
- The right to privacy of home, correspondence and communication is guaranteed and shall not be violated except through due and proper judicial processes;
- Every person has the right to his thoughts, opinions and beliefs. He also has the right to express them so long as he remains within the limits prescribed by law;
- No person may be discriminated against or victimized because of race or colour;
- All persons, whether involved in government or not, are equal before the law and are entitled to equal protection of the law.

These are a few of the ideals and norms set by Islam as it works for justice and for the protection of true religion, life, mind, honour, and property. The strength of Islamic law is there to safeguard these values. But in the first instance, the method of Islam is to appeal to the natural goodness of the human conscience to prevent injury and harm to others. The Qur'anic statements and the noble Prophet's advice are simple, clear and direct:

> "Do not seek to work corruption on earth. God does not like the corrupters."
> (28: 77)
> "Walk not exultantly on earth. God does not like any arrogant boaster."
> (31:18)
>
> *And the noble Prophet has said:*
>
> "Let there be no harm and no reciprocating of harm."
> "Make things easy for people and not difficult."
> "If anyone walks with an oppressor
> to strengthen him
> knowing that he is an oppressor
> he has gone forth from Islam."

Education and intellectual development

Apart from the basic freedoms mentioned above, every person has the right to a minimum education. As we have mentioned before because of the demands of faith, no man and no Muslim in particular can afford to live in a state of illiteracy and barbarity.

Again, there are millions in the world today who cannot read and write or who cannot use these skills with enough ease for practical purposes. These are the "total" or "functional" illiterates. There are about one billion illiterate adults in the world today, many of them in Muslim societies. These are usually condemned to live limited lives, easy prey to superstition and deprivation of many kinds. (This is not to say that there are many erudite intellectuals who are also seized by moral blindness and ignorance and who also live limited and diminished lives.)

One of the greatest gifts of Islam and Muslim civilization to many parts of the world has been the gift of literacy.

The first word which began Muhammad's prophetic mission was "Read!"

> "Read in the name of your Lord
> Who created
> Who created man from a germ-cell.
> Read! for your Lord is most bounteous,
> Who taught the use of the pen,
> Taught man that which he knew not." *(The Qur'an, 96: 1-5)*

Even though Muhammad, peace be on him, was an unlettered prophet, the emphasis on a literate culture (in addition to the strengths of an oral culture and tradition) is striking and accounts for among other things, the historical sense of the Muslims and the preservation and transmission of knowledge. The Prophet's concern for having his followers literate can be demonstrated by a single fact. Any person who had the unfortunate lot of becoming a prisoner of war was immediately offered his freedom by the Prophet if he was literate on condition that he taught some Muslims how to read and write.

Each community and society in the world needs to have a campaign to promote universal education. One of the minimum requirements of this education should be functional literacy.

Apart from their mother tongue, Muslims need to be literate in Arabic, for knowing Arabic may bring one closer to the Qur'an, and being close to the Qur'an means being close to God.

The provision of such a minimum education universally is one of the greater challenges facing an "enlightened" world.

Beyond this of course lies the far greater task of re-shaping knowledge so that it enhances truth and justice and serves God's purposes for man and the universe. The intellectual leadership of mankind must pass from the materialists and those who promote corruption on earth to those who are committed to the long-term welfare of mankind and the global environment.

ENVIRONMENT & ECOLOGY

From motives of power and greed and not necessarily from need, and with a technology to match, man this century has depleted the earth's natural resources, produced, and continues to produce waste and pollution on a scale which has never been known. His science and technology and his motives of power and greed have produced stockpiles of enough nuclear, chemical and biological weapons to destroy the earth several times. His economics and his values have led to the concentration of vast human populations in urban environments and the alienation of man from his environment and nature.

The ecological crisis which the world is witnessing and which threatens man's future could not have happened under the Islamic system of morality and law or under its conception of knowledge and its application.

Unfortunately, under the global impact of the West, Islamic values in their environmental aspects are no longer to be seen even in Muslim societies.

Nowhere in Muslim societies is the Shari'ah adhered to in its totality or the Islamic way of life the basis of human action.

Ecology and Islamic values

On land and sea and air, there is a vast variety of plant and animal species and organisms. Each organism has its place and its role to play in the intricate and interdependent network of ecosystems.

As "nations" like ourselves, each species that make up creation enjoys certain rights. For man this creation, or what is often called nature, are signs of God's power and wisdom. To gain knowledge of this creation is to increase our faith in God and acquire a love and a respect for nature. The world is also a gift to man

> "No creature is there crawling on the earth,
> no bird flying with its wings
> but they are nations like yourselves."
> (*The Qur'an*, Surah Al An'aam, 6: 38)

which he is to use for his benefit. Man has been given the authority but also the moral responsibility to work in harmony with the natural environment. This is God's trust or amaanah to man.

The ethics of this trust is illustrated by the following story in which faith in God is naturally and beautifully expressed by the beloved Prophet in love for His creation.

LET THEIR MOTHER BE WITH THEM

It is narrated that a man once came to the Prophet with a bundle and said:

"O Prophet, I passed through a wood and heard the voice of the young of birds, and I took them and put them in my carpet and their mother came fluttering around my head."

"Put them down," said the noble Prophet. And when he had put them down, the mother joined the young.

"Do you wonder at the affection of the mother towards her young?" asked the noble Prophet. "I swear by Him Who has sent me, verily, God is more loving to His servants than the mother of these young birds. Return them to the place from where you took them, and let their mother be with them."

Only faith in God as the Creator and Sustainer of everything, can generate and sustain the kind of reverence and respect for everything created. In contrast, pantheism or man's worship of nature. degrades man before nature. Scientism or man's arrogant and reckless use of knowledge and technology, turns him into a sadistic exploiter of God's creation.

LOOKING TO THE FUTURE

As a human being, your relationship to the environment is not based on your immediate want and needs but is shaped by your consciousness of the needs of future generations. This is well illustrated in the saying of the Prophet:

"If the Hour is imminent and anyone of you has a palm shoot in his hand and is able to plant it before the Hour strikes, then he should do so and he will be rewarded for that action."

This hadith shows that in Islam improving the quality of this life for others brings several rewards both to the doer of good and those who benefit from his action. It also shows that it is never too late in your life to do good, and that there is a close connection between this world and the Hereafter.

ANIMAL RIGHTS IN ISLAM

Animals should be well fed and well-looked after. The blessed Prophet said: "Fear God in respect of these animals who do not speak (our tongue). Ride them when they are in a good condition and retire them in good health." He admonished a person when he found that he had been inadequately feeding his camel and putting him to excessive work. On another occasion, he told his followers to let them graze well if the deserts are green, but travel fast if they are parched and dry, so that the animal would arrive quickly at its destination and be saved thirst and hunger on the way.

"God has prescribed proficiency and the most suitable way of doing everything... Do it well when you slaughter an animal. And each one of you should sharpen his knife, give comfort to the animal, slaughter it in such a way that its life departs quickly and and it is not left to suffer for a long time."

If a person unjustly killed a sparrow or even a smaller bird (other than for food) he will have to answer for it before God. One is not allowed to kill only for the sake of sport or game.

The blessed Prophet forbade shooting arrows at any cattle or bird which is tied or held up. He banned hitting or marking the animal on its face.

The Prophet saw someone had caught the small chicks of a bird. He ordered him to release the chicks. He found someone had burnt an ant's nest. He told him the prerogative to punish with fire belonged only to God.

The blessed Prophet forbade fighting the animals against one another.

He, peace be on him, said: "Showing kindness to an animal—any animal—is an act which is rewarded by God. He was praising a traveller who found a thirsty dog, went down a well, filled his leather socks with water and offered it to the dog.

Each individual, each community and each society for the sake of self-interest and survival needs to be concerned with the global fate of mankind and the environment on which man and other creatures of God have their being. But there is above all the satisfaction, pleasure and reward of fulfilling his amaanah or trust that must impel man to have a more active concern for the human condition and the integrity of creation.

What is needed

As we have seen, Islam provides the values for creating a better world.

You need to be aware of these values and know how to apply them to your own life, to the lives of those around you and to your environment. When the Qur'an says, for example, "Eat and drink but do not waste for God does not love those who waste". You need to work out how much resources (if any) you waste and how to put these resources to better use by sharing with others.

You need to be aware of developments not only in your neighbourhood but in the wider society in which you live, and also developments on a global level. For the reasons we have mentioned about the increasing inter-connectedness of the world, you need to think globally. No man is an island unto himself and no community can afford to live in a ghetto.

Develop strategies for dealing with specific problems. Tackle problems according to a scale of priorities. Start with situations that are closest to you: while you think globally, start by acting locally. For example, in regard to cleanliness and hygiene, look after your own person, and try to ensure that your home, and your neighbourhood are also clean. Organise campaigns to reduce pollution and see that waste is properly disposed of. In regard to education, take steps to ensure that people in your household are literate and skilled and then people in your own local community and then wider afield, if you have the talents and can organise the resources to do so.

Organise with others; acquire the administrative skills to spread information, to conduct campaigns, to consult and interact with people, to manage finance and resources, to mobilize and transport resources, food, clothing, medicine and equipment where they are needed.

Be prepared to engage in organised effort and struggle to ensure that not only the symptoms of problems are tackled but that their root causes are eliminated. It may not be enough to organise continuous food supplies to a starving people when that starvation is deliberately brought on by an oppressive government to bring about a people's submission. The struggle should aim therefore at dealing with the oppressive government (and in some cases with their external supporters), using first of all persuasion to bring about a change to a more humane policy or in the final resort adopting measures, preferably peaceful, to change the government. The sanction of force is not to be ruled out but if at all used, it must be applied according to fixed principles. All this is in keeping with the Qur'anic injunction to enjoin the good and forbid the evil. It has been well said that all that is needed for evil to triumph is that good men should do nothing.

In the attempt to help people and bring about changes in habits and lifestyles, it is best initially to spend time and effort trying to educate people and create understanding rather than to scold and condemn. There are golden rules in the method of the Prophet which need to be applied in dealing with people as for instance the command to "Make things easy and not difficult for people," and his reminder that "He who is not merciful will have no mercy shown to him."

Finally, it is important to remember that while Islam may have the solution to the range of problems and crises facing mankind, it is not content merely with tinkering at unjust and oppressive systems. It is concerned to reorient man in a direction that is in keeping with his innate values and needs, and equip him to discharge his God-given amaanah or trust on this earth. When this happens, it is the exploiters, the squanderers, the arrogant and the unjust who will need to worry.

TEN

YOU *and* YOUR HEREAFTER

Just as there was a period of time in which man was "not even a thing mentioned" so, after man's present life, time will continue into what the Qur'an refers to as *Al-Aakhirah* or the Hereafter. The major difference is that your Aakhirah as an individual is very closely bound up with, and indeed shaped by, your present life.

Al-Aakhirah is often translated as life after death. It has also been interpreted as the "ends of life" as opposed to the "dunya" or the here-and-now of life.

Al-Aakhirah begins with the resurrection of man, after which there will come a moment when every human will be shaken as he is confronted with his intentions and his deeds, good and bad, and even by his failure to do good in this life.

On the basis of these deeds and misdeeds you will be judged. You will be rewarded or punished according to the unerring justice and mercy of the Master of the Day of Judgement.

The fact of this life after death, of resurrection, judgement, and of just recompense, is an integral part of the Islamic view of reality. Qur'anic statements on the reality of the Hereafter are intended to show that the Hereafter is desirable and necessary and also possible.

THE HEREAFTER: desirable and necessary

Without the idea of the Hereafter—of resurrection and judgement and just recompense, God would not be the just and wise and merciful God that He is.

God created people and made them responsible for their actions. Some behave well and others do not. On earth the virtuous are often in a wretched state while the wicked often seem to have the good things of life. Innocent people often suffer at the hands of exploiters and criminals who seem to gain rather than suffer by their crimes in this world.

If there is no future life in which the virtuous are rewarded and the vicious suffer loss, there would be no justice. There would be no purpose in creating people with a sense of responsibility and in sending prophets to them to remind them of these responsibilities.

"What, does man think that he is to be left aimless?" (75: 36)

"Or do those who commit evil deeds suppose that We shall make them as those who believe and do good works, the same in life and death? Bad is their judgement. And God has created the heavens and the earth with truth, and that every soul may be repaid what it has earned." (45: 21-22)

"We have not created heaven and earth and all that is in between them without meaning and purpose, as is the surmise of those bent on denying the truth...Would We treat those who have attained to faith and do righteous deeds in the same manner as (We shall treat) those who spread corruption on earth? Would we treat the God-conscious in the same manner as the wicked?" (38: 27-28)

Justice and fairness require that there must be a Hereafter. But the Hereafter is also necessary to clarify the true purposes of life so that men may see clearly the real "ends" of life and what they have been striving for. All intentions which precede acts will need to be transparent if, for example, the human moral plague of doing good things for wrong motives is to be exposed. All matters that were disputed in this world, differences between people and their worldviews, differences in beliefs and orientations will need to be, and will be settled to determine what was right and what was wrong. This is why the Hereafter is called in the Qur'an, the "Day of Truth" and the "Day of Decision" when all man's self-deceptions or *ghuruur* will be laid bare and "you will come to know with the eye of certainty".

Your consciousness of these truths of the Hereafter will have important effects on your attitudes, emotions and actions in this world.

It will give meaning and purpose to your life. Your life will not be limited to worldly desires and your own greed. Your life, therefore, will not be a materialistic life because you know that this life will not end with your death.

You will have as a result greater emotional and psychological balance. You would be better able to face challenges, difficulties and trials because you have confidence in the wisdom, mercy and justice of the Master of the Day of Judgement. You will be less afflicted by anxiety, sadness and fear. Frustration will not be a part of your mental make-up.

You will be determined not only to avoid bad, obnoxious and criminal acts, but to use all your resources to the best of your ability to do good for indeed, as God says in the Qur'an, "He has created death and life to test which one of you is best in conduct".

How is the Hereafter possible?

It is therefore necessary and desirable that there should be the Hereafter. But how is it possible?

While some people may believe in a Supreme God, they cannot conceive that their dead and decayed bodies will be resurrected and that they will be called to account for their actions on earth. The secular Quraysh, and even those with a vague belief in the existence of God, found it difficult to accept the possibility of resurrection. "Who shall bring back the bones to life after they have decomposed and become dust?" they asked. (36: 78)

The Qur'an tells the story of a person who passed by a deserted town. Its roofs were caved in and its inhabitants were dead and buried. The person asked

"O mankind! If you are in doubt concerning the Resurrection, (remember that) verily, We have created (every one of) you out of dust, then out of a drop of sperm, then out of a germ-cell, then out of an embryonic lump complete (in itself) and yet incomplete, so that We might make (your origin) clear unto you. "And whatever We will (to be born) We cause to rest in the (mothers') wombs for a term set (by Us), and then We bring you forth as infants and (allow you to live) so that (some of) you might attain to maturity; for among you are such as are caused to die (in childhood), just as many a one of you is reduced in old age to a most abject state, ceasing to know anything of what he once knew so well. "And (if, O mankind, you are still in doubt as to resurrection, consider this:) you can see the earth dry and lifeless — and (suddenly) when We send down waters on it, it stirs and swells and puts forth every kind of lovely plant! "All this (happens) because God alone is the Ultimate Truth, and because He alone brings the dead to life, and because He has the power to will anything and because the Hour of Judgement is bound to come, beyond any doubt, and because God will indeed resurrect all who are in the graves." (22: 5-7)

"Is Man, then, not aware that it is We who created him out of (mere) drop of sperm yet, behold, he shows himself endowed with the power to think and to argue? "And now he argues about Us, and thinks of us in terms of comparison, and forgets how he himself was created! And so he says, Who could give life to bones that have crumbled to dust?' "Say: He who brought them into being in the first instance will give them life once again, seeing that He has full knowledge of every act of creation: He who produces for you fire out of the green tree, so that, behold, you kindle (your fires) therewith. "Is, then, He who has created the heavens and the earth not able to create (anew) the like of those (who have died)? "Yes, indeed — for He alone is the all-Knowing Creator. His being alone is such that when He wills a thing to be, He but says unto it, "Be" — and it is. "Limitless then in His glory is He in whose hand rests the dominion over all things, and unto Him you all will be brought back." (*Surah Yaa Siin*, 36: 77-83) incredulously, "How could God bring all this back to life after its death?" (2: 259)

The Qur'an also tells of people who "As it is, swear by God with their most solemn oaths, 'Never will God raise from the dead anyone who has died.' (16: 38) This shows that even people who have a vague belief in the existence of God refuse to accept the possibility of resurrection. This is mainly because of their materialistic outlook on life.

Those who are bewildered or scoff at the fact of resurrection are told by the Qur'an that there is no reason for such astonishment and mockery because resurrection is not only a logical but a physical possibility. If it is God who created man in the first place, why should it be impossible for Him to re-create him when he dies.

SCENES OF THE HEREAFTER

The Resurrection

In very vivid, awe-inspiring language, the Qur'an sketches over and over the outline of the Last Day. At a time when God sees fit, the world as we know it will be brought to an end in a terrifying cosmic cataclysm and all will be brought to account.

"When the earth quakes with her (last) mighty quaking,
and when the earth yields up her mighty burdens
and man cries out, "What has happened to her?...
On that Day will all men come forward, cut off from one another, to be shown their past deeds.
And so, he who shall have done an atom's weight of good, shall behold it;
And he who shall have done an atom's weight of evil, shall behold it."
(*Al- Zalzalah* 99: 1-8)

"And so, when the piercing call of resurrection is heard,
On a Day when everyone will flee from his brother, and from his mother and father, and from his spouse and his children,
"On that day, to everyone of them will his own state be of sufficient concern.
"Some faces will on that Day be bright with happiness,
laughing, rejoicing at glad tidings,
"And some faces will on that Day with dust be covered, with darkness overspread,
"These, these will be the ones who denied the truth and were immersed in iniquity." (*'Abasa* 80: 33-42)

The Qur'anic descriptions of Resurrection and the Last Day speak of a complete upset of the present cosmos and a dislocation of the heavens and the earth, and of mankind as being "like scattered locusts and the mountains like carded wool". Nothing, however, will be outside God's control and power for "the earth will be in His hand-grip on the Day of Resurrection and the heavens wrapped up in His right hand" (39: 67). After the upheaval, a transformation will take place out of which will come a new form or level of creation: "We have indeed decreed that death shall be (ever-present) among you; but there is nothing to prevent Us from changing the nature of your existence and bringing you into being (anew) in a manner as yet unknown to you." (56: 60-62)

The Judgement

Just as each person is born as a single individual, so he or she will be raised up and judged individually. A record of each person's deeds on earth will have been kept and will be produced as evidence on the day of judgement. No person will be able to deny the contents of this record and even the parts of his body—his tongue, hands, feet and skin—will testify against him. Many will wish for another chance to make amends, but in vain.

A person will be judged by the preponderance of good or evil in him. It is in this connection that the setting up of a *miizaan* or a balance is mentioned in the Qur'an referring to rules of justice and principles of equity.

> "And We will set up a just balance on the Day of Resurrection, so no soul shall be dealt with unjustly in the least, and though there be the weight of a grain of mustard seed, We will bring it forth, and sufficient are We to take account." (21: 47)
>
> "And the measuring out on that day will be just. Then as for those whose measure of good deeds is heavy, they shall be successful. And as for those whose measure of good deeds is light, these it is that have made their souls suffer loss." (7: 8-9).

Intentions crucial

In the judgement of deeds, a person's intentions in doing any act will be crucial. The noble Prophet has said that "Actions shall be judged only according to intentions." In a *hadith qudsi*, the Prophet has explained how God in His justice and mercy has deeds recorded and judged.

> "God has recorded the good deeds and the bad ones. Then He Himself has explained it by saying that a person who has intended a good deed and has not done it, God records it with Himself as a full good deed, but if he has intended it and has done it, God records it with Himself as from ten good deeds to seven hundred times, or many times over.
>
> "But if a person has intended a bad deed and has not done it, God records it with Himself as a full good deed, but if he has intended it and has done it, God records it as one bad deed."

In the Judgement, there will be no possibility of cover-up or hypocrisy and each person will have to face the stark truth. This is vividly illustrated in another hadith qudsi:

"The first of people against whom judgment will be pronounced on the Day of Resurrection will be a man who has died a martyr. He will be brought and God will make known to him His favours and he will acknowledge them. The Almighty will say: And what did you do about them? He will say: I have fought for You until I died a martyr. He will say: You have lied. You only fought that it might be said of you: He is courageous. And so it was said. Then he will be ordered to be dragged along on his face until he is cast into Hell-fire

Another will be a man who has acquired knowledge and has taught it and who used to recite the Qur'an. He will be brought and God will make known to him His favours and he will acknowledge them. The Almighty will say: And what did you do about them? He will say: I acquired knowledge and I taught it and I recited the Qur'an for Your sake. He will say: You have lied. You only acquired knowledge that it might be said of you: He is a reciter. And so it was said. Then he will be ordered to be dragged along on his face until he is cast into Hell-fire.

Another will be a man whom God had made rich and to whom He had given all kinds of wealth. He will be brought and God will make known to him His favours and he will acknowledge them. The Almighty will say: And what did you about them? He will say: I left no path in which You like money to be spent without spending in it for Your sake. He will say: You have lied. You only did so that it might be said of you: He is generous. And so it was said. Then he will be ordered to be dragged along on his face until he is cast into Hell-fire."

The Recompense

Punishment and Hell

The fruits of ingratitude, disobedience and rebellion against God is disgrace, humiliation and punishment. This punishment, a sign of God's just anger (ghadab) will be visited on the sinners even on earth, as was the case with the people of Sodom. Such punishment applies to commnities and societies in particular and is part of God's natural law governing the rise and fall of nations. There is a saying of the noble Prophet in which he warns that "A community in the midst of which sins are committed and which could be but are not corrected by the community is most likely to be encompassed in its entirely by the punishment of God."

There are different levels or degrees of wrong-doing. There are those who completely deny the existence of God, whose moral sense is blunted and whose hearts have become rusted, who live a life of evil and spread corruption on earth. There are hypocrites who spread dissension and strife while pretending to be doers of good and even to be believers. And there are believers who commit minor lapses or even grave crimes in moments of temptation, weakness or forgetfulness.

Accordingly, there are categories or degrees in Hell. Hypocrites who profess to believe in God, but actually rebel and work against Him, will be in the lowest parts of hell (4: 15) and will be gathered together with those who completely reject God.

> "For, (in the life to come) all shall have their degrees, according to whatever (good or evil) they did; and so, He will repay them in full for their doings and they shall not be wronged.
> "And on the Day when those who were bent on denying the truth are exposed to the Fire (and will be told): You dissipated your good things in your worldly life and you took your enjoyment in them; therefore today you shall be recompensed with the chastisement of humiliation for having gloried on earth in your arrogance, offending against all that is right, and for all your iniquitous doings." (46: 19-20)
>
> "On that day, the ungrateful one who denied the truth will say, 'Would that I were dust!' " (78: 40)

Those who are believers but whose balance of evil deeds outweigh their good deeds will only experience Hell for a period of time. If people sincerely repent for their sins in time, God is Forgiving and Merciful. According to the Qur'an, God may forgive all sins except the sin of shirk or associating others with Him.

The mercy of God encompasses everything and even Hell may not be a permanent place. The Prophet, peace be on him, is reported to have said:

"Surely, a day will come over Hell when it will be like a field of corn that has dried up after flourishing for a while. Surely a day will come over Hell when there shall not be a single human being in it."

Reward and Paradise

The fruits of submission to God, of living in harmony with His will, of living the natural way, is satisfaction (*ridwaan*) in this life (whatever the outward signs of difficulty and hardship or ease and plenty) and eternal happiness in the next.

> "But unto the righteous God will say, "O human being that has attained to inner peace!
> Return unto your Lord and Sustainer, well-pleased (and) pleasing (Him).
> Enter, then, together with My (other true) servants!
> Enter My paradise!" (89: 27-28)
>
> "But those who were conscious of their Sustainer will be urged on in throngs towards Paradise till, when they reach it, they shall find its gates wide-open; and its keepers will say unto them, 'Peace be upon you!'... And how excellent a reward will it be for those who laboured (in God's way)!" (39: 73:74)

Paradise is also a place of degrees and categories. In the lofty parts, there will be the Prophets, those who struggled and died as witness in the path of God, and those who were totally honest and truthful to their trusts in their dealings.

"God has promised believing men and women gardens, underneath which rivers flow, wherein they shall abide, and pleasant abodes in the Garden of Eden — but the pleasure of God with them is greater and that is the great success." (9: 72)

In fairness and justice, those who are believers but who remain inactive in this life will not be rewarded in the same measure as those who showed their commitment through struggle and sacrifice.

> "Such of the believers as remain passive — other than the disabled — cannot be deemed equal to those who strive hard in God's cause with their possessions and their lives. God has exalted those who strive hard with their possessions and their lives far above those who remain passive. Although God has promised the good for all believes, yet God has exalted those who strive hard above those who remain passive by (promising them) a mighty reward — many degrees thereof — and forgiveness of sins and His grace; for God is indeed much-Forgiving, most Merciful." (4: 95-96)

Between Paradise and Hell

The Qur'an speaks of a group of people who were able to discern right and wrong in this life but did not definitely incline to either. These are the indifferent ones. They will be placed in a station between heaven and hell, longing to go to paradise and fearing to be put among the evil-doers.

> "And there will be persons who (in life) were endowed with the faculty of discernment (between right and wrong), recognizing each by its mark. And they will call out unto the inmates of Paradise, 'Peace be unto you!' not having entered it themselves, but longing (for it). And whenever their eyes are turned to the inmates of the Fire, they will cry, 'O Our Sustainer! Place us not among the people who have been guilty of evildoing.' " (7: 46-47)

The Hereafter therefore is no "pie in the sky" or figment of man's imagination. It is desirable, it is necessary, it is possible, it is real. The reality of the Hereafter compels an awareness of our long-term future and the need to work for it, with others, here on earth.

In the Hereafter, you will have no opportunity to change anything, to offer a new performance, or to redeem your failings. The only opportunity for that is here and now, in this life, which is given only once (for the Qur'an does not speak, for example, of cycles of rebirths and deaths). This one life, then, is the only life where you can work and earn or sow those seeds that will bear fruit "in the end".

In practical terms, what do you need to do to avoid loss and humiliation here and in the hereafter? To begin with, you need to take stock of your present life, you need to judge yourself before you face the final judgement:

"Assess and judge yourselves before you are assessed and judged." cautioned the noble Prophet.

This stock-taking is a continuous process, a daily process. You need to ask yourself to which category of mankind your really belong: non-believers, misguided believers, indifferent to right and wrong, passive or superficial believers, or true and committed believers.

Are you among the non-believers who reject and are ungrateful to God, who "enjoy this world and eat as cattle eat" and whose vision remains limited to this world?

Are you among those who believe in God but merely follow the religion and ways of your parents and forefathers, refusing to be guided by your God-given powers of reason and insight, and adopting false beliefs and practices in the process?

Are you among superficial believers who fall a prey to evil influences, transgress all limits, succumb to their lusts and degenerate to lowly wickedness and of whom the Qur'an says, "The Evil One has got the better of them, so he has made them lose the remembrance of God"? (58: 19)

Are you among passive or superficial believers who do no great evil but who, afflicted by laziness, cowardice or miserliness, do less than the minimum of good and are content with being onlookers at life?

Or are you among the true and committed believers who sincerely submit to truths and realities, who exert themselves to purify their souls and discharge their responsibilities on earth? Of such the Qur'an says: "And they who have attained to faith, and who have forsaken the domain of evil and are striving hard in God's cause, as well as those who shelter and succour them — it is they who are truly believers. Forgiveness of sins awaits them and a most excellent sustenance." (8: 74)

In the process of stock-taking, as a first step, you need to undertake the task of *islaah* or reform. Recognise and admit the wrongs you have done to your own self and to others which jar against your naturally good nature: the lie you may have told, the promise you have broken, the trust you have undertaken and have betrayed or have not fulfilled, the hurt caused by a malicious, backbiting or racist tongue, the steps taken to a disreputable place or meeting. Take stock of the way you have earned your livelihood — the ounce less in weight on goods sold, the rotten vegetables concealed in a pile of attractive produce, the chicken forced-fed to weigh more at the time of selling, the defective piece of machinery, the bribe given to secure a contract, the idle hours while the supervisor was away. Take stock of how you spend your money and resources — the articles you don't really need but bought for "conspicuous consumption" or to show off and other aspects of spending which you know to be *israaf* — wasteful and extravagant. Take stock of your time and how you spent it — the long hours and even days wasted in trivial pursuits. Such a process of stock-taking and reform requires complete honesty with yourself which can be extremely difficult in the face of such consuming sins as pride or egoism. Recognising and keeping away from the bad is the first step to reform.

There are sins of commission (wrongs that you may have done) and sins of omission (good deeds that you have failed to do). Review therefore the opportunities that you have missed for doing good: the morning Salaat that you constantly miss on time, the Zakaat that you fail to pay, the fast that you consciously miss for no good reason, the theft or embezzlement that you saw and failed to correct, the neighbour in distress you ignored, the hungry person you could have fed but failed to feed.

Genuinely repent for these wrongs committed or duties omitted. Pray to God for forgiveness and resolve not to repeat these errant ways in the knowledge that God is forgiving and merciful and that He rejoices in your repentance or tawbah which will take you back to your naturally good condition and to Him.

> "God is more pleased with the repentance of His servant than any of you would be, if he were on a journey in the desert and lost his riding camel which was carrying his food and drink, and after despairing of it and lying down in the shade of a tree, the camel came back and he saw it standing there."
> (Hadith)

Such steps as the above are merely the minimum for avoiding degradation and loss in this life and the Hereafter. More than this, each one of us would like to improve our performance, to grow in stature and degrees, to pass from the confines of hell and the no-man's land reserved for those who can recognize right from wrong, but remain indifferent and passive, refusing to uphold right or combat wrong.

Aiming at excellence

There still remains the task of seeking to attain God's satisfaction or *ridwaan* and realising true contentment. This can only be done by aiming for and being committed to right doing and excellence in everything—to *ihsaan*.

Ihsaan, as described by the noble Prophet, peace be on him, is "that you worship God as if you see Him, for while you do not see Him, He certainly sees you". This implies therefore being always conscious of your responsibilities before God. It implies striving hard with all the resources of body and possessions to fulfil these responsibilities. It implies not only goodness but a commitment to excellence in all that you do. It implies the willingness to make the ultimate sacrifice for achieving God's purposes for mankind and the rest of creation. One who acts in this fashion is a *muhsin*, of whom the Qur'an says:

"Whoever submits his whole self to God and is a muhsin, his reward is with God." (2: 112)

These purposes are to see, together with others, that the natural values of truth, goodness, beauty and justice are paramount in the world and that falsehood, evil and injustice are resisted. When there is a coming together and a harmony between man's belief, the submission of "his whole self to God" and his striving, a person attains a state of inner contentment, peace and happiness. God is satisfied with his performance in this life and says to him:

> O you tranquil soul
> Return to your Lord and Sustainer
> Satisfied, and He well satisfied with you.
> Enter then among My servants
> Enter My Paradise!"

To attain this state, your worldview, your attitudes and your aspirations should be illumined by such as the following supplication of the noble Prophet, may God bless him and grant him peace, which he often offered in the stillness of the night before dawn:

> "All praise is due to You, O God! You are the Sustainer of the heavens and the earth and whatever is in them.
> All praise is due to You. Yours is the domain of the heavens and the earth and whatever is in them.
>
> All praise is due to You. You are the light of the heavens and the earth and whatever is in them. Praise be to You.
>
> All praise is due to You. You are the Truth. Your promise is true, meeting with You is true, Your word is true. Paradise is true. Hell-fire is true. Prophets are true. Muhammad (may blessings and peace be on him) is true. The hour of Judgement is true.
>
> O God! Unto You do I submit. In You do I believe. Upon You do I depend. Unto You do I turn. For You do I contend. Unto You do I seek judgement. So forgive me for what I did and will do, for what I concealed and what I declared, and for that of which You are more knowledgeable than I.
>
> You are the Expediter and You are the Deferrer.
> There is noone worthy of worship but You.
> And there is no ability or power except by the permission of God."

And let the following supplication not only strike a chord in your heart but sustain your whole being in its journey along the natural, God-given way:

"O Lord!
Direct me aright in my faith
which is the guardian of my affairs
and
direct me aright in my life
in which I have my being
and
set right my Hereafter
which is my resort
and
make my life filled with every type of good and
make my death a comfort from all ill."

Glossary

'Aalim (plural: 'ulamaa'). One who knows; a learned person; scientist. Commonly used for someone who has a thorough knowledge of Islam and its sources, the Qur'an and the Sunnah. An important characteristic of an 'aalim, according to the Qur'an, is that he is deeply conscious of God and stands in awe of Him.

'Aashuuraa. The tenth day of Muharram, the first month of the Islamic calendar. Muslims are recommended to fast on this day following the practice of Prophet Muhammad and of Prophet Moses.

Aayah (plural: aayaat). 1. A sign. 2. A message. 3. A verse of the Qur'an. Each verse or aayah of the Qur'an is considered a sign of God's bounty and a Divine message for mankind.

Adab. Discipline; etiquette, manners, training. Refers in general to the discipline that comes from recognising one's proper place in relation to one's self, family, community and society. It also refers to the etiquette or manner of carrying out particular actions, for example, the adab of reading the Qur'an, the adab of greeting, the adab of eating. Loss of adab implies loss of proper behaviour and discipline and a failure to act with justice.

Adhaan. The call to Salaat or Prayer. It includes the main statements of the Islamic worldview — that God is One and Supreme and that Muhammad is the Messenger of God. It calls people to "Come to Success" through Prayer and devotion to God. The Adhaan is in Arabic. Its form was agreed upon by the Prophet in preference to the use of bells or horns.

Ahl al-Kitaab. Literally, the People of the Book or the People of the Scripture. Refers to the followers of Divine revelation prior to the Qur'an. It refers in particular to the Banii Israa'iil (The Children of Israel) to whom God sent Prophets with Scriptures to guide them — Moses with the Tawrah and Jesus with the Injiil. The term thus refers in particular to Jews and Christians. By extension, it could also refer to any people to whom a Prophet was sent with a Scripture.

Akhlaaq. (Plural of Khuluq). Morals or Ethics. Significantly, the word comes from the word khalaqa which means "God created". Akhlaaq can thus be taken to mean the natural or innate morals or values such as truth, honesty, goodness, justice with which man has been created.

Allah. The Arabic word for the One True God, Creator and Sustainer of all being. The word Allah is unique in that it can have no plural or gender connotation.

Al-Amiin. The Trustworthy. Description by which Muhammad was known in Makkah before his call to Prophethood. This description shows that a true Prophet must be known to be a person of good and unblemished character.

Al-Asaas. The Foundation. Name by which the Opening Chapter of the Qur'an is known in as much as it is regarded as the "foundation" of the Qur'an.

Al-hamdu lillaah. All Praise is due to God. A Qur'anic phrase repeated by the Muslims in all situations in life.

Al-Kanz. The Treasure. Name by which the Opening Chapter of the Qur'an is known.

Allahu Akbar. God is Most Great. A phrase which is uttered in many of the practices of Islam signifying that man is only a creature of God and that God is Supreme.

Al-Aakhirah. The Hereafter; life after death; the "ends" of life. Refers to another existence after the life of this world. A person's hereafter is shaped by the way he conducts his life in this world. The Hereafter begins with the Day of Resurrection

(*Yawm al-Qiyaamah*). This will be followed by the Day of Judgement (*Yawm ad-diin*) or the Day of Recompense (*Yawm al-Jazaa'*) where everyone will be treated with the mercy and absolute justice of the Creator. In the Hereafter, Paradise (*al-Jannah*) will be the reward of those who do good and Hellfire (*Jahannam*) will be the fate of those who do evil. According to Islam, the Hereafter is not only possible, it is necessary and desirable.

Amaanah. Trust; responsibility. Refers to the trust given by God to man to live in and manage this world with justice and goodness and to fulfil all his natural rights and obligations and the rights of all God's creation. Refers also to any undertaking a person makes to another; it is a requirement of faith that a Muslim should discharge all his trusts faithfully and should not act carelessly or treacherously.

Amiir al-Mu'miniin. Literally, Commander of the Believers. The title was first given to any commander of a military mission but was later used specifically for the Khaliifah or Head of the Muslim State.

Amr bi-lMa'ruuf. Commanding what is good — an individual and collective duty of the Muslim community. A community can only be strong and vigorous if it fulfils this and the corresponding duty to forbid what is wrong. (See also **ma'ruuf** below).

Ansaar. Literally, Helpers. Name given collectively to the Muslims native to Madinah during the time of the Prophet.

'Asabiyyah. Tribal loyalty, partisanship; group solidarity; racism; nationalism. Whoever advocates, fights for or dies for 'asabiyyah does not belong to the Muslim community, according to a saying of the Prophet.

As-Saadiq. The Truthful. Description by which Muhammad was known in Makkah before his call to Prophethood. This description shows that a true Prophet must be known to be a person of good and unblemished character. Many people believed in the mission of Muhammad because they knew him to be always truthful.

As-salaamu alaykum. Peace be on you. The Islamic greeting which enhances the feelings of love and brotherhood among people. In the Qur'an it is mentioned as the greeting used by the keepers of Paradise to welcome those who have done well in this life.

Astaghfirullah. I seek God's forgiveness. One of the phrases used by a Muslim to repent for wrongs committed knowingly and unknowingly and which brings a person back to his naturally good and pure state.

'Awrah. The parts of the body which are not to be exposed to the view of others. The 'awrah of a man extends from his navel to his knees. The 'awrah of a woman is her whole body with the exception of her face, hands and feet.

Banii Israa'iil. Literally, the Children of Israel or the Jews. Israa'iil (Israel) was another name for the Prophet Ya'quub (Jacob), the son of Prophet Ishaaq (Isaac) and the grandson of Prophet Ibraahiim (Abraham). Another word used for Jews in the Qur'an is Yahuud.

Baatil. False; Falsehood as opposed to *Haqq* or the Truth. According to the Qur'an, Truth will prevail over Falsehood which is impermanent by nature.

Bismillaah. In the name of God. All actions of a Muslim should begin with Bismillaah to ensure good and meritorious conduct.

Biya'. Monasteries of Christians. The Qur'an stresses that these should be respected by Muslims as places where God's name is remembered and as an expression of Muslim tolerance.

Caliph. See **Khaliifah.**

Darar. Injury, harm. One of the principles of Islamic behaviour and jurisprudence is that a person's actions should not cause harm or injury to others.

Da'f. Weakness, pettiness. This is mentioned in the Qur'an as one of the negative qualities of human beings which lead them to forget God and fall prey to temptation and wrongdoing.

Da'wah. Invitation; Call. Refers to the duty on Muslims to invite or call others to return to the straight and natural path of Islam or submission to God. This, according to the Qur'an, has to be done with wisdom and beautiful advice. The "most excellent speech'' is that of a person who calls others to God. Da'wah is addressed to both Muslims and non-Muslims.

Dhabh. The prescribed manner for slaughtering an animal for food. The animal must be well-fed and watered. It must not be slaughtered in the presence of other animals. There must be no pre-stunning of an animal as this is not only cruel but prevents the maximum drainage of blood. An extremely sharp knife must be used. The words *Bismillaah, Allaahu Akbar (In the name of God, God is Most Great)* must be pronounced before cutting to stress that all life belongs to God and that the animal is being killed only for food. The cut must be sharp and quick to induce a massive hemorrhage and quick onset of unconsciousness. The neck of the animal must not be completely severed and the carotid artery should be left intact so as to facilitate the maximum drainage of blood from the flesh, which is necessary for wholesome meat. The dhabh method is the most efficient, wholesome and humane method of preparing animals for food.

Dhikr. Remembrance, in particular, of God. Every action or utterance made for the sake of God can be considered dhikr.

Dhimmi. A person who lives under the protection of the Muslim state but is not a Muslim. He is exempt from many duties imposed on Muslims like the payment of Zakaat and military service. Instead, he is liable to pay a special tax called *jizyah* or military exemption tax in return for enjoying the security of the State. If the State feels it is unable to protect the Dhimmi, it is obliged to return to him the amount paid.

Dhu-l Hijjah. The last month of the Islamic calendar during which the Hajj or the pilgrimage is performed.

Diin. 1. Faith, Religion, Way of life, Worldview; 2. Judgement and Recompense. Diin has the primary sense of a ''return to man's inherent nature''. Therefore, the true Diin is Islam or submission to God.

''The (true) diin in the sight of God is Islam'' (3: 19). ''And who is better in diin than the one who submits (*aslama*) his whole self to God and is a doer of good'' (4: 125). True diin brings life to a body otherwise dead ''just as the rain which God sends down from the skies, and the life which He gives therewith to an earth that is dead'' (2: 164).

Islam is referred to in the Qur'an as ''the diin of God'', ''the diin of Truth'', ''the one ever-true diin (*ad-diin al-qayyim*)''. Man-made religions or systems of belief and living are also referred to as diin but must not be mixed up with the true Diin of Islam. The Prophet Muhammad is told in the Qur'an to say to those who reject God: ''To you your diin and to me my diin.'' It also says: ''And whoever follows other than Islam as a diin, it will not be accepted from him'' (3: 85). ''Those who fragmented their diin and made themselves into sects, you have nothing to do with them''(5: 159). ● **Yawm ad-diin** — the Day of Judgement or Recompense; this also has the primary meaning of the day of ''Return'' when man will go back to His Lord to be judged and requited. Those who followed the true diin in this life will receive a good return on his good deeds.

Diraar. Reciprocating or perpetuating harm or injury.

Dunya. The present world as opposed to the next world or the Aakhirah. ● **Hayaat ad-dunya** — the life of this world described in the Qur'an as ''sport and amusement'' and of ''passing benefit''. However, while not forgetting your ''portion'' in this world you should seek, by means of what God has granted you, the (good of the) life to come (28: 79).

Du'a. Supplication, calling upon God, prayer. A means of showing gratitude to and dependance on the Creator for guidance and the good things of life. ''Your Lord and Sustainer says, Call upon Me, (and) I shall respond to you!'' (40: 60). Du'a, unlike Salaat, may be said in any language.

Eid. Celebration, Festival. ● **Eid al-Fitr** — the festival of the breaking of the fast of Ramadaan, which occurs on the first of the month of Shawwal. ● **Eid al-Adhaa** — the festival of sacrifice which commemorates Prophet Ibraahiim's obedience of God and his sacrifice and also the steadfastness of his son, Ismaa'iil. This Eid is on the 10th of Dhul Hijjah.

Faatihah, al-. The Opening. the name of the first chapter of the Qur'an which is regarded as the Essence of the Book.

Falaah. Success, Felicity, Happy state. True success or happiness comes only to those who believe in God and act accordingly (24: 1) while those who are unjust (the zaalimuun) will not achieve such success (6: 31).

Fard. Compulsory duty. Not to perform a fard is a sin of omission and is therefore blameworthy. ● **Fard 'Ayn** — a duty which is imposed on every adult and sane individual which cannot be discharged by anyone else, eg fasting in the month of Ramadaan, the daily Salaat. ● **Fard Kifaayah** — a duty which is imposed on the Muslim community as a whole which is considered discharged if carried out by some in the community. If it is not discharged, the whole community bears the responsibility and the blame, eg the duty of jihaad or protecting the community.

Fasaad. Corruption, chaos. ● **Fasaad fi-lArd** or corruption on earth, a Qur'anic expression which means any state of moral, social or political lawlessness that comes from straying from the straight path; it is contrasted with *islaah* or rectification.

Fitrah. Natural disposition; nature; natural moral sense which enables a person to distinguish between good and bad; innate, inborn or essential state of any person or of any aspect of creation; pure and unsullied state. Each being follows its own fitrah or natural and inbuilt laws with which God created it. All nature is the creation of God. Nature does not create of itself. It is therefore false to refer to "Nature" with a capital "N" as if it creates or sustains life and as if it is another word for God.

Ghuruur. Deception, fallacy, illusion. Refers in particular to the fallacy of treating life in this world as the only existence and being unmindful of the Hereafter; also refers to the persistent worship of false gods and regarding what is good and natural as bad and unnatural, and vice versa.

Ghusl. Washing, Bathing. A complete bath performed in the manner taught by the noble Prophet which is necessary under certain conditions and recommended in others. It requires first the washing of the private parts, the performance of wuduu (feet excepted). the washing of the head, right and then left side of the body three times each and then the washing of the feet. It is necessary on attaining maturity, after intercourse, emission of seminal fluid, after menstruation and childbirth. It is recommended on Fridays, the day of congregational Prayer, and at least once in every seven days.

Hadith (plural: **ahaadiith**). Saying of the noble Prophet. ● **Hadith Qudsi.** Literally, a sacred Hadith. Words whose authority is traced back not to the Prophet but to the Almighty but which the Prophet expressed in his own words. Hadith Qudsi differ from the Qur'an in that the latter comprise the exact words of God.

Hajj. Literally, effort. Pilgrimage to the House of God in Makkah which is compulsory once in a lifetime for Muslims who have the means to perform it. It is the fifth "pillar" of Islam.

Halaal. Lawful, Permissible. Only that which is good and beneficial for man and creation is regarded as halaal in Islam. The basic assumption in Islam is that everything is halaal unless it has been declared or is deemed to be haraam or forbidden.

Haraam. Unlawful, Prohibited. Only that which is bad or harmful for man and creation is regarded as haraam in Islam.

Hijrah. Migration. The act of leaving a place to seek sanctuary or freedom of worship in another or for any other purpose. Also the act of leaving a bad practice to adopt a righteous way of life. Specifically, the Hijrah refers to the Prophet's journey from Makkah to Madinah in the twelfth year of his mission corresponding to June 622 CE. The Islamic calendar begins from this event.

Hisbah. The institution for supervising and safeguarding the right norms of public behaviour. Its purpose is to enforce what is right and good (*ma'ruuf*) and forbid what is wrong and bad (*munkar*).

Huduud (plural of **hadd**). Literally, limits or boundaries. Refers to the limits which God has set which man must not transgress or violate. If someone violates them, he is to be punished according to certain fixed penalties. These penalties are also called huduud.

'Ibaadah. Worship. True worship is only for God. All actions of a person which are in accordance with the will of God and intended for the pleasure of God is regarded as worship. For example, earning an honest livelihood, living a chaste life and performing Salaat are all considered as worship in Islam. Man is also warned to keep clear of the worship of false gods including his own passions and desires .

Ihsaan. Goodness, Excellence, Proficiency. This is regarded as one of the major distinguishing characteristics of an ideal person. It accompanies *imaan* (faith), *islaam* (submission to God), and *taqwa* (deep consciousness of God). Ihsaan is right-doing and is an expression of correct knowledge and belief. It also implies aiming at excellence in everything which can only come from a constant awareness of God. When asked what is Ihsaan, the noble Prophet replied: ''That you worship God as if you see Him. For if you do not see Him, He surely sees you.''

Iithaar. Preference. The quality of unselfishness which makes one look after other people's needs before one's own, even if this results in personal hardship. The Ansaar of Madinah are praised in the Qur'an in this respect for their support of the noble Prophet and the Emigrants from Makkah. It was an outstanding quality of the Prophet himself, his family and many of his companions.

'Ilm. The totality of knowledge derived from both Revelation and reason; includes knowledge of truth as against falsehood, right as against wrong, of the right or proper place for a thing or being to be which is a condition of justice, of the frontiers or the limits of knowledge. Since proper knowledge precedes right belief and right action, it is rightly given a most important position in Islam — in the Qur'an alone there are over eight hundred references to knowledge. The concept of knowledge in Islam does not generate such tensions as between religion and science or religion and politics or the sacred and the secular.

Imaam. Leader. Refers to the leader of the Congregational Prayer or Salaat and in a wider context to the Head of the Muslim State.

Imaan. Faith based on knowledge; firm belief and trust in God which is the natural and reasonable attitude for man to adopt.
• **Arkaan al-Imaan** — the articles of faith: to believe in God with all His attributes, in His angels, His scriptures, His messengers, and the Hereafter.

Islaah. Reform, rectification; a process which individuals and communities must undergo to keep to the straight path. The opposite of Islaah is *fasaad* or corruption.

Islaam. 1. Submission to God. 2. The religion (diin) of God. All creation at one level exists in a state of islaam or submission to their inbuilt laws. In addition, man has been given the freedom to acknowledge and obey God and live naturally in accordance with His religion or Islam.

Israaf. Extravagance, Waste (of talents and resources); regarded as sinful and leading towards a refusal to acknowledge the bounties of God. The one who is wasteful (*musrif*) is linked in the Qur'an to the one who denies (*kadhdhaab*) or doubts (*murtaab*) the Truth.

I'tikaaf. Retreat. In particular, retreating to the mosque during the last ten days of Ramadaan for contemplation, worship and attempting to get nearer to God.

Jamaa'ah. 1. Group. 2. Congregation. 3. Organised community of believers. The minimum number for a jamaa'ah is three. Each jamaa'ah, even if it is a group of people travelling together, has a duty to appoint an *amiir* or leader and to run its affairs on the basis of mutual consultation or *shuura*.

Janaazah, Salaat al-. The Funeral Prayer for Muslims which is a *fard kifaayah* (see above).

Jihaad. Literally, striving. Any earnest striving in the way of God, involving either personal effort, material resources or arms, for righteousness and against evil, wrong-doing and oppression. Where it involves armed struggle, it must be for the defence of the Muslim community or a just war to protect even non-Muslims from evil, oppression and tyranny.

Jumu'ah. Friday. ● Salaat al-Jumu'ah — The Friday Congregational Prayer which takes the place of the Zuhr (Mid-day) Prayer. The Khutbah or the Sermon is a vital part of the Congregational Prayer. Friday is not a holy day as such or a compulsory day of rest and worshippers may disperse and go about their business and other activities.

Ka'bah. A cube-shaped structure in Makkah which is described in the Qur'an as the first house of worship built for mankind. Muslims in whatever part of the globe they are align themselves in the direction of the Ka'bah for Prayer. This is a sign of unity and solidarity. The Ka'bah of course is not worshipped or venerated. To do so would be to commit the unforgivable sin of shirk or associating something in worship with God.

Khaliifah. 1. Steward; Vicegerent. 2. Successor. Man is referred to in the Qur'an as the khalifah or steward of God on earth. As a khaliifah, he has been given an amaanah (see above) or trust to discharge. In consequence, he has been given freewill and responsibility and has an important status above other creation. Man has the capacity to be faithful to his trust but he can also be foolish and arrogant enough to abort his mission on earth.

The word Khaliifah was used after the death of the noble Prophet Muhammad to refer to his successor, Abu Bakr, as head of the Muslim community. Later it came to be accepted as the designation for the head of the Muslim State. Anglicized as Caliph.

Khilaafah. The designation of the political system of the Muslim State after the noble Prophet. Anglicized as Caliphate.

Khutbah. Speech, sermon.

Kufr. Ingratitude to God and disbelief in Him and His religion. It has the primary meaning of concealing, that is concealing one's natural inclination to acknowledge God and be grateful for His innumerable bounties. All people who incline to kufr have been described by the Prophet as belonging to one nation or community.

Mahr. Dowry. Amount paid by the bridegroom to the bride as part of the Muslim marriage contract. It is meant to be a security for the bride and could be in the form of education, money or property. A Muslim woman at the time of the Prophet considered as her dowry the acceptance of Islam by her husband-to-be.

Makruuh. Disliked but still permissible, an example of which is divorce.

Ma'ruuf. Literally, that which is known. Right; Good. The human being has the natural capacity to know or sense what is right and good.

Mashrabiyyah. Lattice-work window covering to 'let in light but maintain privacy — a common feature of Muslim architecture.

Masjid. A place of prostration, a mosque. According to a saying of the Prophet, the whole earth is a masjid which makes it easy and natural to perform Prayer at any time. As an institution, the masjid is a vital part of any Muslim neighbourhood or community and fulfils many religious, social, economic and other functions.

Millat. Nation or community which is based on religious affiliation; for example, Jews and Christians are described in the Qur'an as each comprising a millat. Under the Islamic system of government each religious community is given freedom to practice its religion and autonomy in the running of its affairs. This is in accordance with the Constitution of Madinah which the Prophet drew up on his arrival in the city.

Minbar. Raised platform in a mosque from which the Khutbah is delivered.

Miizaan. Balance. Measure. Scale of justice and equity. Denotes the measure or the inbuilt laws or balance with which God created everything. Mankind is admonished (55: 8) never to transgress the measure of what is right and just. Also denotes the weighing of each person's deeds on the day of judgement.

Mubaah. That which is allowed in Islamic law. Failure to do what is mubaaah does not bring any blame. Doing what is mubaah does not merit any special reward.

Muhaajir. A person who undertakes hijrah (see above).

Muhsin. One who acts with ihsaan (see

above).

Muhtasib. One who is responsible for carrying out the duties of *hisbah* (see above).

Mukallaf. Obligated, responsible. One who has reached the age of responsibility. It begins with the onset of maturity (*buluugh*). From this age on, a person whether male or female is under obligation to carry out all the duties of Islam. He or she is responsible for any acts of omission. that is, omitting or failing to perform duties such as Salaat or Fasting in the month of Ramadaan. He or she is also accountable for any acts of commission, that is, for committing any act which is forbidden in Islam.

Murabbi. One who carries out the task of *tarbiyyah* (see below).

Muslim. One who submits to or obeys the laws of God. At one level, all creation can be said to be muslim, functioning according to the natural laws with which each was created. A conscious Muslim is one who consciously submits to God and follows the religion of God or Islam.

Mustahabb. That which is recommended but not compulsory in Islamic law. Failure to perform it is not regarded as sinful. It is however beneficial to perform it, for example, brushing of the teeth before every Salaat.

Muttaqi. Someone who possesses *taqwa* (see below) and is deeply conscious of God and careful in not overstepping the limits set by God.

Mu'aakhaah. The act of linking two persons in brotherhood. A unique arrangement which the noble Prophet made between individual Muhaajirs from Makkah and Ansaar from Madinah in order to create a closely-knit and caring society.

Mu'min. A true believer in God. One who possesses imaan (see above). The opposite of a mu'min is a *kaafir*, one who rejects and is ungrateful to God.

Qard. Loan. ● **Qard hasan** — a loan given for a good cause for the sake of God, without interest and without any expectation of profit.

Rabb. Lord and Sustainer. One who owns something and looks after it well.

Rak'at. A unit of Salaat. Begins from the standing position with the utterance of *Allahu Akbar* and includes the recitation of Al-Faatihah and another portion of the Qur'an, bowing (*rukuu'*) and prostrations (*sujuud*) in the manner shown by the noble Prophet.

Ramadaan. The ninth month of the Islamic calendar. The month of fasting. The month in which the Qur'an was revealed.

Riba. Usury. Fixed interest on a loan which is prohibited in Islam. The Qur'an distinguishes between riba and legitimate profit.

Ridwaan. Pleasure, satisfaction. A person's most natural and sublime aim in life is to seek the pleasure (ridwaan) of God and avoid being alienated from Him.

Saalih. Righteous, upright, good. ● **Saalihaat** — good or righteous deeds.

Sabr. Constancy, Patience, Perseverance, Endurance. One of the important qualities of a believer in dealing with the "tests" of life.

Sadaqah. 1. Charity. 2. Dowry or *mahr* (see above). ● **Sadaqah Jaariyyah** — continuous charity, charitable endowment. ● **Sadaqatu-l Fitr** (also called **Zakaatu-l Fitr**): compulsory amount paid by the head of a household at the end of the fast of Ramadaan for the benefit of the poor.

Salaat. The second pillar of Islam. Prayer performed in the particular manner as taught by the noble Prophet, at particular times and under particular conditions. It includes set movements and postures which correspond to the natural attitudes of worship — respect, reverence and obeisance to God alone.

Shahaadah. 1. Testimony, Witness. 2. Declaration of faith. 3. Martyrdom. The words of the Shahaadah or declaration of faith are: *Ash-hadu an laa ilaaha illa Allah wa ash-hadu anna Muhammad Rasuul Allah* — I testify that there is no god but Allah and I testify that Muhammad is God's messenger.

Shari'ah. The moral and legal code of Islam. The two main sources of the Shari'ah are the Qur'an and the Sunnah (see below) of the Prophet Muhammad.

Shirk. Associating others in worship with God. Regarded in the Qur'an as a "mighty injustice" and the only sin which will not be forgiven.

Shuura. Decision-making through consultation which the Muslim community is required to observe.

Sinn. Age. ● **Sinn al-Buluugh** — the age of maturity which everyone is presumed to have reached at the age of fifteen but which could be earlier. A person at this age assumes all the duties and responsibilities of an adult. ● **Sinn al-Muraahaqah** — the age of puberty normally between the age of 10 and 14. ● **Sinn at-Tamyiiz** — the age of discretion normally between the age of 7 and 10.

SubhaanAllah. Glory be to God — an expression used often in oral *dhikr* or remembrance of God. Also used to express astonishment.

Suffah. Raised platform or bench. Part of the Prophet's mosque in Madinah used as a sort of reception point for newcomers to the city and destitute persons.

Sunnah. Literally, path or example. Refers in particular to the Example of the Prophet Muhammad and includes what he said, what he did and what he agreed to.

Surah. A chapter of the Qur'an. There are 114 surahs in the Qur'an.

Tajdiid. Renewal. Reform. Refers to the renewal and reform of individuals and of society and implies a recommitment to live by the values of Islam and strive towards its goals.

Taqwa. Consciousness of God; being careful not to transgress the limits of God in order to stay as close as possible to one's originally good and unsullied state. One who is so deeply conscious of God is called a *muttaqi*.

Tarbiyyah. Education, Training, Nurturing. Looking after, cherishing and being sensitive to the needs of the one being educated.

Tawbah. Literally, returning. Repenting and seeking forgiveness for one's sins in order to return as close as possible to one's originally good and unsullied state.

Tawhiid. Belief in or affirmation of the Oneness of God. Tawhiid is the correct human attitude to Reality. ● **Tawhiid ar-Rububiyyah:** affirming that only God is the Creator and Sustainer of all the worlds. ● **Tawhiid al-Uluhiyyah:** affirming that only God deserves to be worshipped.

Tawraah. Scripture revealed to Prophet Moses.

Tazkiyyah. Purification. Growth. The total process of purifying knowledge, beliefs and behaviour of an individual or community in order to return to and stay on the Straight Path of correct guidance — in addition to growth and development along this line.

'Ulamaa. Plural of *'aalim* (see above).

Ummah (plural: **umam**). Community, nation. Specifically, the community of Believers or the universal Muslim community. Other species or groups in creation are referred to in the Qur'an as "umam" (nations).

Waliimah. Wedding feast, partly serving as a public announcement of a marriage.

Waqf (plural: **awqaaf**). Charitable endowment or trust. One of the recommended ways of spending surplus funds or resources.

Wuduu. Purification that must precede the Salaat or Prayer and such acts as the reading of the Qur'an. It is recommended that a person should try to remain as much as possible in a state of wuduu.

Zakaat. The compulsory "purifying" tax on wealth which is one of the five pillars of Islam. The word Zakaat is derived from the word meaning purification, growth and sweetening.

Zina. Sexual relations outside marriage, including both adultery and fornication, which are probibited in Islam.

Zulm. Injustice, tyranny. Not placing anything or any being in its proper place and according it its due rights is zulm. Zulm may be against God (eg by associating partners with Him), against oneself, against other human beings, animals or any other of God's creation. The opposite of zulm is *'adl* or justice and equilibrium.

Further Reading

Translations of the Qur'an

Abdullah Yusuf Ali, *The Holy Qur'an: Text, Translation, Commentary*, available in various editions.

Arthur J Arberry, *The Koran*, OUP, Oxford, 1985

Muhammad Asad, *The Message of the Qur'an*, Dar al-Andalus, Gibraltar, 1980

Muhammad Marmaduke Pickthall, *The Meaning of the Qur'an*, various editions available.

(Translations of Qur'anic verses in this book have been taken variously from the above. No single translation was used throughout. In some cases, renderings were combined or some modifications made.)

Hadith

Sahih al-Bukhari, translated into English by Muhammad Muhsin Khan, Hilal Yayinlari, Ankara, 1976

Sahih Muslim, translated into English by Abdul Hameed Siddiqui, Kitab Bhavan, New Delhi, 1984

Hadith Database, Islamic Computing Centre, London, 1986

General Introductions to Islam

Suzanne Haneef, *What Everyone Should Know about Islam and Muslims*, Kazi Publications, Chicago

Hammudah AbdalAti, *Islam in Focus*, American Trust Publications, Indianapolis, 1975

Abdur-Rahman Azzam, *The Eternal Message of Muhammad*, Quartet, London, 1979

Abul A'la Mawdudi, *Towards Understanding Islam*, UKIM, London, 1980

Altaf Gauhar (ed.), *The Challenge of Islam*, Islamic Council of Europe, London, 1978

Khurshid Ahmad (ed.), *Islam its Meaning and Message*, Islamic Foundation, Leicester, 1976

Salem Azzam (ed.), *Islam and Contemporary Society*, Longmans, Islamic Council of Europe, 1982

Alija Ali Izetbegovic, *Islam Between East and West*, ATP, Indianapolis, 1984

Richard Tames, *Approaches to Islam*, John Murray, London 1982

Gamal Badawi, *Basic Teachings of Islam* (in question and answer format) on video and audio cassettes, Ottowa, Canada

Said Ramadan, *Ma'aalim at-Tariiq*, Al-Asr al-Hadiith, Beirut, 1987. Translated into English as *What We Stand For*, Geneva

Yusuf al-Qardawi, *Al-Khasaa'is al-'Aammah li-l Islaam* (General Characteristics of Islam), Maktabah Wahbah, Cairo, 1981

Hasan Ayyub, *Tabsiit al-'Aqaa'id al-Islaamiyyah* (Islamic Beliefs Simplified), IIFSO, Beirut, 1980

Chapter One: Face to Face with Reality

Jaafer Shaikh Idris, *Islam the Basic Truths*, Muslim Welfare House, London

Murtaza Mutahhari, *Fundamentals of Islamic Thought - God, Man and the Universe*, Mizan Press, Berkeley, 1985

C S Lewis, *Mere Christianity*, Collins, Glasgow, 1986. Chapter One: Right and Wrong as a Clue to the Meaning of the Universe

Ninian Smart, *The Religious Experience of Mankind*, Collins, Glasgow, 1984

Ronald Duncan & Miranda Weton-Smith (eds.), *The Encyclopaedia of Ignorance*, Pergamon, Oxford, 1982

Noel G Coley & Vance Hall (eds.), *Darwin to Einstein — Primary Sources on Science and Belief*, Longman/Open University, 1980

J R Ravetz, *Scientific Knowledge and its Social Problems*, Oxford University Press, Oxford, 1971

Fazlur Rahman, *Major Themes of the Qur'an*, Bibliotheca Islamica, Chicago, 1980
Chapter One: God; Chapter Two: Man as Individual.

Suzanne Haneef, *What Everyone Should Know About Islam and Muslims*, op. cit.

Abdur Rahman Azzam, *The Eternal Message of Muhammad*, London, 1979

Said Ramadan, 'Islam a Liberating Force' in *Towards Freedom and Dignity*, London Islamic Circle, 1970

Chapter Two: You and Your Condition

Syed Muhammad Al-Naquib Al-Attas, *Islam and Secularism*, Muslim Youth Movement, Kuala Lumpur, 1978. Chapters 3 and 4.

Abdul Latif Tibawi, *Islamic Education*, Luzac, London, 1972

Abdullah, *Education: A Qur'anic Outlook*, Umm al-Qura University, Makkah, 1980

The Qur'an

Khurram Murad, *Way to the Qur'an*, Islamic Foundation, Leicester, 1986

Adeleke Dirisu Ajijola, *Qur'an in the Classrooom*, Islamic Publications, Lahore, 1977.

Fazlur Rahman, *Major Themes of the Qur'an*, op cit.

Ahmad von Denffer, *'Ulum al-Qur'an*, Islamic Foundation, Leicester, 1983

Arabic

Abdul Wahid Hamid, *Easy Steps in Arabic* (A course in reading and writing the Arabic script with self-study manual, workbooks & audiocassettes), MELS, London, 1987

David Cowan, *Modern Literary Arabic*, Cambridge University Press, 1958

Hans Wehr, *Arabic-English Dictionary*, Spoken Language Services, New York, 1976

Hadith

Ahmad von Denffer, *A Day with the Prophet*, Islamic Foundation, Leicester, 1982 (Sayings and practices of the noble Prophet on various aspects of daily living).

Umran Publications, *Hadith* (an introductory selection), London, 1981

Forty Hadith (selected by Imam an-Nawawi), translated by Ezzedin Ibrahim and Denys Dohnson-Davies

Forty Hadith Qudsi (selected and translated by Ezzeddin Ibrahim and Denys Johnson-Davies

Siirah

Abdur Rahman Azzam, *Eternal Message of Muhammad*, op. cit.

Ahmad Muhammad Assaf, *Qubusaat min Hayaat ar-Rasuul*, Dar li Ihyaa al-'Uluum, Beirut, 1979

Martin Lings, *Muhammad: his life based on the earliest sources*, Allen & Unwin, London, 1983

Zakaria Bashier, *The Meccan Crucible*, FOSIS, London, 1978

The Life of Muhammad (video), text by Khurram Murad, Islamic Foundation, Leicester

Abdul Wahid Hamid, *Companions of the Prophet*, 3 vols, MELS, London, 1985

Sunnah
Sayyid Saabiq, *Fiqh as-Sunnah* (Understanding the Sunnah), Arabic, 3 vols, Cairo. English translation of part available as: *Fiqh as-Sunnah: 1 - Purification and Prayer*, American Trust Publications, Indianapolis, 1985

Shari'ah
Said Ramadan, *Islamic Law: Its Scope and Equity*, Geneva, 1970
AbdulWahhaab Khallaaf, *'Ilm Usuul al-Fiqh*, eleventh impression, Dar al-Qalam, Kuwait, 1977
Ziauddin Sardar, *Islamic Futures: the shape of ideas to come*, Mansell, London, 1985. Chapter 5: The Shari'ah as a Problem-solving methodology.
Aa'idah AbdulAziim AlBannaa, *Al-Islam wa-t Tarbiyyatu-s Sihhiyyah*, (Islam and Health Education), Riyadh, 1983
Ghulam Mustafa Khan, *Personal Hygiene*, The Muslim, 8 6-7 (121-125) March-April 1971
Muhammad alGhazaali, *Khuluq al-Muslim* translated into English as *Muslim's Character*, IIFSO, Beirut, 1983
Muhammad Amra (ed), *Islamic Training Programme Manual*, Muslim Youth Movement of South Africa, Durban, 1981
Muhammad Ghulam Muazzam, *Medical Research and al-Quran: Alcoholism, Gambling, Fasting*, HaMeem Publications, Dhaka, 1985
Omar Austin, 'Understanding Muslim Prayer', *The Muslim*, London, 11 1 (3-7) October November 1973
Khurshid Ahmad, 'Some Aspects of Character-Building in Islam', *The Muslim, 8 (1) 9-15 (1970) and 8 (2) 39-42 (1970)*
Gamal Badawi, *Selected Prayers: A Collection of Du'a from the Qur'an and the Sunnah*, Taha, London, 1979

Chapter Three: You and Your Livelihood
Yusuf al-Qardawi, *The Lawful and the Prohibited in Islam*, Shorouk, London, 1985. Chapter 2, Section 4 and Chapter 4 Section 2
Sabahaddin Zaim, 'The Attitude of Muslim Man in Economic Life', *The Muslim, 13 5-6 (102-106) 1976*
Sadiq al-Mahdi, *'The Economic System of Islam' in Islam and Contemporary Society*, op. cit.
Ziauddin Sardar, *Islamic Futures: The Shape of Ideas to Come*, op. cit. Chapter 9: Islamic Economics: From Partial to Axiomatic Approach.
Syed Nawab Haidar Naqwi, *Ethics and Economics: An Islamic Synthesis*, Islamic Foundation, Leicester, 1981

Chapter Four: You and Your Family
Abdullah Naasih 'Ulwaan, *Tarbiyyatu-l Awlaad fi-l Islam* (Education and Training of Children in Islam), 2 vols., Aleppo, 1981
Abd Ghalib Ahmad 'Isa, *Aadaab al-Mu'aamalah fi-l Islam* (The Etiquette of Inter-relationships in Islam), Dar al-Fikr, Khartoum,1985
Hammudah Abdalati, *Family Structure in Islam*, American Trust Publications, Indianapolis
— — — — *Islam in Focus*, American Trust Publications, Indianapolis, 1975. Chapter Four
Jaafar Shaikh Idris, 'Sex, Society and Morality', *The Muslim*, London, 7 3 (55-56) December 1969
Jaafar Shaikh Idris, 'Marriage and Morals — a Complete View', *The Muslim*, London, 7 7 (148-151) April 1970

Chapter Five: You and Your Neighbourhood

Murtaza Mutahhari, *Social and Historical Change*, Mizan Press, Berkeley, 1986
Abd Ghalib Ahmad Isa, *op cit.*
Ibn Taymiyya, *Public Duties in Islam: the Institution of the Hisba*, Islamic Foundation, Leicester, 1982
Frank Feathers, (ed.), *Through the 80's: Thinking Globally, Acting Locally*, World Future Society, Washington, 1980
Hussein Atesin, *Al-'Imaarah*, unpublished Ph.D thesis, University of Sheffield, 1987

Chapter Six: You and Your Community

Muhammad Asad, *The Principles of State and Government in Islam*, Dar al-Andalus, 1980
Merryl Wyn Davies, *Knowing One Another*, Mansell, London, 1988
Muhammad El-Awa, *On the Political System of the Islamic State*, American Trust Publications, 1980
Islamic Council of Europe, *Model of an Islamic Constitution*, London
Sayyid Qutb, *Social Justice in Islam*, Octagon Books, New York, 1970
Sayyid Abul A'ala Mawdudi, *The Islamic Movement, Dynamics of Values Power and Change*, edited by Khurram Murad, Islamic Foundation, Leicester, 1984
Tayeb Abedin, "The Practice of Shura", *The Muslim*, 7 7 (159-161), April 1970
Charles B Handy, *Understanding Organizations*, Penguin, London, 1979

Chapter Seven: You and the Universal Ummah

Murtaza Mutahhari, *Social and Historical Change*, op cit
Abul Fazl Ezzati, *The Spread of Islam*, News & Media, London, 1978
Thomas Arnold, *The Preaching of Islam*, Ashraf, Lahore, 1968
Sayyid Abu'l Ala Mawdudi, *Witnesses unto Mankind: the Purpose and Duty of the Muslim Ummah*, (edited and translated by Khurram Murad), Islamic Foundation, Leicester, 1986
Isma'il Faruqi and Lois Lamya Faruqi, *The Cultural Atlas of Islam*, Macmillan, 1986

Chapter Eight: Face to Faiths

Isma'il Faruqi, *The Cultural Atlas of Islam*, op.cit., chapters 9 and 10
– – – –, 'Islam and Other faiths: the need for Humane Universalism' in *The Challenge of Islam*, Islamic Council of Europe, London, 1978
Jaafar Shaikh Idris, 'Jesus in the Qur'an', *The Muslim*, 7 4 (87-89) January 1970
Said Ramadan, 'Communism', *The Muslim*, London, 7 3 (59-62) December 1969
Murtaza Mutahhari, *Social and Historical Change*, op. cit.
'Christian Mission and Islamic Da'wah' *International Review of Mission*, 65 260. October 1976
Mindy Raffel, 'The Realisation of the Islamic Self' in *Islam and Sociological Perspectives*, Abu Bakr Bagader (ed.), Muslim Youth Movement, Malaysia, 1983

Chapter Nine: You and Global Issues

Ziauddin Sardar, *The Future of Muslim Civilization*, Croom Helm, London, 1979. Chapter 4: World Systems and the Muslim System
Syed Muhammad Nagib al-Attas, *Islam, Secularism and the Philosophy of the Future*, Mansell, London, 1985
Frank Feathers, (ed.) *Through the 80's: Thinking Globally, Acting Locally*, World Future Society, Washington, 1980
Gamal al-Manna, 'Freedom from Fear and Hunger', *Islamic Cultural Centre Newsletter*, London, Jan 1985
Gulzar Haidar, 'Habitat and values in Islam', in *The Touch of Midas*, edited by Ziauddin

Sardar, University of Manchester Press, Manchester, 1984
E F Schumacher, *Small is Beautiful*, Blond and Briggs, London, 1975
Islamic Council of Europe, *Universal Islamic Declaration of Human Rights*, Paris, 1981

Chapter Ten: You and Your Hereafter
Jaafar S Idris, *Islam the Basic Truths*
Fazlur Rahman, *Major Themes in the Qur'an*. Chapter Six: Eschatology.
Ajijola, *Qur'an in the Classroom*. Chapters 4 & 5: Life after Death & Paradise and Hell
Altaf Gawhar, 'The Concept of Tawbah in the Qur'an', *The Muslim*, London, 10 5 (99-104) May-June 1973
Gamal Manna', 'Death — the Journey Beyond', (lecture at University College, London, February 1988, on audiocassette)
— — — —, 'The Final Reckoning', *Islamic Cultural Centre Newsletter* 16, May 1986
— — — —, 'Growth and Decay', *Islamic Cultural Centre Newsletter* 11, Nov 1985.

Note: *Books listed above can be obtained through*
MELS — 61 Alexandra Road, Hendon, London NW4 2RX.

Index

Other MELS publications

EASY STEPS IN ARABIC

An attractive course in reading and writing the Arabic script
and reading the Qur'an.
Well-graded and extensively tested, the course makes learning the Arabic
script easy, quick and enjoyable.
Now used by many schools and madrasahs throughout the world.
The course is suitable for self-study, or for use in classrooms or in short,
intensive courses.

The course comprises:
- **Alphabet Poster.** Large (A2 size) and in colour.
  For letter recognition. Attractive for classrooms and for homes.
- **Arabic Alphabet Song.**
  A delightful song on cassette for children, and even adults.
  For use with the Alphabet Poster at home or in the classroom.
- **Arabic Flashcards.**
  42 cards with all letters in their separate forms and some in joined forms.
  Used to master letter recognition and for games.

- **Easy Steps in Qur'an Reading (Pupil's Book).** 64 pages.
  A carefully graded reader covering all the elements and rules of reading.
- **Easy Steps in Qur'an Reading (Teacher's/Self-study manual).** 120 pages.
  Contains full explanatory notes in English for each page of the Arabic text.
  Also, suggestions on how to use the course, and teaching techniques.
- **Two audiocassettes** (running time: 60 min. each).
  Contain the full text of *Easy Steps in Qur'an Reading.* Each line of the text
  is identified to make it easy to follow text and tape.
- **Easy Steps in Arabic Handwriting** (Workbooks One & Two). 32 pages each.
  Well-graded. Begin with patterns to encourage right to left movement.
  Special techniques to show how words are built up from individual letters.
  Adequate space for tracing and copying.
  Enjoyable exercises: word building, word search games.
  All words used in the workbooks, except two, are from the Qur'an.
- **Arabic Alphabet Summary Chart.** A4 size.
  A special and important feature of the course. Sets out letters in their
  various forms. Introduces letters in words in a graded sequence.
  Indispensable for ready reference and useful for quick revision.

Companions of the Prophet, Books 1, 2 & 3
by Abdul Wahid Hamid.

"narrated in an attractive manner...
"many lively dialogues...
"will certainly be well-received by both younger and older readers."
The Muslim World Book Review, Leicester.

The series provides an easy and lively introduction to early Muslim history and inspiring models for Muslim values, attitudes and behaviour.
The lives of the Sahabah or Companions of the Prophet, may God bless him and grant him peace, is a rich storehouse of knowledge, guidance and inspiration. The sixty men and women whose stories are told in these books helped to lay the foundations of a new world order and it is only fitting that they should be more widely known.
The series should be read with enjoyment in every home and may also be used in Islamic Studies or Islamic History programmes. They may even be used as supplementary readers in English language arts programmes.

Fatimah — Daughter of Muhammad ﷺ (Book with audio cassette). 24 pages. Cassette running time: 22 minutes.

The true and inspiring story of Fatimah's life — a story of simple living, of love and devotion, of faith and courage, of pain and joy.
Suitable for children aged eight and over.

The Book of Muslim Names.

Everyone has a right to a beautiful and honourable name. This books describes what are the best names in the Muslim tradition and gives easy to follow guidance in the spelling and pronunciation of Arabic Islamic names.
Contains about 500 female and 700 male names. Each name is written in elegant Arabic calligraphy and its meaning given in English.